Decision analysis based on uncertain data is natural in many real-world applications, and sometimes such an analysis is inevitable. In the past years, researchers have proposed many efficient operations research models and methods, which have been widely applied to real-life problems, such as finance, management, manufacturing, supply chain, transportation, among others. This book series aims to provide a global forum for advancing the analysis, understanding, development, and practice of uncertainty theory and operations research for solving economic, engineering, management, and social problems.

More information about this series at http://www.springer.com/series/11709

Xiang Li • Xiaofeng Xu
Editors

Proceedings of the Seventh International Forum on Decision Sciences

Springer

Editors
Xiang Li
School of Economics and Management
Beijing University of Chemical Technology
Beijing, China

Xiaofeng Xu
College of Economics & Management
China University of Petroleum
Qingdao, Shandong, China

ISSN 2195-996X ISSN 2195-9978 (electronic)
Uncertainty and Operations Research
ISBN 978-981-15-5719-4 ISBN 978-981-15-5720-0 (eBook)
https://doi.org/10.1007/978-981-15-5720-0

This Springer imprint is published by the registered company Springer Nature Singapore Pte Ltd.
The registered company address is: 152 Beach Road, #21-01/04 Gateway East, Singapore 189721, Singapore

Contents

Third Party's Extended Warranty Design Strategy in Supply Chain

Ma Jianhua, Zhang Weifeng, Pan Yanchun, and Yang Wen

Abstract This paper investigates how a third party designs its extended warranties in a decentralized supply chain with one manufacturer and one exclusive retailer. The manufacturer produces a single product and sells it through its exclusive retailer with a wholesale price contract. In order to get incremental profit from the supply chain, a third party provides extended warranty to the related product, that is to say, the third party is the provider of the extended warranty. The third party incurs the repair costs of failed products. Moreover, the third party also makes decisions on the retail channel of the extended warranty. The third party can sell extended warranty either by itself or by a reseller. Either manufacturer or retailer may be the reseller of the extended warranty. It is meaningful to figure out when the third party prefers to delegate the retail of the extended warranty to the manufacturer or the retailer, and when the manufacturer or the retailer prefers to be a reseller. We reveal the third party's dominant extended warranty design strategy by considering a game model conducting by a manufacturer, a retailer and a third party.

Keywords Third party · Extended warranty · Supply chain management

1 Introduction

Nowadays, the global economy is developed significantly, which is boosting the demand for durable goods such as household appliances, digital electronic products, and automobiles. With the huge scale of the potential market size, the extended warranty market derived from the related product market also has a potential large scale size. As a result, manufacturers, retailers and third parties all prefer to provide extended warranties to gain incremental profit. Comparing with third parties, the

---

M. Jianhua (✉) · Z. Weifeng · P. Yanchun · Y. Wen
College of Management, Shenzhen University, Shenzhen, Guangdong, China
e-mail: majh@szu.edu.cn; panyc@szu.edu.cn; wenyang@szu.edu.cn

X. Li, X. Xu (eds.), *Proceedings of the Seventh International Forum on Decision Sciences*, Uncertainty and Operations Research,
https://doi.org/10.1007/978-981-15-5720-0_1

manufacturers and retailers are shown many deficiencies in their professional experience and innovation when they providing extended warranties. Hence, it is more dominant in business practice that more and more extended warranties are provided by professional third parties.

When a third party provides the extended warranty, he should provide the maintenance service of the failed products and hence incur the involved repair costs. Moreover, the third party also should determine how to design the retail channel of his extended warranty. There are three possible retail channel strategies for the third party to choose. The third party could sell the extended warranty by itself, or delegate the retail of his extended warranty to the manufacturer or the retailer (in this case the manufacturer or the retailer is called reseller). What kind of extended warranty retail channel can bring more increment profit? When will the third party prefer to delegate the retail of the extended warranty to the manufacturer or the retailer? When will the manufacturer or the retailer prefer to be a reseller? In this paper, we will compare three kinds of extended warranty design strategies for a third party's in a supply chain. We try to figure out the third party's dominant extended warranty design strategy by considering a game model conducting by a manufacturer, a retailer and a third party.

This paper is organized as follows: Section 2 reviews the related literature. Section 3 introduces the model and describes the rules of the game. Section 4 deduces the equilibrium outcomes. Section 5 analyzes the dominant design strategy of the third party. Section 6 concludes the paper.

2 Literature Review

The research on design and analysis of extended warranties is a relatively new development in operations management. For example, Li et al. [1] analyzed how to design extended warranties in a supply chain game model consisting of one manufacturer and one retailer. Desai and Padmanabhan [2] conducted a study of how extended warranties influenced the price coordination for one supply chain that was producing and selling a durable product. Jiang and Zhang [3] discussed how a retailer's extended warranty policy affected the original base warranty policy offered by the manufacturer. He et al. [4] studied how to design extended warranty strategies in a dual supply channel by considering customer channel preferences. Mai et al. [5] investigated how to design extended warranties to coordinate the quality decisions of store-brand products. Heese [6] explored how a common retailer's extended warranties impact its two competing manufacturer's base warranties. By constructing a three-echelon competing online shopping supply chain game model, Qin et al. [7] studied how to design extended warranty strategies for online shopping supply chain to gain more profit. Ma et al. [8] revealed how retailers extended warranty polices affect the channel structure choice game equilibrium for competing supply chains.

Although all of the models in this literature have highlighted the factor of extended warranties, most of them have not directly addressed how a third part designs its extended warranty strategy. Li et al. [1] have considered when the retailer or the manufacturer prefers to be a reseller of the extended warranties provided by a third party. But they also didn't investigate the third party's dominant strategy of the extended warranty in a supply chain. Our research differs from previous papers in that we consider the issue of a third party's extended warranty design strategy by constructing a game model among a third party, a manufacturer and a retailer.

3 The Model

Let p and q denote the retail price and quantity demanded for the product of the supply chain. We use the following demand function as $q = a - bp$, where a ($a > 0$) is the potential market size of the product and b is the price sensitivity parameter. Let x and t denote the extended warranty price and extended warranty length of the product. The price per unit length of coverage x/t is an effective measure for comparing different extended warranties. Let d denote the sensitivity of the extended warranty demand to x/t. Following Li et al. [1], the demand for the extended warranty of product i is

$$Q = q - dx/t, \text{ where } t > 0. \tag{1}$$

Let k and λ denote the unit repair cost and failure rate of the product, respectively. According to Li et al. [1] and Ma et al. [8], the extended warranty-related cost of each product over the extended warranty duration t can be given as ct^2Q, where $c = k\lambda^2$. Without loss of generality, we assume that the marginal production cost of each manufacturer is 0. Moreover, in order to focus our research on extended warranty design strategy, it is assumed that the length of the base product warranty which is provided by the manufacturer is normalized to zero. Denote T, M, R and π as the third party's profit, manufacturer's profit, retailer's profit and total chain's profit.

4 Equilibrium Outcomes with Various Extended Warranty Retail Channel

4.1 The Centralized Supply Chain (C)

We first consider the centralized case in which one centralized decision maker provides the product as well as the extended warranty, which acts as the benchmark. The optimization problem faced by the centralized decision maker is given by

$$\max_{p, p_e > 0} \pi^C = p(a - bp) + \left(p_e - ct^2\right)\left(a - bp - \frac{dx}{t}\right).$$

The decisions under the centralized supply chain can be concluded as follows.

$$p^C = \frac{2ad-abt+bcdt^2}{b(4d-bt)},\ p_e^C = \frac{t\left(d+2cdt-bct^2\right)}{4d-bt},\ \pi^C = \frac{d\left(a^2-abct^2+bdc^2t^3\right)}{b(4d-bt)}.$$

In order to guarantee the existence and non-negativity of the equilibrium outcomes, we assume that $0 < t < 2d/b$ and $a > a^C = ct(2d - bt)$ in centralized supply chain system model.

4.2 The Third Party Provides and Sells the Extended Warranty Directly (3T)

In this section, we consider the case in which the third party provides the extended warranty as well as sells the extended warranty directly. Denote superscript $3T$ as the index of $3T$ structure. In the first stage, the manufacturer decides on wholesale price in order to maximize its profit. The optimization problem faced by the manufacturer is given by:

$$\max_w M^{3\mathrm{T}} = w\,(a - bp)\,.$$

In the second stage, the retailer and third party take the manufacturer's wholesale price as given, and decide on the product retail price and the extended warranty retail price respectively. The optimization problems faced by the retailer and the third party are given as follows.

$$\max_{p>0} R^{3\mathrm{T}} = (p - w)\,(a - bp)\,,$$

$$\max_{p_e>0} T^{3\mathrm{T}} = \left(p_e - ct^2\right)\left(a - bp - \frac{dx}{t}\right).$$

By backward induction, the equilibrium outcomes under $3T$ structure can be concluded as follows.

$$p^{3\mathrm{T}} = \frac{3a}{4b},\ w^{3\mathrm{T}} = \frac{a}{2b},\ p_e^{3\mathrm{T}} = \frac{at + 4cdt^2}{8d},$$

$$M^{3\mathrm{T}} = \frac{a^2}{8b},\ R^{3\mathrm{T}} = \frac{a^2}{16b},\ T^{3\mathrm{T}} = \frac{t(a - 4cdt)^2}{64d}.$$

In order to guarantee the existence and non-negativity of the equilibrium outcomes, it is required that $a > a^{3T} = 4cdt$ in centralized supply chain system model.

4.3 Results: The Third Party Provides and the Manufacturer Resells the Extended Warranty (3M)

In this section, we derive the equilibrium outcomes for the case that the third party is an extended warranty provider and the manufacturer is the reseller. Denote superscript $3M$ as the index of $3M$ structure. The third party first decides on the extended warranty wholesale price to maximize its profit, and the optimization problem faced by the third party is given by:

$$\max_{w_e} T^{3\mathrm{M}} = \left(w_e - ct^2\right)\left(a - bp - \frac{dx}{t}\right).$$

In the second stage, the manufacturer takes the third party's decision as given, and decides on the product wholesale price and extended warranty price respectively. The optimization problem faced by the manufacturer is given as follows.

$$\max_{p_e>0, w} M^{3\mathrm{M}} = w\left(a - bp\right) + \left(p_e - w_e\right)\left(a - bp - \frac{dx}{t}\right).$$

In the third stage, the optimization problem faced by the retailer is given by:

$$\max_{p>0} R^{3\mathrm{M}} = \left(p - w\right)\left(a - bp\right).$$

The equilibrium outcomes under 3M structure are summarized as follows.

$$p^{3\mathrm{M}} = \frac{(48d - 7bt)\,a + 4bcdt^2}{8d\,(8d - bt)},\ w^{3\mathrm{M}} = \frac{(16d - 3bt)\,a + 4bcdt^2}{4d\,(8d - bt)},$$

$$w_e^{3\mathrm{M}} = \frac{at + 4cdt^2}{8d},\ p_e^{3\mathrm{M}} = \frac{(12d - bt)\,a + 16cd^2t - 4bcdt^2}{8d\,(8d - bt)},$$

$$M^{3\mathrm{M}} = \frac{32a^2d - 3a^2bt - 8abcdt^2 + 16bc^2d^2t^3}{32d\,(8d - bt)},$$

$$R^{3\mathrm{M}} = \frac{256a^2d^2 - 32a^2dbt + a^2b^2t^2 - 128abcd^2t^2 + 8ab^2cdt^3 + 16bc^2d^2t^4}{409bd^2 - 1024b^2dt + 63b^3d^2},$$

$$T^{3\mathrm{M}} = \frac{a^2t - 8acdt^2 + 16c^2d^2t^3}{128d - 16bt}.$$

That is to say, $T^{3\mathrm{T}} > T^{3\mathrm{R}} > T^{3\mathrm{M}}$ *for* $t < 1.55d/t$ *and* $a > a^{\mathrm{T}}_{3\mathrm{R}-3\mathrm{T}}$. *Otherwise* $T^{3R} > T^{3T} > T^{3M}$.

By Proposition 3, we know that the third party can profit more from model 3T for small extended warranty length and large potential market size. Otherwise the third party can profit more form model 3R. The third party's profit under 3M is always the smallest. It is the reason why in practice a third party prefers to delegate the retail of the extended warranty to a retailer rather than a manufacturer.

Proposition 4 *The manufacturer's profit under 3R is the largest, and the manufacturer's profit under 3T is the smallest. That is to say* $M^{3\mathrm{R}} > M^{3\mathrm{M}} > M^{3\mathrm{T}}$.

By Proposition 4, we know that the manufacturer profits more from model 3R, and the manufacturer's profit under 3*T* is always the smallest. As a result, the manufacturer in a decentralized supply chain prefers to model 3R.

Proposition 5 *The retailer's profit under 3R is the largest and the retailer's profit under 3T is the smallest. That is to say* $R^{3\mathrm{R}} > R^{3\mathrm{M}} > R^{3T}$.

By Proposition 5, we know that the retailer profits more from model 3R, and the retailer's profit under 3T is always the smallest. As a result, the retailer in a decentralized supply chain prefers to model 3R.

By Proposition 3–5, it is implied that in a decentralized product channel in which the manufacturer and retailer propose wholesale price contract, if the extended warranty length is short and the potential market size is large enough, the third party prefers to provide and sell the extended warranty directly, which is not preferred by both manufacturer and retailer. Otherwise, the third party prefers to provide the extended warranty directly and delegate the retail of the extended warranty to the retail, which is also preferred by both of the manufacturer and retailer.

6 Conclusions

This paper investigates how a third part designs its extended warranties to gain more profit. It is assumed that the manufacturer and retailer propose wholesale price contract to sell a single product. If the extended warranty length is short and the potential market size is large enough, the third party prefers to provide and sell the extended warranty directly, which is not preferred by both manufacturer and retailer. Otherwise, the third party prefers to provide the extended warranty directly and delegate the retail of the extended warranty to the retail, which is also preferred by both manufacturer and retailer. This research helps to explain the observed industry practices, and it offers useful guidelines for third parties in a supply chain to design their extended warranties.

Acknowledgements This research is supported by the National Natural Science Foundation of China (Grant nos. 71402101, 71402102, 71472126 and 71572114).

References

1. Li K, Mallik S, Chhajed D (2012) Design of extended warranties in supply chains under additive demand. Prod Oper Manag 21(4):730–746
2. Desai P, Padmanabhan P (2004) Durable goods, extended warranty and channel coordination. Rev Mark Sci 2(2):1–23
3. Jiang B, Zhang XB (2011) How does a retailer's service plan affect a manufacturer's warranty. Manag Sci 57(4):727–740
4. He Z, Huang D, He S (2018) Design of extended warranty service in a dual supply channel. Total Qual Manag Bus Excell 29(9–10):1089–1107
5. Mai DT, Liu T, Morris MS et al (2017) Quality coordination with extended warranty for store-brand products. Eur J Oper Res 256:524–532
6. Heese HS (2012) Retail strategies for extended warranty sales and impact on manufacturer base warranties. Decis Sci 43(2):341–367
7. Qin XH, Su Q, Huang SH (2017) Extended warranty strategies for online shopping supply chain with competing suppliers considering component reliability. J Syst Sci Syst Eng 26(6):753–773
8. Ma JH, Ai XZ, Yang W et al (2019) Decentralization versus coordination in competing supply chains under retailers' extended warranties. Ann Oper Res 275(2):485–580

Multi-channel Structure Selection Model for Minor Enterprises

Li-hong Deng, Jing He, and Yuan Li

Abstract Traditional channel structure model and multi-channel structure model based on Stackelberg game are established on the issue that whether minor enterprises should choose latter or not. The optimal pricing model of the multi-channel structure is obtained under the consideration that the potential demand of the market is influenced by the new channel. And then if minor enterprises establish the multi channel structure, the boundary conditions that they should satisfied with are calculated under the condition that the channels are interacted with each other strongly. Results illustrate that the total profit that minor enterprises can obtain changes significantly as the potential market demand increases while the profit of the middleman changes slowly with the market share of traditional channels decreases. And when the boundary value is reached, the middleman may be forced to exit the multi-channel structure. So that minor enterprises cannot get more profits until they can control the market share of direct channel and the traditional channel well.

Keywords Minor enterprises · Channel conflict · Multi-channel structure · Stackelberg game

1 Introduction

With the rapid development of China's socialist market economy, all kinds of small and medium-sized enterprises grow rapidly, and play a vital role in promoting the development of the national economy. However, SMEs need to face development bottlenecks such as short life and low income. The key to break through this bottleneck is to expand existing marketing channels. Due to the limitations of enterprise scale and capital chain, SMEs need to pay more attention to the timing

---

L.-h. Deng · J. He (✉) · Y. Li
School of Economics and Management, Harbin Engineering University, Harbin, China
e-mail: denglihong@hrbeu.edu.cn

X. Li, X. Xu (eds.), *Proceedings of the Seventh International Forum on Decision Sciences*, Uncertainty and Operations Research,
https://doi.org/10.1007/978-981-15-5720-0_2

and the relationship between SMEs and traditional channels when establishing dual-channel marketing structure. Otherwise, it will backfire and even lead SMEs to bankruptcy.

The research on dual channel issues mainly focuses on the introduction of direct selling channels and the establishment of a dual channel marketing structure coordination strategy. Around the introduction of channels, Webb proposed that the introduction of electronic channels will make channel conflicts more complicated, but the dual channel management method still applies to the dual channel marketing structure with electronic channels [1]. Chiang and Cattani used game theory to find that the introduction of direct sales channels is not always harmful to retailers, demonstrating the possibility of establishing a dual-channel marketing structure under certain conditions [2, 3]. From the perspective of manufacturers, Park and Hendershott found that establishing direct sales channels will increase market demand, increase manufacturers' profits, damage retailer profits, and increase total channel profit, indicating that manufacturers have the motivation to establish a dual-channel marketing structure [4, 5]. Zhuang Guijun pointed out the changes and characteristics of the dual-channel marketing structure design and management in the electronic environment [6]. Zhu Cuiling and others used the classic Hotelling linear city model, thus indicating that it is not always beneficial for the manufacturer to establish a dual channel marketing structure [7]. From the perspective of consumer purchase price and service quality, Dumrongsiri and others found that establishing direct sales channels will increase manufacturers' profits [8]. Yan Nina and others used the Steinberg game model to explore the conditions for manufacturers to establish a dual-channel marketing structure, and given the necessary conditions for establishing a dual-channel marketing structure [9]. Yan et al. proved that increasing the direct sales channel will have an incentive effect on traditional channels and improve the service and profit of traditional channels [10]. Liu Hanjin also proposed that the introduction of direct sales channels under certain conditions is beneficial to both retailers and manufacturers. If the conditions are not met, it may only be beneficial to manufacturers [11]. Focusing on the pricing and coordination strategy of dual-channel structure, Cattani et al. used utility theory to coordinate network direct sales channels and traditional marketing channels from the perspective of procurement, pricing and distribution of three key elements of channel structure [12]. Qin et al. established a dual-channel marketing structure model under stochastic demand conditions [13]. Wang Hong and Huang respectively make decision-making research on the dual-channel marketing structure under different price models, and conclude that the price-consistent model is not the most favorable pricing model [14, 15]. Hoseininiaa et al. also derive the equilibrium solution of the Steinberg dynamic game model from the perspective of inventory [16]. Zhao Liqiang et al. constructed a shared contract to achieve Pareto improvement, and enabled the dual channel marketing structure to develop harmoniously [17]. Zhang Xizheng and other researches on the degree of product substitution also established a sharing contract mitigation channel [18]. Matsui and other researchers found that not only the pricing model has an impact on dual channels, but also the timing of pricing will have an impact on the profitability of the dual-channel marketing structure [19].

This paper will combine the characteristics of SME sales channels, and under the condition that the direct sales channel has certain influence on the potential demand of the existing market, establish a selection model of SMEs' dual-channel marketing structure, and study the different influences and traditional channels of the direct sales channels on the potential demand of the market. In the case of a different share, the change in profits obtained by SMEs is intended to provide a reference for SMEs to choose different channel structures.

2 Problem Description and Model Assumptions

In today's increasingly fierce market competition, SMEs are beginning to introduce direct sales channels to adopt dual-channel marketing structure to sell goods in order to gain greater market share. However, the establishment of direct sales channels by SMEs will conflict with the existing traditional marketing channels. If the channel conflicts cannot be solved well, it will most likely cause the middlemen to withdraw from the channel structure. Therefore, SMEs need to establish direct sales channels under the condition that the middlemen do not withdraw from the channel structure, and control the direct selling channel product prices and traditional channel product prices, as well as the market share of each channel. In order to better analyze the profit changes obtained by SMEs, agents, wholesalers, retailers, etc. are now analyzed as a profit group. In the dual-channel marketing structure, considering the establishment of direct sales channels will have a certain impact on market demand, so this paper refers to the demand model of [15] and makes reasonable improvements. The demand function for each channel is as follows:

When there are only traditional marketing channels, traditional channel needs:

$$Q_{T0} = S\left(1 - \beta P_{T0}\right) \tag{1}$$

In the dual channel marketing structure, the traditional channel needs:

$$Q_{T1} = \mu\,(S + S_1)\,(1 - [\beta/\,(1 - \theta)]\,P_{T1} + [\beta\theta/\,(1 - \theta)]\,P_{E1}) \tag{2}$$

In the dual channel marketing structure, the demand for direct sales channels:

$$Q_{E1} = (1 - \mu)\,(S + S_1)\,(1 + [\beta\theta/\,(1 - \theta)]\,P_{T1} - [\beta/\,(1 - \theta)]\,P_{E1}) \tag{3}$$

The symbolic description of this article: the lower corner note 0 indicates that there is only a single channel marketing structure of the traditional channel, the lower corner note 1 indicates the dual channel marketing structure after the introduction of the electronic channel, the lower corner note T indicates the traditional channel (intermediary), the lower corner E indicates the electronic channel, and the lower corner note M. Representing SMEs, the top note d indicates unified decision making, the upper note S indicates decentralized decision making; The potential demand for the market is S, the potential demand for new market after the introduction of electronic channels is S_1, and the influence coefficient of price on actual demand is β (S, S_1 and β are positive real numbers); the sales price of products is P, the wholesale price for SMEs to distribute to middlemen is W, the market share for traditional channels is $\mu(0 < \mu < 1)$, the production cost for unit products is C, and the cost of input for electronic channels for SMEs is F. θ is cross-elasticity $(0 < \theta < 1)$, that is, the influence of the price change of one channel product on the demand of another channel, the value of the value is related to the characteristics of the product being sold.

When using the above functional model, the following assumptions should be established: (1) The sales price exceeds the boundary cost. (2) The actual market demand is not negative. (3) The potential demand of the market will not change with the price of any channel. In order to ensure that the above three assumptions are established, it is necessary to constrain the coefficients in the model as follows:

Constraint 1: The demand is not negative, that is $C\beta < 1$.

Constraint 2: The price coefficient in the demand function is non-negative, that is, there is a traditional channel market share μ and cross-elasticity of price demand between channels θ. The following relationship is satisfied: $\{\theta \leq (1 - \mu)/\mu, \theta \leq \mu/(1 - \mu)\} \rightarrow \{\theta/(1 + \theta) \leq \mu \leq 1/(1 + \theta)\}$.

3 Comparison of Traditional Channel Marketing Structure and Dual Channel Marketing Structure

3.1 *Analysis of Traditional Marketing Channel Structure Profit*

Considering that in the traditional channel marketing structure, if SMEs and intermediaries can make unified decisions, the entire channel structure can be regarded as a vertically integrated decision-making system, which can maximize the total profit of the channel structure.

However, in reality, it is difficult for SMEs and middlemen to make unified decisions. They all start from their own interests and attempt to obtain more benefits from the channels. This will lead to the two channels of price increases through the channel structure, and the pursuit of maximum benefits. Intermediaries will not purchase the optimal number of products for SMEs, which will eventually create a double marginalization problem. In this decentralized decision-making situation, SMEs influence the distribution of benefits in the channel by controlling the wholesale price, treating SMEs as leaders in the traditional channel structure, intermediaries as followers, and establishing the Stankelberg game model:

$$\begin{cases} \max\limits_{W_0^s} G_{M0}^s = \left(W_0^s - C\right) S \left(1 - \beta P_{T0}^s\right) \\ s.t. P_{T0}^s = \arg\left(\max G_{M0}^s\right) \\ \max\limits_{P_{T0}^s} G_{T0}^s = \left(P_{T0}^s - W_0^s\right) S \left(1 - \beta P_{T0}^s\right) \end{cases} \quad (4)$$

Solve the optimal strategy for the game model:

$$WS * 0 = (1 + C\beta) / 2\beta \quad (5)$$

$$PS * T0 = (3 + C\beta) 4\beta \quad (6)$$

In the case of decentralized decision-making, the parties gain profits:

$$GS * T0 = S (1 - C\beta) 2/16\beta \quad (7)$$

$$GS * M0 = S (1 - C\beta) 2/8\beta \quad (8)$$

$$GS * 0 = 3S (1 - C\beta) 2/16\beta \quad (9)$$

Comparing the results of unified decision making and decentralized decision making:

Corollary 1: The total profit of the channel under decentralized decision-making is reduced by a quarter compared with the total profit of the channel under unified decision-making.

Proof: From the calculation results, we can see the total profit of the channel structure under unified decision Gd* 0 = S(1 − Cβ)2/4β better than the total profit of the channel structure under decentralized decision making GS* 0 = 3S(1 − Cβ)2/16β, Compare two formulas GS* 0 and Gd* 0, the relationship is: GS* 0 = 3/4 Gd* 0, in addition Gd* 0 > GS* 0 > 0, therefore, the total profit of the channel structure under decentralized decision-making is reduced by a quarter compared with the total profit of the channel structure under unified decision-making.

Corollary 2: Under the decentralized decision, the total profit of the channel structure is optimal when the wholesale price is WS 0 = (1 + 3Cβ)/4β.

Proof: The model knows that the sales volume is related to the sales price. SMEs can reduce the retail price by adjusting the wholesale price W to increase the sales volume of the products to ensure their own interests are not damaged. At this point, the balance point between the SMEs and the middlemen to reach profits also makes the channel's total profit the largest.

3.2 Analysis of the Profit of Dual Channel Marketing Structure After the Introduction of Direct Sales Channels

Similar to the traditional marketing channel structure analysis, considering the actual situation under decentralized decision-making, the Steinberg game model is used to analyze the profit distribution of the dual-channel marketing structure. In this model, SMEs establish a direct sales channel to obtain more profits, and SMEs control the profit distribution of the entire channel by setting wholesale price WS 1and direct selling price PS E1 in the model. The middleman decides how much profit he gets from the channel structure by deciding on the retail price of PS T1. Reference [17] pointed out that the development of electronic direct sales channels will directly lead to a reduction in the market share of traditional retailers, that is, the traditional channels of the products sold and the direct sales channels have a greater impact on each other. This article sets θ to 1/2.

At this point, the optimal profit for SMEs is:

$$GS * M1 = [(S + S1)\,(24\mu 2 - 15\mu - 9\mu 3)\,(1 - C\beta)\,2] \,/\, [8\beta\,(7\mu 2 - 7\mu) + 2\beta] - F \tag{10}$$

The optimal profit obtained by the middleman is:

$$GS * T1 = [9\,(S + S1)\,\mu\,(4\mu - 1)\,2\,(1 - C\beta)\,2\,(1 - \mu)\,2] \,/\, [2\beta\,(28\mu 2 - 28\mu + 1)\,2] \tag{11}$$

The total profit of the dual channel structure is:

$$\begin{aligned} GS * 1 = {} & [3\mu\,(1 - \mu)\,(S + S1)\,(1 - C\beta)\,2\,(18\mu 3 - 38\mu 2 + 58\mu - 1)] \,/ \\ & [\beta\,(28\mu 2 - 28\mu) + 1] - F \end{aligned} \tag{12}$$

3.3 Dual Channel Marketing Structure Establishment Conditions

Comparing the traditional channel marketing structure with the profit analysis of the dual channel marketing structure: *PS T1<PS E1*. Through analysis, the following propositions are obtained.

Proposition 1 When $1/3 < \mu < 2/3$, the ratio of the potential demand of the dual channel marketing structure to the potential demand of the traditional channel marketing structure meets the conditions: $(S+S_1)/S > (28\mu^2 - 28\mu + 1)^2/36\mu(1 - 4\mu)^2 (1 - \mu)^2$, The Chamber of Commerce continues to work with SMEs.

Prove: (1) Obtained by the constraint 2 in the model $\{\theta/(1+\theta) \leq \mu \leq 1/(1+\theta)\}$, So when θ is 1/2, μ effective range is $1/3 < \mu < 2/3$. (2) If SMEs want intermediaries to continue to work with them, then it must be ensured that the profits of the middlemen will not be reduced after the introduction of the direct sales channel. That is, the conditions are met: $S(1 - C\beta)^2/8\beta \leq [9(S + S_1)\mu(1 - 4\mu)^2(1 - C\beta)^2(1 - \mu)^2]/[2\beta(28\mu^2 - 28\mu + 1)^2]$,the ratio of potential requirements for both structures is available: $(S + S_1)/S > (28\mu^2 - 28\mu + 1)^2/36\mu(1 - 4\mu)^2(1 - \mu)^2$.

Proposition 2 When $1/3 < \mu < 2/3$, the potential demand after the introduction of the direct sales channel and the cost of establishing the direct sales channel met the conditions: $(S + S_1)/F \geq [\beta(28\mu^2 - 28\mu + 1)^2]/[(1 - \mu)(1 - C\beta)^2(18 - 21\mu)(11 - 10\mu)]$, The cost of establishing direct channel investment can be recovered.

Prove: Through calculations, the maximum profit obtained by direct sales channels under the decentralized decision-making of SMEs is:

$$G_{ME1}^{S*} = (1 - \mu)(1 - \beta C)^2 (S + S_1)\mu^2 \frac{(18 - 21\mu)(11 - 10\mu)}{\beta(28\mu^2 - 28\mu + 1)^2} - F \quad (13)$$

4 Numerical Simulation

Considering that SMEs are subject to various conditions, the following assumptions are made for the coefficients in the model. Assume that $S = 10{,}000$, $\beta = 0.02$, $C = 20$, by the constraint two, the parameter μ has a value range of $1/2 < \mu < 2/3$, and the S, β, C parameter value is substituted into three propositions. According to Proposition 1, the curve is shown in Fig. 1. From the curve in the figure, it can be seen that as μ becomes larger, S_1 caused by direct sales channels is gradually reduced. It can be seen that when the market share of traditional channels is larger, the impact of SMEs establishing direct sales channels on intermediaries will be smaller. This shows that for SMEs, it is very important for the operation of traditional channels before establishing direct sales channels. Only when the sales and sales of traditional channels are better, the threshold for SMEs to establish direct sales channels will be lower. Therefore, SMEs need to control the market share of direct sales channels within a certain range, so that the dual channel structure can develop harmoniously.

In order to more clearly see that the middlemen get profit $GS\,T1$ with the potential demand of the new market S_1 and the market share of the traditional channel μ, the S,β,C parameters are brought into (10) to get Fig. 2, the surface is the dual channel marketing structure. The middleman obtains the profit surface, and the plane is the profit that the middleman obtains in the traditional channel structure $GS{*}\,cT0$. Because the market has no relationship with S_1 and μ, $GS{*}\,cT0$ is a constant. It can be seen from the trend of the curved surface in Fig. 2 that when the value of μ is small, the profit growth of the middlemen is slow as the potential demand of the new

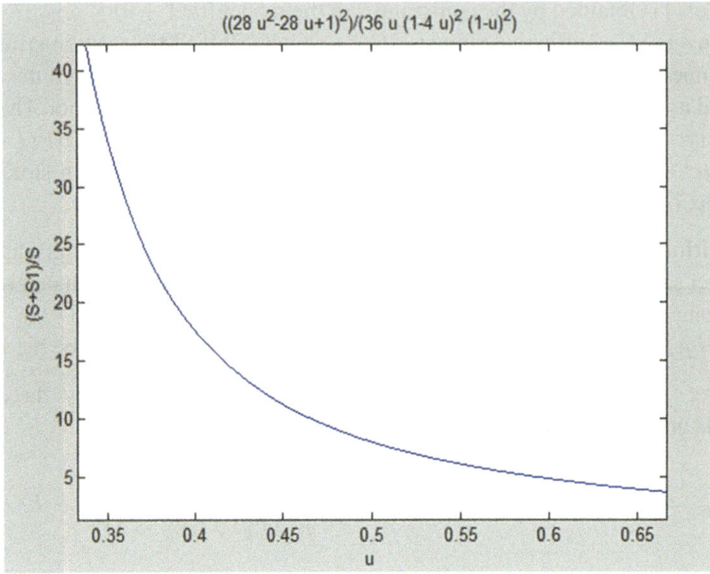

Fig. 1 The relationship of $\frac{S+S_1}{S}$ and μ

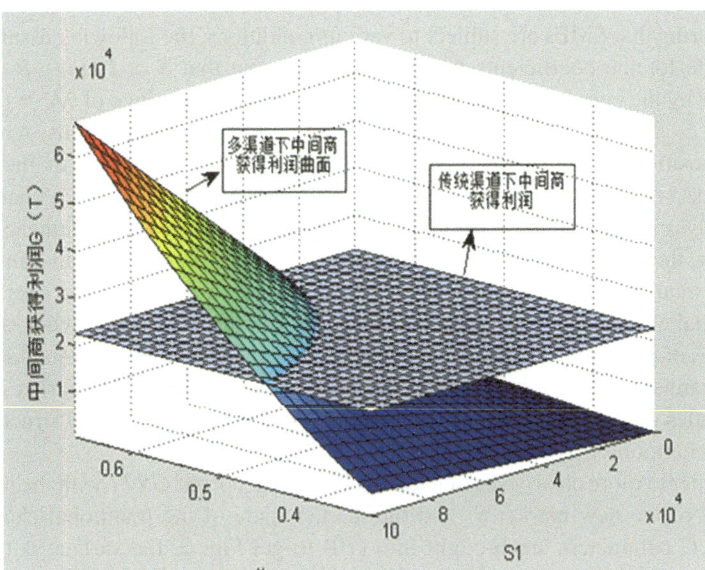

Fig. 2 The middleman gains profits under the two channel structures

market increases. Conversely, the profit earned by the middle quotient will increase substantially as S_l increases. Comparing the plane and the surface, it can be seen that μ and S_l reach a certain critical value. At this time, the broker's profit will be greater than the original profit, and the middleman will not be negatively affected by the establishment of the direct sales channel. When μ and S_l exceed the critical value, the middlemen will prefer SMEs to establish a dual-channel marketing structure to generate more profits.

5 Conclusion

This paper establishes the traditional channel marketing structure and the dual channel marketing structure Steinberg game model from the perspective of small and medium-sized enterprises. Under the situation of large influence between channels, the analysis draws the boundary conditions for SMEs to establish a dual-channel marketing structure: the market share of controlling direct sales channels does not exceed the boundary value to ensure that the middlemen do not withdraw from the channel structure; The ratio of the original potential demand is greater than the specific coefficient, and the ratio of the potential demand to the investment in establishing the direct channel is greater than a certain value, and the capital paid for the establishment of the direct selling channel can be recovered; according to the potential demand and the market share of the traditional channel, the establishment of the direct selling channel can be invested. It lays a solid foundation for the research of dual-channel selection of SMEs, and has a certain guiding role for the marketing channel selection of SMEs.

References

1. Webb KL (2002) Managing channels of distribution in the age of electronic commerce. Ind Mark Manag 31:95–102
2. Chiang WYK, Chhajed D, Hess JD (2003) Direct marketing, indirect profits: a strategic analysis of dual-channel supply-chain design. Manag Sci 49(1):1–20
3. Cattani K, Gilland W, Heese HS et al (2006) Boiling frogs: pricing strategies for a manufacturer adding a direct channel that competes with the traditional channel. Prod Oper Manag 3:40–57
4. Park SY, Keh HT (2003) Modelling hybrid distribution channels: a game-theoretic analysis. J Retail Consum Serv 10:155–167
5. Hendershott T, Zhang J (2006) A model of direct and intermediated sales. J Econ Manag Strategy 15:279–316
6. Guijun Z, Yilian Z (2006) Marketing channel management in electronic network environment. J Manag 3(4):443–450
7. Zhu C, Lin W, Xujin P (2006) Research on the judgment model of manufacturers constructing dual-channel retail model. J China Univ Sci Technol 36(7):788–793
8. Dumrongsiri A, Fan M, Jain A et al (2008) A supply chain model with direct and retail channels. Eur J Oper Res 187:691–718

9. Nina Y, Xiaoyuan H, Bing L (2007) A master-slave strategy model for supply chain dual source channels in the electronic market environment. Chin Manag Sci 15(3):98–103
10. Yan RL, Pei Z (2009) Retail services and firm profit in a dual-channel market. J Retail Consum Serv 16:306–314
11. Hanjin L, Xiaojun F, Hongmin C (2015) Research on dual channel pricing strategy under retailer Price leadership structure. Chin Manag Sci 23(6):91–99
12. Cattani KD, Gilland WG, Swaminathan JM (2004) Coordinating traditional and internet supply chains. In: Simchi-Levi D, Wu SD, Shen ZJ (eds) Handbook of quantitative supply chain analysis. International series in operations research & management science, vol 74. Springer, Boston, MA, pp 643–677
13. Qin G, Mallik S (2007) Inventory competition and allocationin a multi-channel distribution system. Eur J Oper Res 182:704–729
14. Huang W, Swaminathan JM (2009) Introduction of a second channel: implications for pricing and profits. Eur J Oper Res 194:258–279
15. Wang H, Jing Z (2009) Research on decision making of dual-channel supply chain under different price models. Chin Manag Sci 17(6):84–89
16. Hoseininiaa M, Esfahania MMS, Didehvarb F et al (2013) Inventory competition in a multi channel distribution system: the Nash and Stackelberg game. Sci Iranica 20(3):846–854
17. Liqiang Z, Xu J (2014) Contract design of dual channel conflict and coordination in supply chain based on electronic market. Chin Manag Sci 2(6):61–69
18. Xizheng Z, Wei L, Renlong Z (2016) Pricing and coordination of dual-channel supply chain based on alternative product competition. Soft Sci 30(3):121–126
19. Matsui K (2017) When should a manufacturer set its direct price and wholesale price in dual-channel supply chains? Eur J Oper Res 258:501–511

Crude Oil-Import Portfolio Optimization Based on Interval Prediction Data

Xiaolei Sun, Jun Hao, and Jianping Li

Abstract The optimization of crude oil-import portfolio is a hot research issue in the field of energy security, which is related to the implementation of national strategy and development of economy. Forecasting the demand of crude oil-import is the basis for portfolio optimization. Therefore, this paper innovatively introduces the decomposition hybrid interval prediction method and proposes a multi-objective programming model so as to provide decision-making support for the formulation of crude oil-import portfolio scheme. Under the constraints of volume, price and risk, the minimum cost and risk of importing crude oil are achieved. Furthermore, by introducing optimization parameters and risk preference factors, and setting different scenarios for numerical simulation, the results show that (1) the decomposition hybrid prediction methods perform better in predicting the import demand of crude oil. Since the prediction accuracy of the decomposition hybrid prediction method is much higher than the single prediction model, in terms of MAPE and RMSE test; (2) NSGA-II algorithm can effectively solve the multi-objectives problem of crude oil-import portfolio.

Keywords Energy security · Country risk · Decomposition hybrid methodology · Interval prediction · Multi-objective programming

---

X. Sun · J. Hao
Institutes of Science and Development, Chinese Academy of Sciences, Beijing, China

School of Public Policy and Management, University of Chinese Academy of Sciences, Beijing, China
e-mail: haojun181@mails.ucas.ac.cn

J. Li (✉)
Institutes of Science and Development, Chinese Academy of Sciences, Beijing, China

School of Economics and Management, University of Chinese Academy of Sciences, Beijing, China
e-mail: ljp@casipm.ac.cn

X. Li, X. Xu (eds.), *Proceedings of the Seventh International Forum on Decision Sciences*, Uncertainty and Operations Research,
https://doi.org/10.1007/978-981-15-5720-0_3

1 Introduction

The optimization of crude oil-import portfolio is a hot research issue in the field of energy security [1]. As an important and strategic industrial raw material, crude oil plays a significant role in promoting the development of economy and carrying out the national strategies. Meanwhile, the supply of crude oil is closely related to national economic, political and military security [2]. Due to the rapid development of industries, more and more crude oil have been consumed, however, the self-sufficiency ability of crude oil is limited, so China needs to import a large amount of crude oil to insure the satisfy of economic development [3]. As reported, China became the world's largest importer of crude oil (over 462 million tons), with an external dependence of 70.9% in 2018 (BP). The higher the external dependence of crude oil, the lower the national energy security [4]. However, the major countries of China's crude oil-import are concentrated in the volatile regions, such as Middle East and Africa. More than 90% of crude oil transports to China through long-distance maritime system, which will face various risks such as pirate attacks, geographical environment and climate factors. In front of such problems, it is necessary to conduct in-depth analyze and research on the optimization of crude oil import portfolio so as to actively respond to and alleviate national energy security issues.

2 Mathematical Model

2.1 Problem Statement

Based on forecasting data of crude oil demand, this paper studies the optimization of crude oil-import portfolio with cost, risk and resource constraints. In the whole process of crude oil import, it mainly involves procurement and transportation stage. The procurement process requires decision makers to select suitable exporting countries from a number of alternatives and determine the quantity of imported crude oil. The transportation phase determines the transportation risks of crude oil imports, which vary with transportation routes. The crude oil export price P varies with the quality of crude oil and transportation distance of each exporting country to China. Meanwhile, the export volume of crude oil E varies by the different capacity of the crude oil production and the domestic demand level. In addition, country risk RC can vary with political, economic and financial risks of crude oil exporting countries. Therefore, the key point in this paper is to select a set of proper crude oil exporting countries which meet the following three objectives: First, the total exporting volume of crude oil meets the national energy demand; Second, the total importing cost of crude oil is the minimize; Third, the total importing risk of crude oil is the lowest under the condition of limited export of crude oil.

Table 1 Mathematical symbols involved in the optimal model

Symbol	Description
n	The number of crude oil exporting countries that can be selected
D	Quantity of crude oil import demand
E_i	The largest crude oil export volume of country i
P_i	CIF price of crude oil imported from country i
l_{ij}	Driving distance from country i to j
b_{ij}	The number of key nodes between countries i to j
rc_i	Country risk of the ith crude oil exporting country
rt_{ij}	The transportation risk from ith country to jth
x_i	The volume of crude oil imported from country ith

Note: CIF: cost, insurance, freight as included in a price

2.2 *Optimization Model*

The formulation of the crude oil-import portfolio optimization scheme is a NP-hard problem, and a series of influencing factors including cost, risk and volume need to be considered in the process of portfolio optimization. According to the actual crude oil-import problem, an oil-import portfolio optimization model is established with the minimum import cost and the lowest risk as the objective functions. The parameters and variables involved in this paper are shown in Table 1.

$$f_{\cos t} = \sum_{i=1}^{n} p_i * x_i \tag{1}$$

$$f_{\text{risk}} = w * \sum_{i=1}^{n} rc_i * x_i + (1 - w) * \sum_{i=1}^{n} rt_i * x_i \tag{2}$$

$$rc_i = \log\left(100 - icrg_i\right)/10 \tag{3}$$

$$rt_{ij} = \log l_{ij} * \log b_{ij} \tag{4}$$

$$\sum_{i=1}^{n} x_i \geq D \tag{5}$$

$$0 \leq x_i \leq E_i \tag{6}$$

3 Decomposition Hybrid Interval Prediction Method

Due to the complexity of crude oil import demand, the "decomposition hybrid" strategy is introduced [5–8]. According to the principle of "decomposition hybrid", it first needs to introduce a specific decomposition process to formulate DHIPM (abbreviation of Decomposition hybrid interval prediction method) for crude oil import demand.

3.1 *Ensemble Empirical Mode Decomposition*

The EEMD method involves four steps [9]:

Step 1: adding a Gaussian white noise sequence with a small relative root mean square $n_m(t)$ to the original time series $x(t)$;

Step 2: decomposing time series $x_m(t)$ into k IMF components $c_{im}(i = 1, 2, \cdots, k)$ using EMD method [10];

Step 3: adding different white noise sequences with equal root mean squares for each decomposition, repeating steps (1) and (2), so that n sets of IMF components can be obtained;

Step 4: calculating the mean of the IMF components of the n groups, and using the mean of the IMF $c_i = \sum_{m=1}^{n} c_{i,m}/n$ as the final decomposition result of the EEMD method.

3.2 *Extreme Learning Machine*

The ELM (abbreviation of Extreme Learning Machine) is a simple and an efficient algorithm that does not require tuning parameters and has extremely fast learning speeds [11]. The network of ELM training model is a single hidden layer feed forward neural network structure. The ELM algorithm randomly generates the threshold of the hidden layer neuron and the connection weight between the input layer and the hidden layer. When training with the ELM algorithm, it only needs to set the number of hidden layer neurons to obtain a unique optimal solution and there is not necessary to artificially adjust the parameters [12].

4 Experiment Research

4.1 Data Description

This paper selects 27 crude oil exporting countries for empirical analysis. In the past 5 years, more than 90% of crude oil in China has been imported from these countries, which means they can effectively characterize the actual situation of China's crude oil imports. Moreover, these countries are scattered throughout the regions worldwide, such as Asia Pacific, Eurasia, Middle East, Oceania, South America and Africa (East, Southern, North and West). The crude oil CIF price of each crude oil exporting country is represented by the ratio of annual import volume to total import volume. Country risk is obtained by firstly accumulating ICRG's monthly risk and then averaging them to the annual. The largest export volume of crude oil countries comes from BP World Energy Statistical Yearbook; the node and route distance come from BLM-Shipping. The data sources are shown in Table 2.

4.2 Results Analysis

4.2.1 Forecasting Analysis

Figure 1 shows the prediction accuracy criterions of three different prediction methods. EEMD-ELM-ELM and EEMD-ELM-SA perform better than ELM in the prediction precision (MAPE&RMSE), and EEMD-ELM-SA achieves a higher accuracy than EEMD-ELM-ELM. This paper performs a 12-step rolling forward prediction based on the EEMD-EML-SA method. Through this method, the import demand volume of crude oil for each month in 2019 can be predicted, and then the prediction interval at the 95% confidence level can be calculated, which are shown in Table 3.

Table 2 Sources of basic data for crude oil imports

Parameter	Data sources
CIF price	International Trade Center http://www.trademap.org/Country_SelProduct_TS.aspx
Country risk comprehensive index	International Country Risk Guide, ICRG http://www.prsgroup.com/
Crude oil production	BP World Energy Statistical Yearbook https://www.bp.com/en/global/corporate/energy-economics/statistical-review-of-world-energy.html
Nodes and route distance	BLM-Shipping

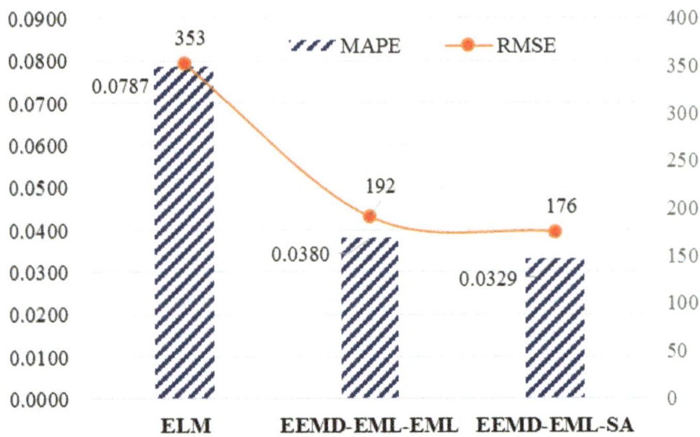

Fig. 1 MAPE and RMSE of different prediction method

Table 3 Prediction interval of each month using the EEMD-EML-SA method

Month	Predictive value	Prediction interval (95%)	
		Lower bound	Upper bound
Jan-2019	4139	3745	4628
Feb-2019	4110	3658	4586
Mar-2019	4013	3469	4658
Apr-2019	4096	3716	4543
May-2019	4071	3686	4602
Jun-2019	4150	3723	4655
Jul-2019	4157	3760	4613
Aug-2019	4150	3750	4609
Sep-2019	4152	3823	4592
Oct-2019	4165	3876	4499
Nov-2019	4142	3758	4512
Dec-2019	4154	3854	4500
Total	49,499	44,818	54,997

4.2.2 Oil-Import Portfolio

In this paper, we set target optimization parameter 0.2, and use the NSGA-II algorithm to solve the multi-objective problem. In the NSGA-II algorithm, setting Pareto Fraction = 0.50, Population = 100, Generations = 300 to get the Pareto front in three different scenarios, as shown in Fig. 2. The Pareto front shows that NSGA-II can effectively solve the multi-objectives problem of crude oil-import portfolio. The optimal import portfolio optimization scheme is shown in Table 4.

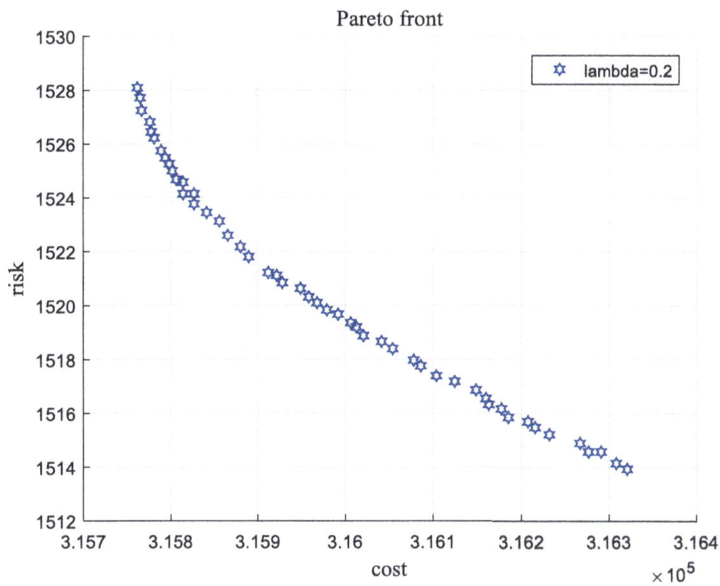

Fig. 2 Pareto front in three different scenarios

Table 4 Optimization scheme of crude oil import portfolio in three different scenarios

Country	Volume	Country	Volume
Angola	22	Nigeria	22
Argentina	22	Norway	2
Australia	19	Oman	35
Brazil	24	Qatar	22
Congo	18	Russian	28
Equatorial Guinea	8	Saudi Arabia	22
Gabon	9	Sudan	8
Indonesia	24	Thailand	14
Iran	19	UAE	25
Iraq	22	UK	22
Kazakhstan	22	Venezuela	24
Kuwait	22	Viet Nam	15
Libya	31	Yemen	9
Malaysia	23	Total	530

Acknowledgements This work was supported by National Natural Science Foundation of China (No. 71771206 and 71425002) and President's Youth Foundation of the Institutes of Science and Development, CAS (Y7X111Q01).

References

1. Wang J, Sun X, Li J, Chen J, Liu C (2018a) Has China's oil-import portfolio been optimized from 2005 to 2014? A perspective of cost-risk tradeoff. Comput Ind Eng 126:451–464
2. Augutis J, Krikštolaitis R, Martišauskas L, Pečiulytė S, Žutautaitė I (2017) Integrated energy security assessment. Energy 138:890–901
3. Sun W, Xu Y (2017) Research on China's energy supply and demand using an improved Grey-Markov chain model based on wavelet transform. Energy 118:969–984
4. Bompard E, Carpignano A, Erriquez M, Grosso D, Pession M, Profumo F (2017) National energy security assessment in a geopolitical perspective. Energy 130:144–154
5. Yu L, Zhao Y, Tang L (2014) A compressed sensing based AI learning paradigm for crude oil price forecasting. Energy Econ 46:236–245
6. Montgomery JM, Hollenbach FM, Ward MD (2015) Calibrating ensemble forecasting models with sparse data in the social sciences. Int J Forecast 31:930–942
7. Wang S, Yu L, Tang L, Wang S (2011) A novel seasonal decomposition based least squares support vector regression ensemble learning approach for hydropower consumption forecasting in China. Energy 36:6542–6554
8. Yu L, Wang S, Lai KK (2008) Forecasting crude oil price with an EMD-based neural network ensemble learning paradigm. Energy Econ 30:2623–2635
9. Li L, Qu X, Zhang J, Li H, Ran B (2018) Travel time prediction for highway network based on the ensemble empirical mode decomposition and random vector functional link network. Appl Soft Comput 73:921–932
10. Liang X, Wu Z, Yang M, Wang S (2020) Air passenger demand forecasting based on a dual decomposition strategy and fuzzy time series model. Chin J Manage Sci. https://doi.org/10.16381/j.cnki.issn1003-207x.2019.1100 (In Chinese)
11. Huang G-B, Zhu Q-Y, Siew C-K (2006) Extreme learning machine: theory and applications. Neurocomputing 70:489–501
12. Hao J, Sun X, Feng Q (2020) A novel ensemble approach for the forecasting of energy demand based on the artificial bee colony algorithm. Energies 13:550. https://doi.org/10.3390/en13030550

Portfolio Optimization of Material Purchasing Considering Supply Risk

Jun Hao, Jianping Li, Dengsheng Wu, and Xiaolei Sun

Abstract In order to better cope with the problem of material procurement, this paper establishes a multi-objective optimization model in a systematic analysis framework for material procurement considering supply risk. This paper firstly combs and identifies the influencing factors of supply risk, and constructs a supply risk evaluation system from the dimensions of quality, price, delivery, service and technology. Secondly, based on the linguistic scale and fuzzy theory, this paper measures the supply risk of the candidate suppliers, and estimates the relevant parameters of the multi-objective optimization model by using the triangular fuzzy numbers. In addition, traditional intelligent algorithms are easily falling into a local optimal solution when solving programming problems. Through numerical simulation experiments, it is verified that the optimization model established in this paper can effectively simulate the operation of the enterprise in actual business. At the same time, the proposed model is feasible and useful for the selection of candidate suppliers and the portfolio optimization of material procurement.

Keywords Multi-objective optimization · Supply risk · Material procurement · NSGA-II algorithm

---

J. Hao · D. Wu · X. Sun (✉)
Institutes of Science and Development, Chinese Academy of Sciences, Beijing, China

School of Public Policy and Management, University of Chinese Academy of Sciences, Beijing, China
e-mail: haojun181@mails.ucas.ac.cn; wds@casisd.cn

J. Li
Institutes of Science and Development, Chinese Academy of Sciences, Beijing, China

School of Economics and Management, University of Chinese Academy of Sciences, Beijing, China
e-mail: ljp@casipm.ac.cn

X. Li, X. Xu (eds.), *Proceedings of the Seventh International Forum on Decision Sciences*, Uncertainty and Operations Research,
https://doi.org/10.1007/978-981-15-5720-0_4

1 Introduction

One of the modern enterprise's challenges is the increase of the number and competitiveness of competitors operating in the same market and providing common types of products and services [1]. A variety of options has spurred customers to seek products with high quality, low cost, short time delivery and tailored service [2]. In this context, enterprises have to satisfy such challenging requirements and improve products and services continuously while remaining efficient in the supply chain. In a sense, competition between modern companies usually depends on supply chain efficiency. The manufacturing companies will focus on their core business and outsource the general operations to upstream and downstream companies, thereby enhancing their competitive advantage [3]. Via maximizing the overall benefits of the supply chain, the competitive advantage of the enterprise can be gained, such as Apple and Toyota. Material procurement is one of the most critical aspects in supply chain management of enterprises. As the starting point of the manufacturing enterprise's production and operation activities, material procurement provides raw materials, auxiliary materials and equipment accessories for the enterprise's manufacturing activities [4]. The quality and price of purchased materials will directly affect that of the final products, and will determine whether the enterprise can attract the terminal customers or not [5, 6]. Therefore, it is of great significance to formulate a reasonable procurement scheme from the perspective of the system, which is effective for enterprises to reduce procurement costs, to increase management flexibility, and to improve the core competitiveness. Besides, how to choose proper suppliers and allocate orders is critical for manufacturing enterprises to reduce supply risks and ensure the realization of production and operation activities.

2 Mathematical Model

2.1 Problem Statement

In the production and operation activities of manufacturing enterprises, the links between enterprises are much closer than ever before due to the continuous reinforcement of specialized division of labor and refined operations. For the same reason, it makes products have more advantage in technology and cost, which means cost-effective. In this context, enterprises will purchase raw materials for processing and production from different suppliers to meet the demand of production operations, so as to maximize the comprehensive benefits. To this end, this paper focuses on the optimal allocation scheme of material procurement considering cost, risk and resource constraints from the perspective of manufacturing enterprises. It is necessary to consider purchasing costs, supply risks, and resource constraints when purchasing materials and selecting suppliers. The manufacturing enterprise has multiple raw material candidate suppliers, and the price and quantity of raw

Table 1 Mathematical symbols involved in the optimal model

Variable type	Notation	Description
Indicator variable	i	Indicates the number of suppliers
	j	Indicates the types of raw material
Decision variables	x_{ij}	Indicates the quantity of *j* raw material purchased from *i* supplier
Parameters	c_{ij}	Indicates the price of the *i* supplier's *j* product
	C_0	Indicates the fixed costs incurred in the procurement process
	r_i	Indicates the supply risk of *i* supplier
	Q_{ij}	Indicates the maximum volume of *j* raw material that *i* suppliers can offer
	$Q_{require}$	Indicates the minimum demand of the manufacturing enterprise

materials provided by each supplier are different, which means that the manufacturing enterprise has multiple procurement portfolio schemes. In addition, different candidate suppliers have different supply risks, which means proper suppliers should be selected to reduce the procurement risks. Therefore, manufacturers need to choose the right suppliers and allocate reasonable orders to guarantee the interests of enterprise. The key issue of this paper is how to select the right supplier and to determine an optimal scheme of material procurement to ensure the lowest overall risk and minimize the procurement cost while satisfying the resource limit.

2.2 Optimization Model

This paper selects the minimum procurement cost and the lowest supply risk as the objectives of decision-making, and builds a multi-objective optimization model of material procurement. In this paper, two important but conflicting objective functions, namely cost and risk, are constructed. Mathematical symbols involved in the optimal model are shown in Table 1.

$$\min C = \sum_{i=1}^{m} \sum_{j=1}^{n} c_{ij} * x_{ij} + C_0 \tag{1}$$

$$\min R = \sum_{i=1}^{m} \sum_{j=1}^{n} r_{ij} * x_{ij} / \left(\sum_{i=1}^{m} \sum_{j=1}^{n} x_{ij} \right) \tag{2}$$

$$\sum_{i=1}^{m} \sum_{j=1}^{n} y_{ij} \leq 1 \tag{3}$$

$$x_{ij} \leq Q_{ij} \tag{4}$$

$$\sum_{i=1}^{m}\sum_{j=1}^{n} x_{ij} \geq Q_{require} \quad (5)$$

$$x_{ij} \geq 0 \quad (6)$$

3 Supply Risk Evaluation

3.1 Evaluation Indicator

Risk factors need to be identified to have an effective assessment of the supply risk of suppliers [7]. Through literature review and using bibliometric method, this paper sorts out five types of risk: quality risk (Q), price risk (P), delivery risk (D), service risk (S) and technical risk (T) and the corresponding influencing factors of each risk are screened out [8–13]. The specific index system in supply risk assessment is shown in Table 2.

Table 2 Supply risk assessment index system

Evaluation system	Risk type	Influencing factor
Supply risk index system	Quality risk (*Q*)	Product quality
		Product inspection
		Internal review
	Price risk (*P*)	Deal price
		Purchase cost
		Financial status
		Cost control
	Delivery risk (*D*)	Punctual delivery
		Production capacity
		Delivery flexibility
		Delivery integrity
	Service risk (*S*)	Order lead time
		Internal communication
		Inventory level
		After sales service
	Technical risk (*T*)	R&D investment
		Experiment apparatus
		Designing ability

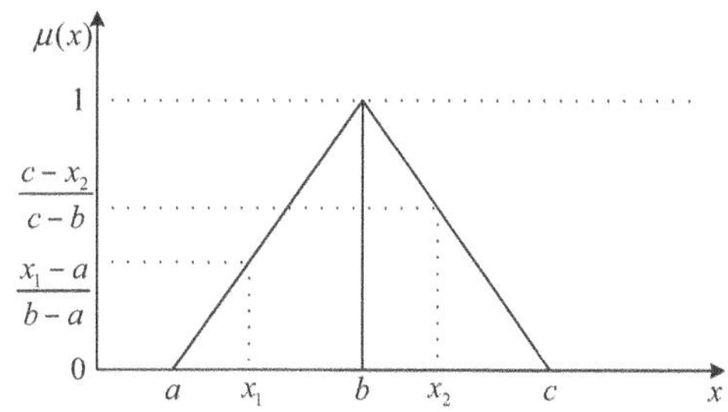

Fig. 1 Triangle fuzzy number

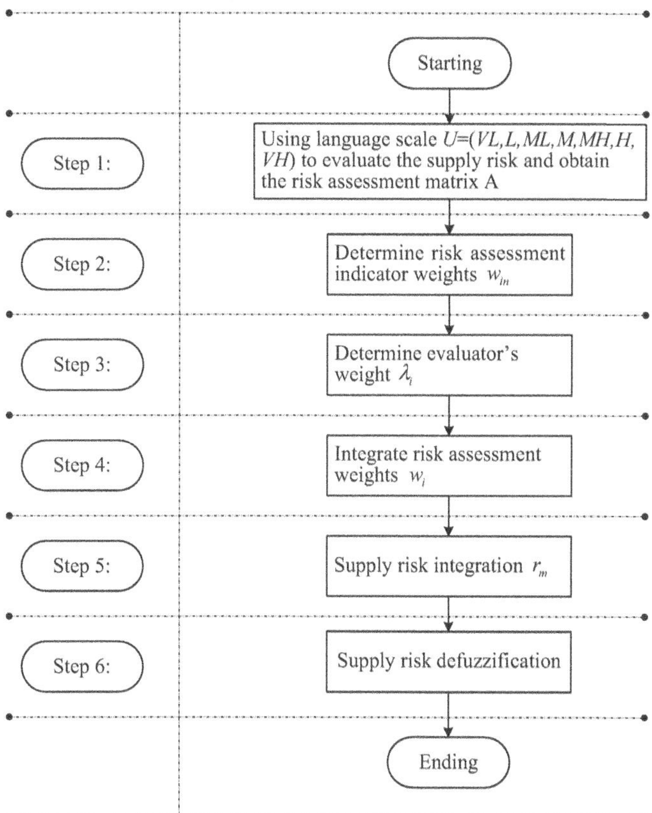

Fig. 2 Supply risk assessment process

3.2 *Process of Evaluation*

The supply risk of supplier is evaluated using language scale and triangular fuzzy number, which are shown in Fig. 1. And then the process of supply risk evaluation is introduced in Fig. 2. Assuming that there are n experts in the risk evaluation team and m candidate suppliers in the supply chain system. Each candidate supplier is evaluated separately by the risk evaluation team.

4 Experimental Analysis

4.1 Data Description

Ten candidate suppliers are considered for the experimental analysis in this paper. The prices and supply risks of materials offered by different suppliers vary due to the differences in product quality, production capacity and technical level. To this end, three experts are invited to form a risk evaluation team to evaluate the supply risk of the candidate suppliers by utilizing the linguistic scale and the triangular fuzzy number. Risk assessment matrix of ten candidate suppliers is shown in Table 3.The weights of risk factors and experts are demonstrated in Tables 4 and 5, respectively. The evaluation results of the supply risks of the candidate suppliers are presented in Table 6. The price and the quantity of materials supplied by the candidate suppliers and the minimum and maximum quantity of the materials purchased by the enterprises are shown in Table 7. In order to solve the multi-objective optimization model of material procurement considering supply risk and analyze the effect of NSGA-II algorithm, we use MATLAB R2016a for encoding.

4.2 Optimal Results

The input parameters are set as follows: the coefficient of the optimal Pareto frontier is 0.5, the population size is 100, and the maximum evolution number is 1000, the deviation of fitness function value is 10^{-100}, the number of iterations to terminate evolution is 1000. After determining the input data, running NSGA-II algorithm on MATLAB R2016a to obtain the Pareto frontier, which is shown in Fig. 3.

The solutions of optimization problem are evenly distributed on the Pareto frontier (shown in Fig. 3), reflecting that the NSGA-II algorithm with elite strategy is effective in solving such optimization problem. At the same time, there is a significant negative correlation between cost and risk. Therefore, it is impossible to find an optimal solution while achieving the minimum cost and the lowest risk objectives, which means that when the risk is reduced, the cost will increase, and vice versa.

Table 3 Risk assessment matrix

Risk factors	Enterprise 1			Enterprise 2			Enterprise 3			Enterprise 4			Enterprise 5		
	E1	**E2**	**E3**	**E1**	**E2**	**E3**	**E1**	**E2**	**E3**	**E1**	**E2**	**E3**	**E1**	**E2**	**E3**
Q	VH	MH	H	MH	M	L	MH	ML	MH	M	VH	MH	H	L	H
P	M	H	M	H	H	ML	H	L	H	H	M	H	M	ML	M
D	M	H	ML	M	H	M	H	ML	M	H	M	H	ML	ML	MH
S	MH	M	M	M	L	M	MH	ML	M	L	MH	M	M	H	ML
T	M	M	L	M	M	H	M	H	M	M	M	M	H	MH	M
Risk factors	**Enterprise 6**			**Enterprise 7**			**Enterprise 8**			**Enterprise 9**			**Enterprise 10**		
	E1	**E2**	**E3**	**E1**	**E2**	**E3**	**E1**	**E2**	**E3**	**E1**	**E2**	**E3**	**E1**	**E2**	**E3**
Q	VH	M	ML	M	MH	L	MH	VH	MH	MH	M	L	H	L	H
P	M	H	L	H	H	ML	H	M	H	H	H	ML	M	ML	M
D	M	H	ML	H	H	M	H	M	H	H	H	ML	ML	ML	MH
S	MH	L	ML	L	MH	M	MH	MH	M	M	L	H	M	H	ML
T	M	M	H	M	M	H	M	M	M	M	M	MH	H	MH	M

Note: VL = (0,0,1), L = (0,1,3), ML = (1,3,5), M = (3,5,7), H = (7,9,10), VH = (9,10,10)

Table 4 Weights of risk factors

Risk factors	EV1	EV2	EV3
Q	H	M	H
P	M	MH	H
D	VH	H	H
S	MH	H	MH
T	H	H	MH

Table 5 The weight of the evaluator

Expert	Experience	Weight
EV1	Good	(10,20,20)
EV2	Medium	(5,10,5)
EV3	Medium	(5,10,5)

Table 6 Supply risk assessment results

Enterprise	a	b	c	DF	Score
Supplier 1	10,210	77,520	178,610	88,780	0.4726
Supplier 2	9170	72,560	170,940	84223.333	0.3459
Supplier 3	10,310	79,200	178,860	89456.667	0.5544
Supplier 4	11,940	87,440	195,860	98413.333	0.9113
Supplier 5	9100	73,040	170,770	84303.333	0.3491
Supplier 6	9890	75,760	174,140	86596.667	0.4404
Supplier 7	11,200	83,360	188,120	94226.667	0.7445
Supplier 8	12,420	90,000	199,500	100,640	1.0000
Supplier 9	10,310	78,160	176,670	88,380	0.5115
Supplier 10	7280	62,160	157,190	75543.333	0.0000

Table 7 Material supply and procurement data

Enterprise	Price	Supply/purchase volume
Supplier 1	(1,6,8)	(450,650,800)
Supplier 2	(2,5,9)	(550,800,950)
Supplier 3	(2,4,7)	(100,350,400)
Supplier 4	(4,5,10)	(200,300,400)
Supplier 5	(3,4,10)	(350,600,800)
Supplier 6	(2,4,9)	(500,800,950)
Supplier 7	(4,7,8)	(100,200,500)
Supplier 8	(2,5,9)	(450,600,900)
Supplier 9	(2,4,8)	(50,200,400)
Supplier 10	(1,5,7)	(400,550,600)
Minimum	—	(2500,3000,3500)
Maximum	—	(4500,5000,5500)

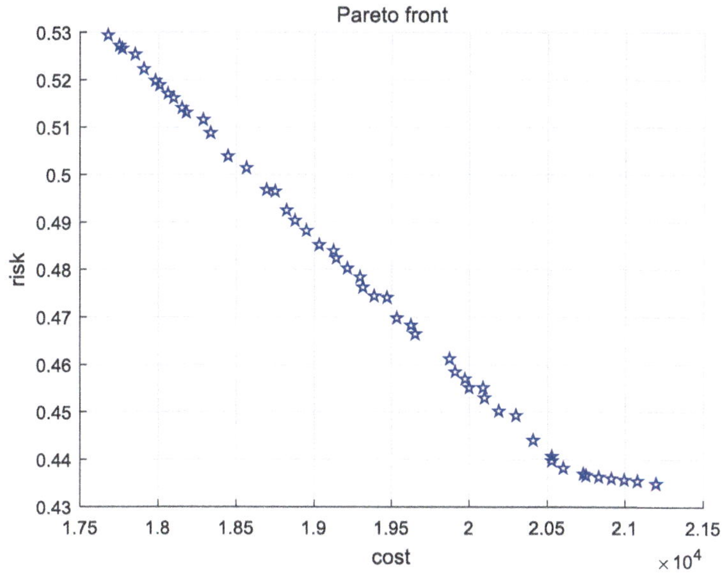

Fig. 3 Pareto frontier of the optimization results

Acknowledgements This work was supported by National Natural Science Foundation of China (No. 71771206, 71425002, and 71571179) and President's Youth Foundation of the Institutes of Science and Development, CAS (Y7X111Q01).

References

1. Cunha AL, Santos MO, Morabito R, Barbosa-Póvoa A (2018) An integrated approach for production lot sizing and raw material purchasing. Eur J Oper Res 269:923–938
2. Lee AHI, Kang H-Y, Lai C-M, Hong W-Y (2013) An integrated model for lot sizing with supplier selection and quantity discounts. Appl Math Model 37:4733–4746
3. Srai JS, Lorentz H (2019) Developing design principles for the digitalisation of purchasing and supply management. J Purch Supply Manag 25:78–98
4. Xu X, Hao J, Deng Y, Wang Y (2017) Design optimization of resource combination for collaborative logistics network under uncertainty. Appl Soft Comput 560(7):684–691
5. Kellner F, Lienland B, Utz S (2019) An a posteriori decision support methodology for solving the multi-criteria supplier selection problem. Eur J Oper Res 272:505–522
6. Xu X, Sun Y (2020) Optimization of task-route matching based on multi-hub and spoke collaborative logistics network. Chin J Manage Sci 27(9):175–182 (In Chinese)
7. Li J, Sun X, Wang F, Wu D (2014a) Risk integration and optimization of oil-importing maritime system: a multi-objective programming approach. Ann Oper Res 234:57–76
8. Kolotzek C, Helbig C, Thorenz A, Reller A, Tuma A (2018) A company-oriented model for the assessment of raw material supply risks, environmental impact and social implications. J Clean Prod 176:566–580
9. Kumar A, Jain V, Kumar S (2014) A comprehensive environment friendly approach for supplier selection. Omega Int J Manag Sci 42:109–123

10. Vilko JPP, Hallikas JM (2012) Risk assessment in multimodal supply chains. Int J Prod Econ 140:586–595
11. Behzadi G, O'Sullivan MJ, Olsen TL, Zhang A (2018) Agribusiness supply chain risk management: a review of quantitative decision models. Omega 79:21–42
12. Achzet B, Helbig C (2013) How to evaluate raw material supply risks—an overview. Resour Policy 38:435–447
13. Liao H, Xu Z, Zeng X-J (2015) Hesitant fuzzy linguistic VIKOR method and its application in qualitative multiple criteria decision making. IEEE Trans Fuzzy Syst 23:1343–1355

Coordination via Revenue and Technology-Cost Sharing in a Two-Supplier and One-Manufacturer Supply Chain System

César Augusto Rodríguez Gallegos, Qingguo Bai, and Mingyuan Chen

Abstract Access to new technologies is a key factor of competitive advantage for many supply chains. In this paper, we explore the impact of technology investment on supply chain coordination. To be specific, we analytically investigate the optimal pricing and technology investment decisions in a system consisting of two complementary suppliers and one manufacturer. On one hand, the suppliers are required to invest in new technologies in order to participate in the supply chain negotiations. On the other hand, the manufacturer acts as the Stackelberg leader, who offers a wholesale price (WS) contract to the suppliers. We compare both the decentralized and centralized settings, and show that if the supply chain members decide to cooperate and coordinate the system, they could increase the overall expected profit by at least 1/3 compared to the non-cooperative scenario. We then find that the cost-revenue sharing (CR) contract is capable of coordinating the two-supplier one-manufacturer supply chain. Interestingly, the CR contract also offers a win-win profit scenario to all parties of the negotiation.

Keywords Supply chain management · Technology investment · Cost and revenue sharing contract · Coordination · Win-win condition

---

C. A. R. Gallegos · M. Chen (✉)
Department of Mechanical and Industrial Engineering, Concordia University, Montreal, QC, Canada
e-mail: ce_r@encs.concordia.ca; mychen@encs.concordia.ca

Q. Bai
Institute of Operations Research, School of Management, Qufu Normal University, Rizhao, China
e-mail: hustbaiqg@alumni.hust.edu.cn

X. Li, X. Xu (eds.), *Proceedings of the Seventh International Forum on Decision Sciences*, Uncertainty and Operations Research,
https://doi.org/10.1007/978-981-15-5720-0_5

1 Introduction

In this globalized economy, the fierce competence in the market, added to the increasingly exigences from customers demanding products with more added value and lower prices, obligate organizations to be always at the vanguard to maintain their positioning in the market. One critical ingredient for maintaining the competitive advantage is the acquisition and implementation of new technologies for achieving product enhancement. This is specially the case for high-tech industries in sectors like aerospace, pharmaceutic and telecommunication, to name but a few. But investment in new technologies is a challenging decision due to its complexity for implementation and the cost involved. Therefore, it is of utmost importance to understand the effect of new technologies on the performance of the acquiring company and on its supply chain.

Although the existence of an ample number of empirical studies that describe the relation between $\mathcal{SC}$ performance and new technologies investment, analytical research on this matter is quite scarce. In this paper, our aim is to model and analyze the impact of new technologies investment on the $\mathcal{SC}$ members performance and to demonstrate how it can lead to the coordination of the $\mathcal{SC}$. Furthermore, we step further from the simple models previously investigated and propose the study of more complex scenarios closer to real industry environments.

2 Literature Review

2.1 Impact of Technology Investment in the Supply Chain

Knowledge stands a step further from information as the accumulation of learning, expertise and know-how useful for the problem solving process but that at the same time poses more difficulties when being managed and shared [1]. It highlighted in [2] that the $\mathcal{SC}$ knowledge consists of four basic components, one of them been the technological component. This latter is the subject of our research. Global competition makes the investment in new technologies crucial for the success of any firm [3]. Due to the increasingly technological complexity and shortened life-cycle of products, organizations are compelled to continually invest in new technologies to maintain their positioning in the market [4]. Technology is seen as a key element for competitive advantage [5] that can lead companies to access wider markets, sales increment, cost reduction, brand enhancement, to name but a few [3, 6]. And its benefits are not limited only to the owner of the technology but they can be translated into the performance improvement of the $\mathcal{SC}$ as a whole [7]. On the other hand, management of new technologies can result challenging because of its complexity and high cost [4, 8], specially for high-tech industries [2]. Firms can access new technologies either through its internal development in their R&D departments [9], or thanks to its acquisition from external sources

[10]. Nowadays, an increasingly number of companies are relying less on their internal resources, and opting to acquire high-tech components from suppliers who invest on innovation [11]. Examples of new technologies in the $\mathcal{SC}$ can be quite diverse. It can refer to any one or the combination of tangible aspects like materials, tools, equipment, machinery; or intangible elements like skills, applied knowledge, methods, intellectual property, among others [5, 6, 12]. An example of analytical research regarding the impact of new technologies on $\mathcal{SC}$ performance can be found in the work of [13]. They study how the investment in new sustainable green technologies can contribute to the carbon emission reduction in a $\mathcal{SC}$. Furthermore, they use contract coordination to determine the necessary conditions to maximize the $\mathcal{SC}$ profit. The authors conceptualize and model the development process of new products between two firms with different R&D capabilities and study how revenue, technological innovation and investment sharing can benefit the overall performance of the $\mathcal{SC}$ system in [4]. In their research the authors establish the conditions at which any of the sharing mechanisms proposed would be of interest for the firms.

2.2 *Supply Chain Coordination*

The field of $\mathcal{SC}$ management has widely examined the $\mathcal{SC}$ coordination. The reader is referred to [14] for a detailed review on this topic. $\mathcal{SC}$ contracts is one of the main mechanisms studied in the literature for achieving coordination. Among these contracts, the cost sharing contract and the cost and revenue sharing contract are well-known and extensively adopted in many organizations. A $\mathcal{SC}$ formed by one retailer and two competing suppliers is studied and how collaborative quality improvement can be of benefit for all the parties is analyzed in [15]. The authors propose different coordination mechanisms to incentive the retailer and suppliers to share the cost on quality investment. Their results show that with the cost-sharing contract the $\mathcal{SC}$ can attain higher quality improvement levels and higher profits compared to the wholesale price contract. The benefit of cost sharing contracts over a supplier-manufacturer $\mathcal{SC}$ negotiation committed towards green initiatives is explored in [16]. Utilizing a game theoretic approach, the authors identify how the proposed contract can influence the product greening levels and profits of the $\mathcal{SC}$ participants. They further prove that implementation of the cost sharing contract results in higher profits for both parties and for the $\mathcal{SC}$ as a whole. The cost and revenue sharing contract is another contract extensively adopted in industry. examine A sustainable $\mathcal{SC}$ formed by one manufacturer and one retailer with deteriorating items and under carbon cap-and-trade regulation is examined in [13]. The authors propose two coordination mechanisms in their research, the revenue and promotional cost-sharing contract and the two-part tariff contract. They demonstrate that both contracts are capable to reach coordination and they determine the win-win conditions for the $\mathcal{SC}$ members. Moreover, the authors prove that the two-part tariff contract is more robust compared to the revenue and promotional cost-sharing contract. A revenue and cost sharing contract as a mechanism to enhance the remanufacturer-retailer $\mathcal{SC}$ is analyzed in [17]. In this study the author investigates the scenario when the retailer is the Stackelberg leader of the negotiation, and the one when the leader is the remanufacturer. Results from the numerical example show that in both cases the proposed contract can achieve a higher expected profit for the two parties.

3 Base Models

3.1 Supply Chain Model

We consider in this paper a supply chain ($\mathcal{SC}$) consisting of two complementary suppliers ($\mathcal{S}_i$, where i=1,2) who sell a component (i) to one original equipment manufacturer (OEM) that uses them to assembly the final product to be sold in the market. It is assumed that both suppliers need to acquire certain level of technology $0 < \alpha_i < 1$ in order to participate in the $\mathcal{SC}$ negotiation. This technology could be required by the suppliers for meeting manufacturing regulations [13], enhance quality level [4, 15], to name but a few. The new technology cost is denoted by η_i and it is considered to be a one-off investment [18]. For analytical simplicity, we assume that the investment on technology does not affect the cost structure of the system. Similar assumptions can be found in the work of [15] and [18]. After receiving the costumer's order, the $\mathcal{OEM}$ sends it to the $\mathcal{S}_i$ that follow a make-to-order (MTO) manufacturing policy. The unit production cost and unit wholesale price for component (i) are c_i and w_i respectively. The unit retail price of the final product is p. In addition, it is established that $p > w_1 + w_2$ and $w_i > c_i$. These inequalities assure the non-negative profit for the parties. It is further considered that the market demand $D(p, \alpha_1, \alpha_2, \xi)$ is stochastic, price dependent [15, 16], and technology dependent [4]. It is formulated as $D(p, \alpha_1, \alpha_2, \xi) = d - \theta p + \beta_1\alpha_1 + \beta_2\alpha_2 + \xi$, where $d > 0$ is the base demand, $\theta > 0$, $\beta_1 > 0$ and $\beta_2 > 0$ are the demand sensitivity coefficient to p, to α_1 and to α_2 respectively, and ξ is the demand uncertainty with $\mathbb{E}[\xi] = 0$ and $\text{Var}[\xi] = \sigma^2$. Similar to the work of [18], we consider that all information is symmetric between the members, and that the market can accurately perceive the technology enhancement in the final product. Finally, for the negotiation the $\mathcal{OEM}$ acts as the leader while $\mathcal{S}_i$ are the followers.

3.2 Profit Objective Functions

With the base supply chain model established, we now proceed to formulate the profit functions for each participant of the $\mathcal{SC}$. First, Eqs. 1 and 2 present the profit and expected profit functions for the $\mathcal{OEM}$:

$$\Pi^{WS}_{\mathcal{OEM}}(p) = (p - w_1 - w_2)(d - \theta p + \beta_1\alpha_1 + \beta_2\alpha_2 + \xi). \tag{1}$$

$$\mathbb{E}_\xi[\Pi^{WS}_{\mathcal{OEM}}(p)] = (p - w_1 - w_2)(d - \theta p + \beta_1\alpha_1 + \beta_2\alpha_2). \tag{2}$$

Similarly, Eqs. 3 and 4 show the profit and expected profit functions for $\mathcal{S}_i$, (i=1,2), respectively:

$$\Pi^{WS}_{\mathcal{S}_i}(w_i, \alpha_i) = (w_i - c_i)(d - \theta p + \beta_1\alpha_1 + \beta_2\alpha_2 + \xi) - \frac{1}{2}\eta_i\alpha_i^2. \tag{3}$$

$$\mathbb{E}_\xi[\Pi^{WS}_{\mathcal{S}_i}(w_i, \alpha_i)] = (w_i - c_i)(d - \theta p + \beta_1\alpha_1 + \beta_2\alpha_2) - \frac{1}{2}\eta_i\alpha_i^2. \tag{4}$$

Finally, Eq. 5 presents the expected profit function for the $\mathcal{SC}$:

$$\mathbb{E}_\xi[\Pi^{WS}_{\mathcal{SC}}(p, w_1, \alpha_1, w_2, \alpha_2)] = \mathbb{E}_\xi[\Pi^{WS}_{\mathcal{OEM}}(p)] + \mathbb{E}_\xi[\Pi^{WS}_{\mathcal{S}_1}(w_1, \alpha_1)] + \mathbb{E}_\xi[\Pi^{WS}_{\mathcal{S}_2}(w_2, \alpha_2)] \tag{5}$$

4 Equilibrium Analysis

4.1 Optimal Decisions for the Decentralized Supply Chain

In this section we derive the optimal pricing and technology-acquisition decisions of the WS contract by exploring the equilibrium of the negotiation game. Because $\mathcal{S}_i$ $(i = 1, 2)$ are the followers, we first find the optimal values for wholesale price and level of technology.

Proposition 4.1 *The $\mathbb{E}_\xi[\Pi^{WS}_{\mathcal{OEM}}(p)]$ is a strictly concave function of p and the optimal retail price p^{WS*} can be expressed as:*

$$p^{WS*} = \frac{(d + \theta(c_1 + c_2))\left(\theta\eta_1\eta_2 - \beta_2^2\eta_1 - \beta_1^2\eta_2\right) + 4d\theta\eta_1\eta_2}{2\theta\left(3\theta\eta_1\eta_2 - \beta_2^2\eta_1 - \beta_1^2\eta_2\right)}. \tag{6}$$

Proposition 4.1 demonstrates the concavity of $\mathbb{E}_\xi[\Pi^{WS}_{\mathcal{OEM}}(p)]$ and therefore the existence of an unique optimal retail price p^{WS*}.

Proposition 4.2 *The* $\mathbb{E}_\xi[\Pi_{S_i}^{WS}(w_i, \alpha_i)]$ *is a strictly concave function of* w_i *and* α_i *and the optimal wholesale price* w_i^{WS*} *and technology level* α_i^{WS*} *can be expressed as:*

$$w_i^{WS*} = \frac{\eta_i\eta_j\left(d-\theta c_j\right)+c_i\left(5\theta\eta_i\eta_j-2\beta_j^2\eta_i-2\beta_i^2\eta_j\right)}{2\left(3\theta\eta_i\eta_j-\beta_j^2\eta_i-\beta_i^2\eta_j\right)}, \text{ where } i \neq j. \tag{7}$$

$$\alpha_i^{WS*} = \frac{\beta_i\eta_j\left(d-\theta\left(c_i+c_j\right)\right)}{2\left(3\theta\eta_i\eta_j-\beta_j^2\eta_i-\beta_i^2\eta_j\right)}, \text{ where } i \neq j. \tag{8}$$

4.2 Optimal Decisions for the Centralized Supply Chain

As a benchmark, we now assume that both $\mathcal{S}_i$ $(i = 1, 2)$ and the $\mathcal{OEM}$ belong to the same centrally coordinated system. Under this assumption, the profit and expected value of profit for the $\mathcal{SC}$ can be expressed as:

$$\Pi_{\mathcal{SC}}(p, \alpha_1, \alpha_2) = (p-c_1-c_2)(d-\theta p+\beta_1\alpha_1+\beta_2\alpha_2+\xi)-\frac{1}{2}(\eta_1\alpha_1^2+\eta_2\alpha_2^2). \tag{9}$$

$$\mathbb{E}_\xi[\Pi_{\mathcal{SC}}(p, \alpha_1, \alpha_2)] = (p-c_1-c_2)(d-\theta p+\beta_1\alpha_1+\beta_2\alpha_2)-\frac{1}{2}(\eta_1\alpha_1^2+\eta_2\alpha_2^2). \tag{10}$$

We proceed now to derive the optimal pricing and technology-acquisition decisions for the $\mathcal{SC}$ in the centralized scenario.

Proposition 4.3 *The* $\mathbb{E}_\xi[\Pi_{\mathcal{SC}}(p, \alpha_1, \alpha_2)]$ *is a strictly concave function of* p *and* α_i *and the optimal retail price* p^* *and technology level* α_i^* *can be expressed as:*

$$p^* = \frac{d\eta_1\eta_2+(c_1+c_2)\left(\theta\eta_1\eta_2-\beta_2^2\eta_1-\beta_1^2\eta_2\right)}{2\theta\eta_1\eta_2-\beta_2^2\eta_1-\beta_1^2\eta_2}. \tag{11}$$

$$\alpha_i^* = \frac{\beta_i\eta_j\left(d-\theta\left(c_i+c_j\right)\right)}{2\theta\eta_i\eta_j-\beta_j^2\eta_i-\beta_i^2\eta_j}, \text{ where } i \neq j. \tag{12}$$

Proposition 4.3 implies that in the centralized $\mathcal{SC}$, the optimal retail price p^* and technology level α_i^* in the Stackelberg equilibrium uniquely exist.

4.3 Comparison of the Decentralized and Centralized Supply Chain Models

A review of both the decentralized and centralized $\mathcal{SC}$ models lead us to the following interesting observations:

Proposition 4.4 *The comparison of both models show that:*

(a) The decentralized model can not coordinate the supply chain.
(b) If the supply chain members decide to cooperate and reach coordination, they can increase the expected optimal profit of the supply chain at least $1/3$ *compared to the decentralized scenario.*

Proposition 4.4.(b) presents a clear incentive for all members to collaborate in the expectation to reach the $\mathcal{SC}$ coordination. Next section shows a contract designed to coordinate the $\mathcal{SC}$. This contract is tested to verify: (1) its ability to coordinate and reach the maximum expected profit for the $\mathcal{SC}$, and (2) the existence of win-win conditions that will lead to an increment of the profit for all members of the $\mathcal{SC}$.

5 Coordination: Technology-Cost and Revenue Sharing Contract

5.1 Model and Optimal Decisions

For the CR contract it is now assumed that the $\mathcal{OEM}$ is willing to share a fraction of the technology cost paid by $\mathcal{S}_i$, i.e. $\frac{\eta_i(1-\phi_i)}{2}$, while on the other hand $\mathcal{S}_i$ agree to share a fraction of its revenue with the $\mathcal{OEM}$, i.e. $w_i(1-\phi_i)$. Equations 13 and 14 present the profit and expected value of the profit for the $\mathcal{OEM}$, respectively:

$$\Pi^{CR}_{\mathcal{OEM}}(p) = (p - w_1\phi_1 - w_2\phi_2)(d - \theta p + \beta_1\alpha_1 + \beta_2\alpha_2 + \xi) - \frac{1}{2}(\eta_1(1-\phi_1)\alpha_1^2 + \eta_2(1-\phi_2)\alpha_2^2). \tag{13}$$

$$\mathbb{E}_\xi[\Pi^{CR}_{\mathcal{OEM}}(p)] = (p - w_1\phi_1 - w_2\phi_2)(d - \theta p + \beta_1\alpha_1 + \beta_2\alpha_2) - \frac{1}{2}(\eta_1(1-\phi_1)\alpha_1^2 + \eta_2(1-\phi_2)\alpha_2^2). \tag{14}$$

Similarly, Eqs. 15 and 16 show the profit and expected profit functions for $\mathcal{S}_i$, (i=1,2), respectively:

$$\Pi_{\mathcal{S}_i}(w_i, \alpha_i) = (w_i\phi_i - c_i)(d - \theta p + \beta_1\alpha_1 + \beta_2\alpha_2 + \xi) - \frac{1}{2}\eta_i\phi_i\alpha_i^2. \tag{15}$$

$$\mathbb{E}_\xi[\Pi_{\mathcal{S}_i}(w_i, \alpha_i)] = (w_i\phi_i - c_i)(d - \theta p + \beta_1\alpha_1 + \beta_2\alpha_2) - \frac{1}{2}\eta_i\phi_i\alpha_i^2. \tag{16}$$

In order to derive the optimal pricing and technology-acquisition decisions of the CR contract, we proceed to find the optimal values for wholesale price and level of technology.

Proposition 5.1 *For $\mathcal{S}_i$, $(i = 1, 2)$, with a given retail price p, its optimal wholesale price w_i^{CR*}, and optimal level of technology acquired α_i^{CR*} can be expressed as:*

$$w_i^{CR*}|_p = \frac{\eta_i \eta_j \phi_i (d - p\theta) + ci\left(\theta\eta_i\eta_j - \beta_j^2\eta_i - \beta_i^2\eta_j\right)}{\left(\theta\eta_i\eta_j - \beta_j^2\eta_i - \beta_i^2\eta_j\right)\phi_i}, \ where\ i \neq j. \tag{17}$$

$$\alpha_i^{CR*}|_p = \frac{\beta_i \eta_j (d - p\theta)}{\theta\eta_i\eta_j - \beta_j^2\eta_i - \beta_i^2\eta_j}, \ where\ i \neq j. \tag{18}$$

5.2 *Comparison of the CR Contract and Centralized Supply Chain Model*

In order to test if the CR contract of the decentralized model can reach coordination, we set $\alpha_i^{CR*}|_p = \alpha_i^*$ and then from these results determine if $p^{CR*} = p^*$.

Proposition 5.2 *We reach to the following observations:*

(a) The CR contract coordinates the supply chain.
(b) $p^{CR*} = p^*$ and $\alpha_i^{CR*} = \alpha_i^*$.

This means that the CR contract can successfully coordinate the $\mathcal{SC}$. Furthermore, it is proved that $p^{CR*} = p^*$ and $\alpha_i^{CR*} = \alpha_i^*$, meaning that the 3 decision variables of the CR contract can coordinate simultaneously. Now, it is analyzed the win-win conditions of this contract. Comparing the optimal expected profit functions of the OEM and $\mathcal{S}_i$ for both the WS and CR contract lead us to the next interesting finding:

Proposition 5.3 *There exist a feasible solution for ϕ_i that offers a win-win condition for the $\mathcal{OEM}$ and the $\mathcal{S}_i$ in the CR contract.*

6 Conclusions

This paper studies the technology investment strategy in a two echelon supply chain consisting of two complementary suppliers and one manufacturer. By comparing a non-collaborative scenario with wholesale price (WS) contract and a collaborative scenario with cost-revenue sharing (CR) contract, we analyze whether a collaborative technology enhancement initiative is beneficial to all supply chain parties. We demonstrate that if the supply chain members decide to cooperate and coordinate the system, they could increase the overall expected profit by at least 1/3 compared to the non-cooperative scenario. We then find that the CR contract is capable of coordinating the two-supplier one-manufacturer supply chain. Interestingly, the CR contract offers also a win-win profit scenario to all parties of the negotiation.

Acknowledgments The authors are grateful for the partial financial support from the Natural Sciences and Engineering Research Council of Canada (NSERC); the National Natural Science Foundation of China under grant 71771138, the Special Foundation for Taishan Scholars of Shandong Province, China under grant tsqn201812061, the Science and Technology Research Program for Higher Education of Shandong Province, China under grant 2019KJI006; and the Secretary of Higher Education, Science, Technology and Innovation of Ecuador (Senescyt).

References

1. Rowley J (2007) The wisdom hierarchy: representations of the dikw hierarchy. J Inf Sci 33(2):163–180
2. Battistella C, Toni AFD, Pillon R (2016) Inter-organizational technology/knowledge transfer: a framework from critical literature review. J Technol Transf 41(5):1195–1234
3. Kumar S, Luthra S, Haleem A (2015) Benchmarking supply chains by analyzing technology transfer critical barriers using ahp approach. BIJ 22(4):538–558
4. Bhaskaran SR, Krishnan V (2009) Effort, revenue, and cost sharing mechanisms for collaborative new product development. Manag Sci 55(7):1152–1169
5. Reisman A (2005) Transfer of technologies: a cross-disciplinary taxonomy. Omega 33(3):189–202
6. da Silva VL, Kovaleski JL, Pagani RN (2019) Technology transfer in the supply chain oriented to industry 4.0: a literature review. Tech Anal Strat Manag 31(5):546–562
7. Kang P, Jiang W (2011) The evaluation study on knowledge transfer effect of supply chain companies. In: International conference on advances in education and management, pp 440–447
8. Gunsel A (2015) Research on effectiveness of technology transfer from a knowledge based perspective. Procedia Soc Behav Sci 207:777–785
9. Tatikonda MV, Stock GN (2003) Product technology transfer in the upstream supply chain. J Prod Innov Manag 20(6):444–467
10. Brunswicker S, Vanhaverbeke W (2015) Open innovation in small and medium-sized enterprises (smes): External knowledge sourcing strategies and internal organizational facilitators. J Small Bus Manag 53(4):1241–1263
11. Wang J, Shin H (2015) The impact of contracts and competition on upstream innovation in a supply chain. Prod Oper Manag 24(1):134–146
12. Liu S, Fang Z, Shi H, Guo B (2016) Theory of science and technology transfer and applications. Auerbach Publications
13. Bai Q, Chen M, Xu L (2017) Revenue and promotional cost-sharing contract versus two-part tariff contract in coordinating sustainable supply chain systems with deteriorating items. Int J Prod Econ 187:85–101
14. Chan HK, Chan FT (2010) A review of coordination studies in the context of supply chain dynamics. Int J Prod Res 48(10):2793–2819
15. Chakraborty T, Chauhan SS, Ouhimmou M (2019) Cost-sharing mechanism for product quality improvement in a supply chain under competition. Int J Prod Econ 208:566–587
16. Ghosh D, Shah J (2015) Supply chain analysis under green sensitive consumer demand and cost sharing contract. Int J Prod Econ 164:319–329

17. Inaba T (2018) Revenue and cost sharing mechanism for effective remanufacturing supply chain. In: 2018 IEEE international conference on industrial engineering and engineering management (IEEM), pp 923–927
18. Yang H, Chen W (2018) Retailer-driven carbon emission abatement with consumer environmental awareness and carbon tax: Revenue-sharing versus cost-sharing. Omega 78:179–191

Intelligent Freight Transportation and Supply Chain Drivers: A Literature Survey

Shervin Espahbod

Abstract Over the last 10 years, Intelligent Freight Transportation (IFT) has significantly transformed the structure of the trucking industry in North America by implementing new digital-dependent policies (e.g. the ELD mandate), digital freight marketplaces (e.g., digital load boards) and intelligent hardware (e.g., autonomous trucks). In this paper, the author reviews the IFT literature in freight transportation from between 2009 and 2019, focusing on the effect of digitization in performance indicators and supply chain drivers. Based on the current gap in the body of literature available, while many behavioral studies in drivers' safety have been conducted, there is a lack of behavioral research on most human-oriented topics (interface with IFT). Moreover, the role of smart contracts in improving sustainability (e.g., GHG reduction) is rarely measured and cited in many IFT frameworks.

Keywords Intelligent Freight Transportation · Trucking · Ground Freight Transportation

1 Introduction

The traditional trucking industry has confronted massive changes over the past two decades. On average, many sensors are installed on each modern truck [1]. With the introduction of autonomous trucks, the number of sensors will be significantly higher. In addition to the necessity of transportation vehicles, in North America, the ELD mandate rules expedite the information technology [2]. Modern freight markets, such as spot markets, have provided new shipping opportunities for individual truckers. Intelligent systems not only specify new markets but also play

---

S. Espahbod (✉)
Department of Operations and Decision Science, Wilfrid Laurier University, Waterloo, ON, Canada
e-mail: Espa9610@mylaurier.ca

X. Li, X. Xu (eds.), *Proceedings of the Seventh International Forum on Decision Sciences*, Uncertainty and Operations Research,
https://doi.org/10.1007/978-981-15-5720-0_6

a key role in estimating freight demand and shipping prices. More than half of all the goods in North American containers are imported. This means that the smallest local company also has the potential to play an important role in the chain of an international commodity. Therefore, any global incidence is a variable that may have a considerable impact on the level of performance of the trucking firm. Despite the advances and developments in transportation industry technology, the author should emphasize that the trucking industry is still inefficient. After a long-haul delivery, at least 10–15% of trucks return to the depot without having any goods [3]. Worst of all, in more than half of the cases, a loaded container is available at or near the return point that could prevent the excess empty container movement.

Is the symptom of empty container repositioning due to the vulnerability of the data collection/analysis or the optimization weakness? From the perspective of fragmented market optimization, the problem of reaching the optimal point has almost been solved. Because of the massive size of the real-world assignment problem, many heuristic and analytic methods have been developed over the past 50 years. But with the rapid development of powerful computations, a trucking assignment problem today is one of the questions that can be solved with the simple methods of integer programming [4]. But the reality is that these technical computations are just solving tools while the bigger problem is being overlooked. The main issue is the strategy and ability of trucking companies and their different capabilities toward market information.

The different capabilities of companies are due to differences in (1) the structure/resources of the company and (2) the structure of their customers. The transportation industry has been critically fragmented in recent years [3]. The size of a carrier company can differ from a single truck to several thousands of tractors. With the growth of the spot markets and the easier shipment exploring of small companies, the author observes the growth of owner-operators at the market level [5]. In terms of the structure of customers, the potential clients of these trucking companies may be loyal, regular or single shot. The amount of companies' investment in collecting data from the market and customers is different. Perhaps the available data in the market could be obtained from data provider companies, but smaller companies, especially owners-operators, are still incapable of analyzing this data and are unable to afford information analysis [6]. Therefore, the majority of these small truckers are faced with two options: (1) along with other companies, going under the data umbrella of non-asset based logistics providers or (2) withdrawing from backhaul's search and coming back empty, since hiring a 3PL (third-party logistics firm) will cut their profit margins [7].

Although profitability is the aim of all transportation companies, the criteria for evaluating the performance of truckers vary, according to their size and strategy. The main performance criteria are (1) financial profitability, (2) service level and (3) safety and quality of delivery. With the epidemic growth of the green supply chain, the fourth criterion of carbon emission has been introduced with respect to the amount of pollutant production compared to the empty repositioning ratio. This criterion was important or insignificant with respect to how much the trucker or even his customer cares about sustainability [8]. It should be considered that in recent years, many companies have been seriously measuring the carbon footprint of their products and it should be noted that an important part of the carbon footprint is due to the trucks' transportation. In the case of the second criterion, truckers also weigh clients differently, depending on the type and relationship. While companies may miss out on their profit margin or go a long empty way for their important customers without any loads, such a blessing will not be used for small and transitory customers. Finally, financial performance is only a criterion of relative similarity in the market.

As in most other areas that are vital to organizations, information technology has significantly changed the aspects of freight trucking companies [9]. Several innovations are directly data-oriented, such as the Internet of Things (IoT) of shipments, while others (e.g., autonomous trucking) benefit indirectly from information technology [10]. The aims of system intelligence in supply chain management can be classified into two groups: uncertainty minimization and performance (efficiency) enhancement. Achieving these goals will lead to new revenue streams and decreasing costs. Uncertainty minimization is the result of improvement of visibility, analytics and transparency across the supply chain.

2 Review of Publications

This study has focused on the top papers of the field between 2009 and 2018 in Web of Science and Scopus. The total number of 147 papers with at least ten citations have exclusively addressed the effect of IFT on ground freight transportation. As of June 2019, the selected paper 9362 times have been selected as the reference. This level of popularity implies the attractiveness of the topic for scholars for different research questions.

Using segmentation technics, the author categories papers as followed: (1) Transportation mean and hardware innovation, (2) price estimation and cost analysis, (3) Transportation network design, (4) Terminals and intramodality and (5) Sourcing strategies and contract design. Figure 1 describes category-specified distributions of the papers in the last decade. The number in the bracket of each category implies the total number of citations for each category. As each paper might cite to multiple selected papers, the analysis of citations is not statistically meaningful.

While there are substantial publications for Transportation means and hardware innovation after 2014, the number of publications about terminal and intermodality has lessened. The publication rate in other categories has remained stable.

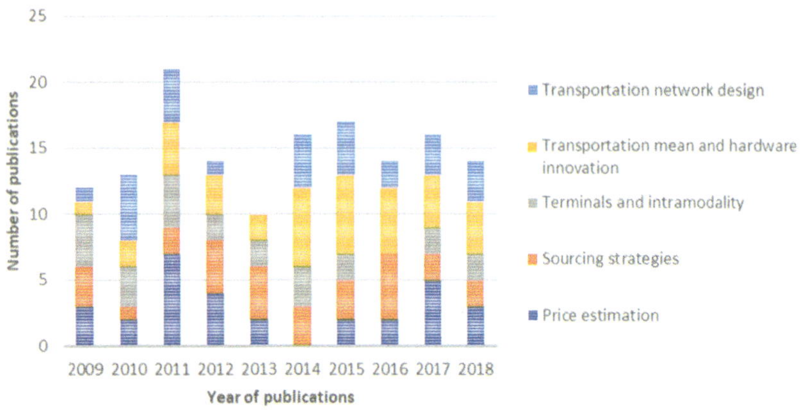

Fig. 1 The distribution of publications between 2009 and 2018

3 Content-Review Based Approach

According to Fig. 2, emerging and developing intelligent technologies (e.g., IoT) not only play their cross-functional roles but also redefine the strategic capabilities of the transportation companies. These capabilities can improve truckers' ideal strategic zones. So, unlike classical frameworks [11], IFT can concurrently decrease the cost and improve the responsiveness.

According to the framework in Table 1, conventional transportation (particularly ground freight transportation) will be significantly disrupted by IFT. A primary

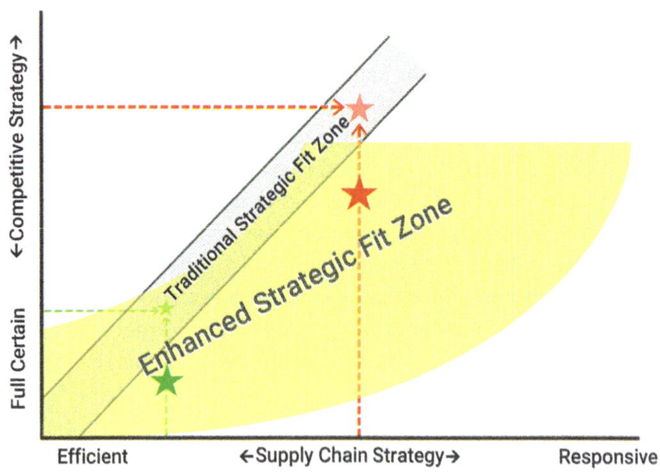

Fig. 2 The enhanced strategic fit zone after IFT improvement. More prominent stars are a modified strategic zone

impact of IFT is currently underway, as human-driven action is being quickly replaced by artificial intelligence [12]. IoT can significantly lower lead-time uncertainty. For example, in the event of delivery delays, IoT will provide details that can be used to identify the cause and aid problem-solving in real-time [8].

By applying IFT in container repositioning, scholars expect demand points to become more visible and certain [15]. Moreover, shipment-related information is going to be symmetric among the carriers. These improvements will significantly reduce the overall empty container movement. The optimal pricing of truckload and less than truckload (LTL) will be more integrated [18]. For instance, the sharing economy and servicing can integrate the carriers [17]. Moreover, the behavior of consumers, such as their loyalty and time-window flexibility, can significantly determine the price of goods and services.

To sum up, IFT-oriented facilities (e.g. smart truck duck stations) use technologies like IoT to provide more transparency and decision support for both customers and truckers [16]. Big data and IoT will play a key role in partnership and collaboration. For instance, truckers can detect any quality issue (e.g. delivery delay, handling damage) even before the container leaves the facility and enters the trucks [16].

Both short-term (e.g., spot markets) and long-term contracts with shippers necessitate a good level of information [5]. By knowing more about the demand, truckers and brokers can enhance their pricing approach [18] and decide whether they are able to find a backhaul load or not. Sourcing can easily reach through an innovative approach, such as crowd-shipping and the sharing economy [19].

4 Findings and Opportunities

Even with advanced IFT, as long as the information monopoly is considered the main source of competitive advantage, it will be hard to share information among truckers. Exterior factors seem to be able to provide quasi-symmetric information such as, policy pressures to minimize emissions through the carbon tax or other deterrent factors in reducing empty container repositioning. These bonus-penalty policies elevate the tendency of companies to try to find backhaul and improve their willingness to share available shipping opportunities. These policies should be smartly deployed with intelligent systems. For example, at this moment, the carbon tax is set at a single unit price on each liter/gallon of fuel. By using an intelligent system, the transparent data is processed in a way where policy can differentiate between the loaded and unloaded kilometers, then a larger penalty can be considered for unloaded transport. Several IFT-related hypotheses can be the backbone of future research:

1. As mentioned in the last section, truck companies are generally reluctant to reveal their demand points. Therefore, collecting third-party information (independent of the trucker and the shipper) can help significantly to predict demand points

Table 1 The effect of IFT on the supply chain drivers of trucking firms and other freight transportation agents

Supply chain driver	Focus of study	Main outcomes of using IFT	Research methods and tools
Transportation mean and hardware innovation	Autonomous trucks [12] Platoon trucks [13] Safety and security [14]	Higher initial investment but safer, faster and more reliable and congestion is expected	Simulation & Modelling Behavioral experiments
Network design	Predictive analytics [8]	IoT and big data will improve visibility and predictability of demand and transportation lead time. Also, IFT improves mobility and traffic management.	Modelling & simulation Machine learning
Pricing	Using IoT dynamic pricing based on the customer and capacity [15]	Know the customers' attributes, competitors' situations and the historical price in order to make the pricing easier	Empirical, modelling Machine learning
Facility/terminal	Collaboration [16] Intermodality/multimodality [10] Co-opetition [8]	Activating cooperative intermodal systems such as vehicle–highway automation	Modelling & simulation
Sourcing	Integrating carriers' decisions [6], sharing economy [17], integrating spot markets [5]	Information sharing with shippers based on the window opportunity of the shipment can improve the overall profit of the market. The application of intelligent systems in contract design is growing.	Modelling & empirical Game theory

and amounts. For example, geospatial intelligence methods can estimate the supply and demand points by analyzing images of the density of containers in the depots, roads and ships. This method is currently being implemented by oil brokers to predict the offshore production of oil rigs [20] through the observation of the ships' transportation. Investigating the field of demand forecasting with this methodology is recommended.

2. The design of transportation contracts based on the sharing economy can result in each truck of a shipping company being deployed at three levels: owner-operator, corporate, or leasehold (uber trucking). Designing the contractual-informational infrastructure for the sharing economy should not have any impact on customer loyalty to the parent company. Also, the profits received by the responsible shipper carrier or broker and the truck operator should be such that both parties are willing to cooperate, taking into account the existing risks of the customer losing or reducing the quality of the transportation (physical damage or delay in delivering the load).
3. Using intelligent systems to coordinate truckers with other modes of transportation can have a significant result in efficient transportation with the help of inter-modality. For example, rail/marine systems can transfer a part of the loads from a region where the supply of trucks is less than the demand to areas with better balance.
4. The role of artificial intelligence in transferring information, determining the optimal price of shipping, and finally, negotiating with a potential customer can significantly reduce the search cost and, consequently, the ordering cost of companies. Comparing behavioral experiments with intelligent systems (e.g. artificial intelligence) and their impacts on other quality aspects of transportation, based on efficiency components, should be analyzed.

Acknowledgements I would highly appreciate my supervisor, Dr. Michael Haughton, who always provided insightful comments on my project.

References

1. Guerrero-Ibáñez J, Zeadally S, Contreras-Castillo J (2018) Sensor technologies for intelligent transportation systems. Sensors 18(4):1212
2. Sharpe, B. (2019). MODERNIZING DATA COLLECTION AND REPORTING METHODS FOR THE SMARTWAY PROGRAM
3. Lafkihi M, Pan S, Ballot E (2019) Freight transportation service procurement: a literature review and future research opportunities in omnichannel E-commerce. Transp Res E Logist Transp Rev 125:348–365
4. Phillips AE, Waterer H, Ehrgott M, Ryan DM (2015) Integer programming methods for large-scale practical classroom assignment problems. Comput Oper Res 53:42–53
5. Lindsey C, Mahmassani HS (2017) Sourcing truckload capacity in the transportation spot market: a framework for third party providers. Transp Res A Policy Pract 102:261–273
6. Gürel Y, Güllü R (2019) Effect of a secondary market on a system with random demand and uncertain costs. Int J Prod Econ 209:112–120

7. Zolfagharinia H, Haughton M (2016) Effective truckload dispatch decision methods with incomplete advance load information. Eur J Oper Res 252(1):103–121
8. Zhao Y, Choi TM, Cheng TCE, Wang S (2018) Supply option contracts with spot market and demand information updating. Eur J Oper Res 266(3):1062–1071
9. Perego A, Perotti S, Mangiaracina R (2011) ICT for logistics and freight transportation: a literature review and research agenda. Int J Phys Distrib Logist Manag 41(5):457–483
10. Shladover SE, Systematics C (2012) Literature review on recent international activity in cooperative vehicle–highway automation systems (No. FHWA-HRT-13-025). United States. Federal Highway Administration
11. Meindl SCP (2016). Supply chain management – strategy, planning and operation. Tsinghua University Press. Wheat soybean others land for no use
12. Fagnant DJ, Kockelman K (2015) Preparing a nation for autonomous vehicles: opportunities, barriers and policy recommendations. Transp Res A Policy Pract 77:167–181
13. Bhoopalam AK, Agatz N, Zuidwijk R (2018) Planning of truck platoons: a literature review and directions for future research. Transp Res B Methodol 107:212–228
14. Alam A, Besselink B, Turri V, Martensson J, Johansson KH (2015) Heavy-duty vehicle platooning for sustainable freight transportation: a cooperative method to enhance safety and efficiency. IEEE Control Syst Mag 35(6):34–56
15. Inderfurth K, Kelle P (2011) Capacity reservation under spot market price uncertainty. Int J Prod Econ 133(1):272–279
16. Scott A (2015) The value of information sharing for truckload shippers. Transp Res E Logist Transp Rev 81:203–214
17. Rauch DE, Schleicher D (2015) Like Uber, but for local government law: the future of local regulation of the sharing economy. Ohio State Law J 76:901
18. Özkaya E, Keskinocak P, Joseph VR, Weight R (2010) Estimating and benchmarking less-than-truckload market rates. Transp Res E Logist Transp Rev 46(5):667–682
19. Standing C, Standing S, Biermann S (2019) The implications of the sharing economy for transport. Transp Rev 39(2):226–242
20. Robards MD, Silber GK, Adams JD, Arroyo J, Lorenzini D, Schwehr K, Amos J (2016) Conservation science and policy applications of the marine vessel automatic identification system (AIS)—a review. Bull Mar Sci 92(1):75–103

Research on Refined Oil Distribution Strategy and Oil Gas Recovery Joint Optimization

Chenglong Wang and Xiaofeng Xu

Abstract There are many times of loading and unloading processes in the refined oil distribution network, and during each process of loading and unloading a large amount of refined oil gas is generated. These gases not only pollute the environment but also cause unnecessary loss of refined oil and cause huge economic losses. Therefore, in this paper the joint optimization of refined oil distribution strategy and refined oil gas recovery strategy is considered from the perspective of refined oil recovery, based on environmental protection requirements. A three-objective model with the lowest distribution cost, the shortest cumulative delivery time, and the highest satisfaction with delivery services is established, solved by the NSGA-III algorithm, and the model is verified based on the distribution data of China Petroleum Guangdong Sales Company. Finally, it is concluded that refined oil gas recovery will indeed reduce refined oil gas losses, economic losses and reduce the cumulative execution time of distribution tasks, reducing the time cost.

Keywords Refined oil gas recovery · VRP · Joint optimization

1 Introduction

Refined oil distribution is the terminal of the energy supply network. However, there are multiple loading-unloading in this process, which emit a lot of oil gas. According to *Sinopec's Compilation for "Oil Gas Emission Control Standards for Refined Oil Marketing Companies"*, the total oil-gas loss rate in this process is about 0.33%. According to the consumption of refined oil in China in 2018, 32.514 million tons, the oil-gas loss amounted to 1.073 million tons, and the value was about 5.4 billion

C. Wang (✉) · X. Xu
School of Economics and Management, China University of Petroleum, Qingdao, Shandong Province, China
e-mail: wcl1175407897@126.com; xuxiaofeng@upc.edu.cn

X. Li, X. Xu (eds.), *Proceedings of the Seventh International Forum on Decision Sciences*, Uncertainty and Operations Research,
https://doi.org/10.1007/978-981-15-5720-0_7

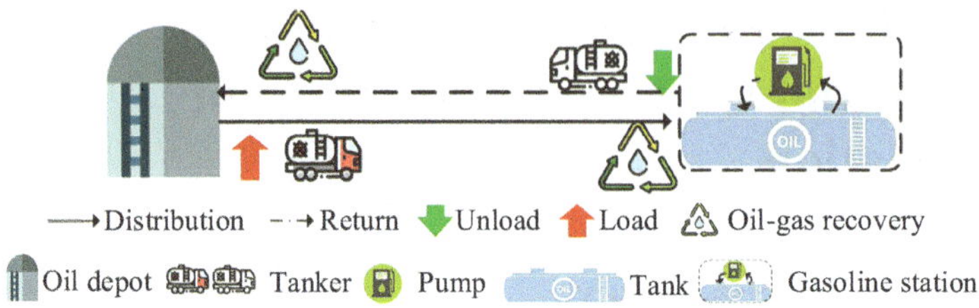

Fig. 1 Terminal process of refined oil distribution and recovery settings

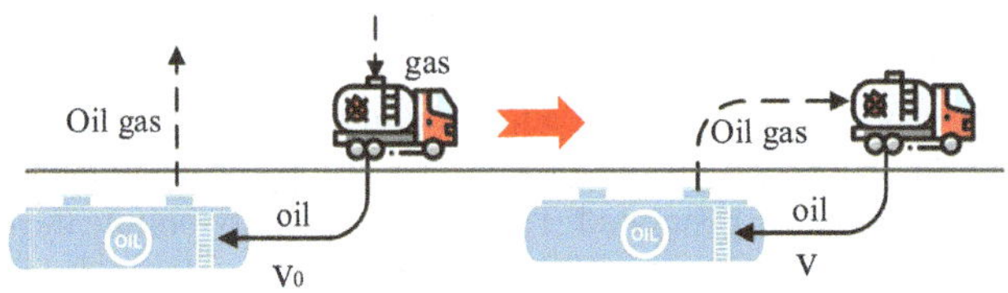

Fig. 2 Changes in loading-unloading methods

yuan. Therefore, the oil-gas recovery needs to be performed during the loading and unloading process of the distribution process of refined oil (shown in Fig. 1). However, currently refined oil marketing companies pay less attention to oil-gas recovery.

We found that, on the one hand, oil-gas recovery can affect the traditional calculation method of the distribution cost of refined oil, on the other hand, oil-gas recovery needs to change the loading-unloading method of refined oil (as shown in Fig. 2), and this will affect the speed of loading-unloading to a certain extent, and thus affect the service time of a single gas station. In addition, according to the *GB 20952-2007 Emission Standards of Air Pollutants for Gasoline Stations*, concentration of oil-gas emission of the gasoline station is not higher than 25 g/m^3, but he actual concentration of emitted oil gas is much greater than 25 g/m^3, so oil-gas recovery in the Refined oil distribution network has become a necessary requirement. Therefore, we proposed the distribution optimization of refined oil considering oil-gas recovery from oil depot to gasoline station based on environmental protection requirements.

2 Literature Review

In this paper, the joint optimization of refined oil distribution and refined oil gas recovery were discussed. The former is a typical application in the actual scenario of Vehicle Routing Problem (VRP), mainly to solve the shortest path or minimum of the vehicle under actual restrictions. The problem of the cost path. The problem of finished oil product distribution was originally proposed by foreign scholars Brown and Graves [1]. Afterwards, a large number of scholars have carried out rich research on the problem of refined oil transportation and expanded the problem accordingly. From the initial single-car path problem to the Multi-Compartment Vehicle Routing Problem (MCVRP), Cornillier et al. [2] studied the multi-stage oil distribution problem in the case of single-tank tanker distribution; Kjetil et al. [3] and Charlotte et al. [4] studied the problem of multi-cabin tanker tank allocation in the field of ship transportation, and solved this problem by mixed integer linear programming and heuristic algorithm respectively; Ostermeier et al. [5]. The MCVRP problem has been studied in the field of general cargo road transportation, and the optimal path is solved by the large neighborhood search algorithm. From a single vehicle path optimization to delivery time, gas station inventory [6, 7], vehicle fuel consumption [8], Joint optimization of carbon emissions [9]; Popovi et al. [10] solved the Inventory Routing Problem (IRP) by variable neighborhood search algorithm; Erdogan and Miller-Hooks [11] proposed Green Vehicle Routing (GVRP) with the goal of minimizing emissions; Poonthalir and Nadarajan [12] extended the problems of Erdogan and Miller-Hooks and studied Greenhouse gas emission problems in the variable speed environment of transportation vehicles, and particle swarm optimization algorithm and greedy algorithm are used to solve this problem; Leggieri and Haouari [13] studied the green vehicle routing problem with the goal of minimizing fuel consumption of transportation vehicles. The solution method has also evolved from the exact algorithm at the beginning to the heuristic algorithm, but with the complexity of the VRP problem, the computational algorithm is violently increasing. The exact algorithm can no longer meet the solution requirements. Genetic algorithm [1, 14] Heuristic algorithms such as immune genetic algorithm [15], ant colony algorithm [16], particle swarm optimization algorithm [17] have become large-scale and complex. The main algorithm of the VRP problem.

At present, from the development of the problem of refined oil distribution, the main research hotspots focus on MCVRP, joint optimization, and algorithm improvement. However, in the MCVRP, the focus is on the pure multi-cabin problem, and there is little research on the MCVRP optimization of the hybrid model. In the joint optimization, the focus is on the green VRP problem such as vehicle fuel consumption and carbon emission and the joint optimization of inventory, but it is specific to the environment. There is little research on the oil and gas losses and recovery required for the finished oil handling process. This paper considers the joint optimization problem of environmental protection requirements and economic benefits of oil and gas loss and recovery in single/multi-cabin model mixing and product oil handling and solves the problem with NSGA-III algorithm.

3 Problem Description

In the refined oil distribution network $G = (V, A)$, $V = \{n|\ 1, 2, 3, \ldots, N\}$ represents the set of nodes in the network, $A = \{(i,j), i,j \in V\}$ represents the set of paths between each node, and d_{ij} represents the distance between any two nodes in the

4.1 Distribution Costs of Oil Depot

To carry out oil-gas recovery under requirements of environmental protection, the primary concern of marketing companies is to minimize the total distribution cost. The total cost consists of the following five components.

Transportation Costs C_s The transportation cost can be divided into two parts, one is a fixed cost that has nothing to do with the volume of refined oil transportation, such as the fixed cost of tanker C_{sc}; the other is the variable cost related to the order quantity q_k, such as the transportation cost C_{sd} of the refined oil. Therefore, the transportation costs of refined oil $C_s = C_{sc} + C_{sd}$, according to the above content:

$$\begin{aligned} C_s &= C_{sc} + C_{sd} \\ &= C_{sc} + \sum_{i,j \in V} \sum_{n=1}^{N} \sum_{m=1}^{M} \sum_{v=1}^{Vm} \sum_{k=1}^{Km} q_k^{mn} C_{sd}^0 x_v^{ij} d_{ij}, (i \neq j) \end{aligned} \tag{1}$$

Loading-Unloading Costs C_{lu} The loading-unloading costs is a variable costs related to the order quantity q_k, expressed by C_{lu}.

$$C_{lu} = \sum_{n=1}^{N} \sum_{k=1}^{Km} C_u^0 q_k^n \tag{2}$$

Penalty Costs and Waiting Costs C_{el} Because each gasoline station has a specified time window for receiving refined oil, if the tanker arrives early, it will incur a waiting cost C_e, and if the tanker is late, it will incur a penalty cost C_l.

$$\begin{aligned} C_{el} &= \begin{cases} C_e, t_{nv} < T_{ne} \\ 0, T_{ne} \leq t_{nv} \leq T_{nl} \\ C_l, t_{nv} > T_{nl} \end{cases} \\ &= \begin{cases} \sum_{v=1}^{Vm} \sum_{n=1}^{N} C_e^0 (T_{ne} - t_{nv}), t_{nv} < T_{ne} \\ 0, \qquad T_{ne} \leq t_{nv} \leq T_{nl} \\ \sum_{v=1}^{Vm} \sum_{n=1}^{N} C_l^0 (t_{nv} - T_{nl}), t_{nv} > T_{nl} \end{cases} \end{aligned} \tag{3}$$

Cost of Oil-Gas Recovery *Cr* If the volume of recovered oil gas is q, the cost of oil-gas recovery *Cr* is as follows:

$$Cr = C_0 q = E_0(\eta)\ P_e q \tag{4}$$

Where C_0 is the cost of unit recovered oil gas, $C_0 = E_0 P_e$, E_0 is the energy consumption for per unit recovered oil gas, $E_0 = E_0(\eta)$, *Pe* is the price of unit energy.

Revenue of Oil-Gas Recovery *Sr* If the price of unit refined oil is P_{oil}, the revenue S_r of oil-gas recovery is:

$$S_r = P_{oil}\frac{q_g \rho_g}{\rho_l} = P_{oil}\frac{\eta q \rho_g}{\rho_l} \tag{5}$$

Where q_g is the volume of recovered oil gas, $q_g = \eta q$, ρ_g is the density of oil-gas, ρ_l is liquid refined oil density, ρ_g is a function related to temperature, but they can be regarded as constant values within a certain temperature variation range.

According to the above five parts of the costs, the objective of the lowest distribution costs is:

$$\min Z_1 = C_s + C_{uw} + C_{el} + Cr - Sr \tag{6}$$

4.2 Distribution Time of Depot-Station

Distribution time can be divided into two parts, one is the time that the tankers travel on the route, the traveling time; and the other is the waiting time that is generated during the distribution process, waiting time.

Traveling time T_r:

$$Tr = \sum_{v=1}^{Vm}\left(\sum_{i,j\in V} x_v^{ij} d_{ij}\right) / V_s, (i \neq j) \tag{7}$$

Waiting time T_w, which can be expressed by $T_w = T_t + T_{uw}$.

Waiting time for unloading T_t, waiting time due to arriving at the gas station early:

$$Tt = \begin{cases} \sum_{v=1}^{Vm}\sum_{n=1}^{N}(T_{ne} - t_{nv}), t_{nv} < T_{ne} \\ 0, \qquad t_{nv} \geq T_{ne} \end{cases} \tag{8}$$

Unloading time T_{uw}

$$T_{uw} = \sum_{n=1}^{N}\left[\left(\sum_{k=1}^{Km} q_k^n / V_u\right)\right] \tag{9}$$

where *Vu* is the loading-unloading speed under oil-gas recovery, which can be measured according to the actual situation.

According to the above two parts of the cost, the total distribution time-consuming objective function can be obtained as follow:

$$\min Z_2 = Tr + Tw \tag{10}$$

4.3 Satisfaction of Gasoline Stations

Due to the limitation of gas station service time window, when the tankers arrive later than the service time window (T_{ie}, T_{il}), it will reduce the satisfaction of gasoline station with the distribution. Therefore, the satisfaction function is a function to describe the extent to which the delivery time of the tanker truck is later than the service time window. Therefore, the satisfaction can be expressed by the delay time. It can be seen that there is a negative correlation between the satisfaction and the delay time. The shorter the delay time, the higher the satisfaction. When the delay time is 0, satisfaction is highest.

Delivery delay time

$$T_{late} = \sum_{i=1}^{n} \max(0, t_{iv} - T_{il}) \tag{11}$$

Satisfaction function

$$\max Z_3 = \frac{1}{T_{late} + c}, c > 0 \tag{12}$$

There are two roles of c in the satisfaction function: since the value of T_{late} is $[0, +\infty)$, when $T_{late} = 0$, it makes the satisfaction function meaningful; the range of the satisfaction function is adjusted to be $(0, 1/c]$, so the closer to $1/c$ the higher the satisfaction, the value of c in this paper is 1.

4.4 Model Setting

In order to solve the above problems, a multi-objective GVRP model is proposed in this paper, which is as follows:

$$\min f\left(Z_1, \frac{1}{Z_2}, Z_3\right) \tag{13}$$

Constraints as follows:

$$u_{vk} \leq Q_{vk}, \forall v, k \tag{14}$$

$$\sum_{n=1}^{N} q_{kv}^{n} \leq u_{vk}, \forall v, k \tag{15}$$

$$\sum_{m=1}^{M}\sum_{n=1}^{N}\sum_{v=1}^{Vm} x_{v}^{nm} = \sum_{m=1}^{M}\sum_{n=1}^{N}\sum_{v=1}^{Vm} x_{v}^{nm} \tag{16}$$

$$\sum_{j\in V}\sum_{v=1}^{Vm} x_{v}^{ji} = \sum_{j\in V}\sum_{v=1}^{Vm} x_{v}^{ij}, \forall i \in V \tag{17}$$

$$\sum_{v=1}^{Vm}\sum_{m}^{M}\sum_{n}^{N} x_{v}^{mn} = Vm \tag{18}$$

$$x_{v}^{ij} = \begin{cases} 1 \\ 0 \end{cases}, \forall v, i, j \tag{19}$$

$$0 \leq \eta < 1 \tag{20}$$

Equation (14) shows that the loading amount of tank v for the oil k does not exceed the maximum capacity; Eq. (15) shows that the total unloading amount of the oil k does not exceed the total amount of the oil k in the tanker v; Eq. (16) shows that after the distribution from the oil depot, all tankers returns to the oil depot, and cannot return to the initial depot; Eq. (17) shows that for any gasoline station, the tankers is balance of in and out; Eq. (18) shows that tankers in the distribution network depart from the oil depot; Eq. (19) shows 0–1 decision variable constraint; Eq. (20) shows the constraint of oil-gas recovery efficiency.

5 Solution Procedure

According to the characteristics of the problem, a three-layer coding is designed to represent the execution of the task in this paper.

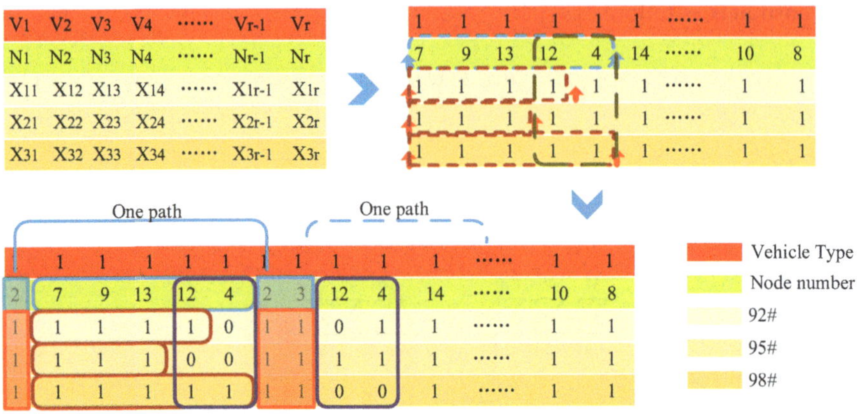

Fig. 4 Chromosome coding

The first layer of code indicates the type of tanker, adopting 0–1 code, 0 for single compartment tanker, 1 for multi compartment tanker, the same value on the same route. The second layer represents the path node number, which is represented by real numbers 1–18. If both numbers in this layer code are the number of the oil depot and there is only the number of the gas station between the two numbers, then this serial number represents the path traveled by a vehicle. The third layer indicates whether the requirements of the gasoline station node are met, adopting 0–1 code, which is divided into three layers of coding, 1 indicates that the gasoline station requirements are met, and 0 indicates that the gas station requirements are not met. In addition, in order to avoid different chromosome lengths, the length of each layer of all chromosomes is required to be the longest chromosome length r, if the length of chromosome is less than r, filled with zero.

Firstly, the nodes of the gas station are randomly sequenced, and the 92#, 95# and 98# refined oil of the gasoline station are accumulated in order. When $sum(q_1, q_2, \ldots, q_{N-1}) < u_v < sum(q_1, q_2, \ldots, q_N)$, the oil depot node is inserted, and the calculation continues from the Nth node until the nodes of the gas station are calculated in order, as shown in Fig. 4, and pseudo code of NSGA-III shown in Table 2.

6 Numerical Example

This article uses the numerical example provided by CNPC sales company, as shown in Table 3. The gas stations in the case are represented by nodes 4–18, and nodes 1 ~ 3 are used to represent three oil depots supplying gasoline stations in data example.

Table 2 The pseudo code of NSGA-III

```
Begin
Initialize chromosomes
Calculation fitness
Non-dominated sorting
For i = 1: Maxgen
Crossover and mutation
Calculation fitness
Non-dominated sorting
Update chromosomes
End
End
```

Table 3 Information on gasoline stations and oil depots

Nodes	Longitude	Latitude	Time window (min)		Demand for refined oil (L)		
					92#	95#	98#
1	113.59	22.97	–	–	–	–	–
2	113.57	22.81	–	–	–	–	–
3	113.88	22.37	–	–	–	–	–
4	114.16	22.68	60.0	120.0	2000	2000	2000
5	113.82	22.97	0.0	60.0	3000	4000	0
6	113.82	22.95	30.0	90.0	4500	2500	2000
7	113.71	22.66	30.0	60.0	2200	2200	0
8	113.89	22.83	60.0	120.0	3500	2200	2200
9	113.63	22.89	0.0	60.0	2000	2500	0
10	114.18	22.82	120.0	180.0	4500	2000	3000
11	113.71	22.82	30.0	90.0	7000	7000	3000
12	113.89	22.93	30.0	90.0	3000	3000	2400
13	113.81	22.89	60.0	120.0	4000	3000	2000
14	113.83	22.73	30.0	90.0	10,000	8000	0
15	113.90	22.98	30.0	90.0	2500	4000	2000
16	113.94	22.83	120.0	180.0	3000	3000	2500
17	113.68	22.96	30.0	60.0	2000	2000	2000
18	113.73	22.92	60.0	120.0	3000	3000	0

According to the energy consumption parameters provided by the oil-gas recovery equipment supplier, the fitting equation of the correlation between the energy consumption per unit of recovered oil gas and the recovery efficiency is $E_0 = 9401.2\eta^3 - 27177\eta^2 + 2619\eta - 8413.1$.

7 Results Analysis

In reality, the temperature has a great influence on the density of oil gas. In order to expand the application scope of this study, we compare the oil-gas recovery under the conditions of high temperature (average temperature in summer in China, 30 °C) and low temperature (average temperature in summer in China, – 10 °C).

Because in the actual production and operation process, only one or several solutions are usually needed, we compare the solutions under different target priorities. The Z1 (yuan), Z2 (min), and Z3 targets are assigned different priorities, for example, Z1Z2Z3 indicates that the priorities of the Z1, Z2, and Z3 are sequentially reduced, as shown in Table 4. In addition, we also made a road map in the case of oil-gas recovery (shown in appendix).

Whether at low or high temperature, oil-gas recovery can reduce the distribution cost and time consuming to a certain extent, but there is no significant improvement in satisfaction.

1. When Z1 has the highest priority, the values of the objectives are the same under the conditions of priorities Z1Z2Z3 and Z1Z3Z2, the distribution cost (Z1) with oil-gas recovery is reduced from 61,972 yuan to 60,538 yuan, saving about 2.3%; the distribution time (Z2) with oil-gas recovery was reduced from 1041 minutes to 1001, saving about 4%.
2. When Z2 has the highest priority, the values of the targets are the same under the conditions of the priorities Z2Z1Z3 and Z2Z3Z1, the distribution time (Z2) with

Table 4 Comparison of multi-objective solutions under different priorities

		NSGA-III (high temperature)		NSGA-III (low temperature)			
Priority level	Recovery	Z1	Z2	Z3	Z1	Z2	Z3
Z1 Z2 Z3	Y	60,238	1004	0.67	60,528	1001	0.67
	N	61,972	1041	0.67	61,972	1041	0.67
Z1 Z3 Z2	Y	60,238	1004	0.67	60,528	1001	0.67
	N	61,972	1041	0.67	61,972	1041	0.67
Z2 Z1 Z3	Y	122,615	915	0.33	122,615	917	0.32
	N	124,649	955	0.19	124,649	955	0.19
Z2 Z3 Z1	Y	122,615	915	0.33	122,615	917	0.32
	N	124,649	955	0.19	124,649	955	0.19
Z3 Z1 Z2	Y	88,876	1213	1	89,076	1215	1
	N	90,510	1245	1	90,510	1245	1
Z3 Z2 Z1	Y	133,022	999	1	133,322	998	1
	N	135,600	1048	1	135,600	1048	1

oil-gas recovery has been reduced from 952mins to 917mins, saving about 3.6%; the distribution cost (Z1) with oil-gas recovery is reduced from 124,549 yuan to 123,015 yuan, saving about 1.2%; the satisfaction (Z3) with oil-gas recovery increased from 0.19 to 0.32, an increase of 68.4%.

3. When Z3 has the highest priority, the optimal value of satisfaction (Z3) can be obtained regardless of whether oil-gas recovery is performed. Under the priority Z3Z1Z2, distribution costs (Z1) and distribution time (Z2) saved 1.6% and 2.4% respectively due to oil-gas recovery; under the priority of Z3Z2Z1, distribution costs (Z1) and distribution time (Z2) saved 1.7% and 4.7% respectively due to oil-gas recovery.

It can be seen that the distribution strategy with oil-gas recovery has certain advantages over the situation without oil-gas recovery in terms of distribution cost, distribution time and satisfaction.

8 Conclusions

Oil-gas recovery has no directly significant effect on gasoline station satisfaction, compared with different objective priorities of GVRP. At the same satisfaction, the oil-gas recovery in closed mode can effectively reduce the total distribution cost and save the total delivery time, compare with the satiation in closed mode. Based on the above analysis, we can conclude that GVRP considered oil-gas recovery in refined oil distribution can not only reduce oil-gas emission and protect the environment, but also decrease the distribution cost by obtaining additional recycling benefits, and save the total delivery time effectively. In addition, there are still some issues needed to consider in future, such as vehicle speed changes in the distribution network, whether distribution nodes are connected, and whether there are congestions in the travel path. The above limitations can be taken as future research directions.

Appendix: Distribution Route

Priority level	Refined oil	Routes (single compartment vehicle)	Routes (three compartment vehicle)					
		2-14-2	2-7-10-2	3-5-9-13-3	2-12-15-6-8-18-3	1-8-18-17-11-16-4-3	2-11-16-4-1	
Z1	92#	1	1-1	1-1-1	1-1-1-0-0	1-1-1-0-0-0	1-1-1	
Z2	95#	1	1-1	1-1-1	1-1-1-1-0	0-1-1-0-0-0	1-1-1	
Z3	98#	0	1-1	1-1-1	1-1-1-1-1	0-0-1-1-1-1	0-0-0	
		2-14-2	2-7-10-2	1-5-13-9-1	1-15-12-6-8-18-1	2-8-18-1711-16-4-3	2-11-16-4-1	
Z1	92#	1	1-1	1-1-1	1-1-1-0-0	1-1-1-0-0-0	1-1-1	
Z3	95#	1	1-1	1-1-1	1-1-1-1-0	0-1-1-0-0-0	1-1-1	
Z2	98#	0	1-1	1-1-1	1-1-1-1-1	0-0-1-1-1-1	0-0-0	
		2-14-2	2-4-10-3	1-5-11-1813-1	2-18-13-9-12-7-17-8-2	2-12-7-17-8-6-15-16-1	2-8-6-15-16-2	2-16-2
Z2	92#	1	1-1	1-1-0-0	1-1-1-0-0-0-0	1-1-1-0-0-0-0	1-1-1-0	1
Z1	95#	1	1-1	1-1-0-0	1-1-1-0-0-0-0	1-1-1-1-0-0-0	0-1-1-1	0
Z3	98#	0	1-1	1-1-1-1	0-0-1-1-1-1-1	0-0-0-0-1-1-1	0-0-0-0	0
		2-14-2	2-8-15-12-1	1-12-6-17-11-2	2-11-5-4-10-16-2	3-10-16-9-18-13-7-2	1-18-13-7-2	
Z2	92#	1	1-1-0	1-1-1-0	1-1-1-0-0	1-1-1-0-0-0	1-1-1	
Z3	95#	1	1-1-1	0-1-1-0	1-1-1-0-0	1-1-1-0-0-0	1-1-1	
Z1	98#	0	1-1-1	0-1-1-1	0-1-1-1-1	0-0-1-1-1-1	0-0-0	
		2-14-2	2-9-12-17-1	1-17-10-16-4-3	2-18-8-6-13-5-1	1-6-13-5-15-11-7-2	1-5-15-11-7-2	2-11-7-2
Z3	92#	1	1-1-1	0-1-1-1	1-1-0-0-0	1-1-0-0-0-0	1-1-1-0	1-1
Z1	95#	1	1-1-1	0-1-1-1	1-1-1-0-0	0-1-1-1-0-0	0-0-1-1	0-0
Z2	98#	0	1-1-0	1-1-1-1	1-1-1-1-1	0-0-0-1-1-1	0-0-0-0	0-0
		2-14-2	2-9-12-17-1	1-17-10-16-4-3	2-18-8-6–13–5–1	1-6-13–5–15-11–7–2	1-5-15-11–7–2	2-11-7–2
Z3	92#	1	1-1–1	0-1-1-1	1-1-0-0-0	1-1-0-0-0-0	1-1-1-0	1-1
Z2	95#	1	1-1-1	0-1-1-1	1-1-1-0-0	0-1-1-1-0-0	0-0-1-1	0-0
Z1	98#	0	1-1-0	1-1-1-1	1-1-1-1-1	0-0-0-1-1-1	0-0-0-0	0-0

References

1. Brown GG, Graves GW (1981) Real-time dispatch of petroleum tank trucks. Manag Sci 27(1):19–32
2. Cornillier F, Boctor FF, Laporte G, Renaud J (2008) A heuristic for the multi-period petrol station replenishment problem. Eur J Oper Res 191(2):295–305
3. Kjetil F (2009) Tank allocation problems in maritime bulk shipping. Elsevier, London
4. Vilhelmsen C, Larsen J, Lusby R (2016) A heuristic and hybrid method for the tank allocation problem in maritime bulk shipping. 4OR 14(4):417–444
5. Ostermeier M, Hübner A (2018) Vehicle selection for a multi-compartment vehicle routing problem. Eur J Oper Res 269(2):682
6. Day JM, Wright PD, Schoenherr T, Venkataramanan M, Gaudette K (2009) Improving routing and scheduling decisions at a distributor of industrial gasses. Omega 37(1):227–237
7. Wang HF, Zheng KW (2010) An optimal run-mode scheduling for oil refinery production – a case study on Taiwan CPC corporation. Prod Plan Control 21(3):301–318
8. Li J, Wang D, Zhang J (2018) Heterogeneous fixed fleet vehicle routing problem based on fuel and carbon emissions. J Clean Prod 201:896–908
9. Jin LI, Zhang JH (2014) Study on the effect of carbon emission trading mechanism on logistics distribution routing decisions. Syst Eng Theory Pract 34(7):1779–1787
10. Popović D, Vidović M, Radivojević G (2012) Variable neighborhood search heuristic for the inventory routing problem in fuel delivery. Expert Syst Appl 39(18):13390–13398
11. Erdoğan S, Miller-Hooks E (2012) A green vehicle routing problem. Transp Res E Logist Transp Rev 48(1):100–114
12. Poonthalir G, Nadarajan R (2018) A fuel efficient green vehicle routing problem with varying speed constraint (F-GVRP). Expert Syst Appl 100:131–144
13. Leggieri V, Haouari M (2017) A practical solution approach for the green vehicle routing problem. Transp Res E Logist Transp Rev 104:97–112
14. Berger J, Barkaoui M (2004) A parallel hybrid genetic algorithm for the vehicle routing problem with time windows. Comput Oper Res 31(12):2037–2053
15. Xu XF, Hao J, Deng YR, Wang Y (2016) Design optimization of resource combination for collaborative logistics network under uncertainty. Appl Soft Comput 56:684
16. Bullnheimer B, Hartl RF, Strauss C (1999) An improved Ant System algorithm for the vehicle routing problem. Ann Oper Res 89(1):319–328
17. Kuo RJ, Zulvia FE, Suryadi K (2012) Hybrid particle swarm optimization with genetic algorithm for solving capacitated vehicle routing problem with fuzzy demand – a case study on garbage collection system. Appl Math Comput 219(5):2574–2588

Decision Analysis Between Government and Competing Enterprises Under E-Waste Take-Back Regulations

Yuyu Chen, Guoqing Zhang, Bangyi Li, and Linbin Guo

Abstract With the rapid technological development, the waste electrical and electronic equipment (WEEE) increase sharply. To manage WEEE, the government has enacted a series of regulations, such as collection rate regulation and tax regulation. Using a stylized equilibrium model, we analyze the problem as a Stackelberg game between the government and two enterprises (a manufacturer and a remanufacturer) under both collection rate and tax regulations. First, we study enterprises' behavior under the two regulations, including production and pricing decisions. Then, we explore how should the government set the optimal collection rate and tax according to the decisions of enterprises.

Keywords Electrical and electronic equipment · Collection · Remanufacturing · Regulation

Y. Chen (✉)
College of Economics and Management, Nanjing University of Aeronautics and Astronautics, Nanjing, China

Supply Chain and Logistics Optimization Research Center, Department of Mechanical, Automotive & Materials Engineering, University of Windsor, Windsor, ON, Canada
e-mail: chenyuyu@nuaa.edu.cn

G. Zhang
Supply Chain and Logistics Optimization Research Center, Department of Mechanical, Automotive & Materials Engineering, University of Windsor Windsor, ON, Canada

B. Li
College of Economics and Management, Nanjing University of Aeronautics and Astronautics Nanjing, China

L. Guo
Mechanical, Automotive and Materials Engineering, University of Windsor, Windsor, Ontario, Canada

College of Information Science and Technology, Beijing University of Chemical Technology, Beijing, China

X. Li, X. Xu (eds.), *Proceedings of the Seventh International Forum on Decision Sciences*, Uncertainty and Operations Research,
https://doi.org/10.1007/978-981-15-5720-0_8

1 Introduction

In recent years, the social, economic and environmental benefits of remanufacturing closed-loop supply chain have received high attention from governments, enterprises and consumers. At the same time, scholars have conducted extensive research on them.

In reality, in view of the lack of management, technology and personnel, few original manufacturers are willing to implement remanufacturing; on the contrary, there are many independent third-party remanufacturers in the market, they are not engaged in the research and production of new products [1]. However, they are keen on recycling and remanufacturing. For example, Hauser's survey of the US remanufacturing market shows that in more than 2000 remanufacturing companies, the original manufacturer accounts for only 6% [2]. In this case, the remanufactured products produced by the remanufacturer will compete with the new products produced by the original manufacturer, thereby eroding the market share and profit of the new product [3]. Then what measures should the manufacturer take to deal with the threat of the remanufacturer and protect his interests? This is an important decision issue for the manufacturer. In response to this problem, scholars have also conducted in-depth research.

Reference [4] formulate A game theoretic model in which the supplier provides the raw material to the manufacturer and the remanufacturer, to investigate the interaction within the closed-loop supply chain. Reference [5] examine the impact of third-party remanufacturing on a forward supply chain. Reference [6] develops a closed-loop supply chain model consisting of a manufacturer and a remanufacturer, and characterizes the equilibrium decisions and profits. Reference [7] explore the impact of patent licensing on operation decisions of a two-period closed-loop supply chain considering the competition between a manufacturer and a remanufacturer.

The above literature has important reference significance for us. However, they all discuss how the manufacturer deals with the threat of the remanufacturer from the perspective of competition between them, but they do not consider the role of government regulation. If the government regulates the behavior of enterprises, how should they make decisions? In recent years, some scholars have studied the decision-making of production operations under different regulations. Reference [8] study the impact of take-back regulation considering the competition of the manufacturer and the remanufacturer. Reference [9] explore a new form of e-waste legislation, and compare it with the traditional form. Reference [10] investigate the collection rate regulation and tax regulation when there is no competition with remanufacturer.

However, the above literature only considers the problems faced by enterprises and ignores the social welfare which the government should pay attention to. In short, the government's decision-making is exogenous. This paper seeks to find optimal decisions of enterprises and government under both collection rate and tax regulations.

2 Notations and Problem Statement

2.1 Notations

The notations of this paper are shown in Table 1, where superscripts $k \in \{R, T\}$, and R(Rate) and T(Tax) represent the collection rate regulation and the tax regulation, respectively.

2.2 Problem Description

Using a stylized equilibrium model, we analyze the problem as a Stackelberg game between the government and duopoly enterprises. There are two enterprises on the market, the manufacturer and the remanufacturer produce new product and remanufactured product, respectively.

Let q_n and q_r denote the quantities of new and remanufactured products offered by the manufacturer and remanufacturer. Consumers' willingness to pay for a new product is θ, where $\theta \in [0,\ 1]$. The remanufactured and new products have same functions, but the former are perceived inferior [11]. Hence, the valuation for remanufactured products is $\delta\theta$, and$\delta \in (0,\ 1)$. The inverse demand functions are $p_n = 1 - q_n - \delta q_r$ and $p_r = \delta(1 - q_n - q_r)$ [12, 13].

In order to realize the recycling of resources and protect the environment, the government has enacted regulations on the collection of used electronic products. Two regulations are analyzed: (i) A collection rate regulation imposes collection

Table 1 Notations

Notation	Description
Decision variables	
p_n, p_r	The prices of new product and remanufactured product
q_n, q_r	The quantities of new product and remanufactured product
τ	Collection rate determined by the government
t	Collection tax determined by the government
Parameters	
ε	Environmental cost of uncollected WEEE
θ	Consumers' willingness to pay for new product
$\delta\theta$	Consumers' willingness to pay for remanufactured product
$c_n,\ c_r$	Production costs of unit new product and remanufactured product
c_k	Collection cost of unit WEEE under regulation k, $k \in \{R, T\}$
Objective functions	
Π_n^k	The profit of the manufacturer under regulation k, $k \in \{R, T\}$
Π_r^k	The profit of the remanufacturer under regulation k, $k \in \{R, T\}$
Π_G^k	Objective function of the government under regulation k, $k \in \{R, T\}$

target on both enterprises and requires them to collect a specified fraction of new products for proper disposal; (ii) A taxation regulation imposes fees on both enterprises, which is similar to the environmental pollution tax, and the government undertakes the collection of e-waste.

First, we study the behavior of enterprises under the two regulations, including production and pricing decisions. Furthermore, we explore how should the government set the optimal collection rate and tax according to the decisions of enterprises.

The decision sequence is as follows: first, the government determines which regulation to adopt, and sets the collection rate in the rate regulation the collection rate and tax in the tax regulation; then the manufacturer and the remanufacturer determine their optimal production and pricing decisions.

3 The Model Analyses

3.1 Equilibrium Outcomes under Collection Rate Regulation (R)

The government is in a dominant position, so he makes decisions first; the enterprises are subordinate, they then make decisions sequentially. Furthermore, the manufacturer and the remanufacturer make decisions at the same time, that is, the Cournot game between enterprises.

The profit function of the manufacturer under collection rate regulation is

$$\max_{\{q_n\}} \Pi_n^R = (p_n - c_n)\, q_n - q_n c_R \tau. \tag{1}$$

The profit function of the remanufacturer under collection rate regulation is

$$\max_{\{q_2\}} \Pi_r^R = (p_r - c_r)\, q_r - q_r c_R \tau. \tag{2}$$

where $p_n = 1 - q_n - \delta q_r$ and $p_r = \delta(1 - q_n - q_r)$.

The government's objective function contains environmental element and does not include economic element, so the expression is

$$\begin{aligned} \max_{\{\tau\}} \ & \Pi_G^R = -\varepsilon\,(1-\tau)\,(q_n + q_r) \\ s.t. \ & 0 \le \tau \le 1 \end{aligned} \tag{3}$$

There is a Stackelberg game between the government and the enterprises, so there is a sequential decision. According to the inverse induction method, the optimal decisions of the enterprises are first analyzed.

Proposition 1 Under the collection rate regulation, the optimal production decisions of the manufacturer and the remanufacturer are $q_n^{R*} = \frac{2-2c_n+c_r-\delta-c_R\tau}{4-\delta}$ *and* $q_r^{R*} = \frac{\delta(1+c_n+c_R\tau)-2c_r-2c_R\tau}{(4-\delta)\delta}$*. The optimal prices are* $p_n^{R*} = \frac{2+c_r+c_n(2-\delta)-\delta+c_R(3-\delta)\tau}{4-\delta}$ *and* $p_r^{R*} = \frac{2c_r+\delta+c_n\delta-c_r\delta+2c_R\tau}{4-\delta}$.

The profits of the manufacturer and the remanufacturer are $\Pi_n^{R*} = \frac{(2-2c_n+c_r-\delta-c_R\tau)^2}{(4-\delta)^2}$ and $\Pi_r^{R*} = \frac{(\delta+c_n\delta-2c_r-c_R(2-\delta)\tau)^2}{(4-\delta)^2\delta}$, respectively.

Then we analyze how the government determines the optimal collection rate according to the decisions of the enterprises under the collection rate regulation. The following conclusion can be drawn.

Proposition 2 Under the collection rate regulation, the optimal collection rate determined by the government is

$$\tau^{R*} = \begin{cases} \frac{2c_R-c_r(2-\delta)+\delta(3-c_n-\delta)}{4c_R}, & \text{if} \quad c_R > \frac{\delta(3-c_n-\delta)-c_r(2-\delta)}{2} \\ 1, & \text{otherwise} \end{cases}.$$

Proposition 2 indicates that, if the collection cost is extremely low, the government set the collection rate as high as possible to reduce the impact of WEEE on the environment. Otherwise, the government should consider the both the collection cost and production cost of enterprises when set the collection rate.

3.2 *Equilibrium Outcomes Under Tax Regulation (T)*

The profit function of the manufacturer under taxation regulation is

$$\max_{\{q_n\}} \Pi_n^T = (p_n - c_n)\, q_n - tq_n. \tag{4}$$

The profit function of the remanufacturer under taxation regulation is

$$\max_{\{q_r\}} \Pi_r^T = (p_r - c_r)\, q_r - tq_r. \tag{5}$$

where $p_n = 1 - q_n - \delta q_r$ and $p_r = \delta(1 - q_n - q_r)$.

The government's objective function contains both environmental and economic elements, so the expression is

$$\max_{\{\tau,\ t\}} \ \Pi_G^T = (t - c_T\tau)(q_n + q_r) - \varepsilon(1-\tau)(q_n + q_r) \qquad (6)$$
$$s.t. \quad 0 \le \tau \le 1, \quad t > 0.$$

Similarly, according to the inverse induction method, the enterprises' optimal decisions are first analyzed.

Proposition 3 Under the collection tax regulation, the optimal production decisions of the manufacturer and the remanufacturer are $q_n^{T*} = \frac{2-2c_n+c_r-\delta-t}{4-\delta}$ *and* $q_r^{T*} = \frac{\delta(1+c_n+t)-2c_r-2t}{(4-\delta)\delta}$. *The optimal prices are* $p_n^{T*} = \frac{2+c_r+c_n(2-\delta)-\delta+t(3-\delta)}{4-\delta}$ *and* $p_r^{T*} = \frac{2c_r+\delta+c_n\delta-c_r\delta+2t}{4-\delta}$.

The profits of the manufacturer and the remanufacturer are $\Pi_n^{T*} = \frac{(2-2c_n+c_r-\delta-t)^2}{(4-\delta)^2}$ and $\Pi_r^{T*} = \frac{(\delta+c_n\delta-2c_r-t(2-\delta))^2}{(4-\delta)^2\delta}$, respectively.

Then we analyze how the government determines the optimal collection rate and the tax according to the decisions of the enterprises under the tax regulation. The following conclusion can be drawn.

Proposition 4 Under the collection tax regulation, the optimal collection rate and tax determined by the government are

$$\left(\tau^{T*},\ t^{T*}\right) = \begin{cases} \left(0,\ \frac{1}{4}(\delta(3-c_n-\delta) - c_r(2-\delta) + 2(\varepsilon + c_T\tau))\right), & if \quad c_T > \varepsilon \\ \left(1,\ \frac{1}{4}(\delta(3-c_n-\delta) - c_r(2-\delta) + 2c_T\tau)\right), & if \quad c_T \le \varepsilon \end{cases}.$$

4 Conclusion

In this paper, based on the Stackelberg game model, enterprises and governments decisions have been analyzed. First, we study enterprises' behavior under the two regulations, including production and pricing decisions. Furthermore, we explore how should the government set the optimal collection rate and tax according to environmental impact of WEEE and the collection cost.

Acknowledgements This work is supported by Natural Sciences and Engineering Research Council of Canada discovery grant (Grant No. RGPIN-2014-03594, RGPIN-2019-07115), the Postgraduate Research Innovation Program of Jiangsu Province (Grant No. KYCX18_0236), and Nanjing University of Aeronautics and Astronautics, short-term program for Ph.D. (Grant No.180611DF09).

References

1. Chen J, Chang C (2012) The co-opetitive strategy of a closed-loop supply chain with remanufacturing. Transportation Research Part E: Logistics and Transportation Review 48(2):387–400
2. Abdulrahman MD, Subramanian N, Liu C et al (2015) Viability of remanufacturing practice: a strategic decision making framework for Chinese auto-parts companies. J Clean Prod 105:311–323
3. Oraiopoulos N, Ferguson ME, Toktay LB (2012) Relicensing as a secondary market strategy. Manag Sci 58(5):1022–1037
4. Wu X, Zhou Y (2019) Buyer-specific versus uniform pricing in a closed-loop supply chain with third-party remanufacturing. Eur J Oper Res 273(2):548–560
5. Jin M, Nie J, Yang F et al (2017) The impact of third-party remanufacturing on the forward supply chain: a blessing or a curse? Int J Prod Res 55(22):6871
6. Wu C (2013) OEM product design in a price competition with remanufactured product. Omega 41(2):287–298
7. Hong X, Govindan K, Xu L et al (2017) Quantity and collection decisions in a closed-loop supply chain with technology licensing. Eur J Oper Res 256(3):820–829
8. Esenduran G, Kemahlıoğlu-Ziya E, Swaminathan JM (2017) Impact of take-back regulation on the remanufacturing industry. Prod Oper Manag 26(5):924–944
9. Mazahir S, Verter V, Boyaci T et al (2019) Did Europe move in the right direction on e-waste legislation? Prod Oper Manag 28(1):121–139
10. Atasu A, Özdemir Ö, Van Wassenhove LN (2013) Stakeholder perspectives on e-waste take-back legislation. Prod Oper Manag 22(2):382–396
11. Chen Y, Li B, Bai Q et al (2018) Decision-making and environmental implications under cap-and-trade and take-back regulations. Int J Environ Res Public Health 15(4):678
12. Ferrer G, Swaminathan JM (2010) Managing new and differentiated remanufactured products. Eur J Oper Res 203(2):370–379
13. Atasu A, Sarvary M, Van Wassenhove LN (2008) Remanufacturing as a marketing strategy. Manag Sci 54(10):1731–1746

Bank Credit Versus Trade Credit: The Preferences of Financial Formats for Supply Chain Members

Feng Tao, Qiuyang Jiang, Yao-Yu Wang, Junsong Bian, and Yan Cheng

Abstract Bank credit and trade credit are two types of financial formats in a supply chain. We consider a two-echelon supply chain with one supplier and one capital constrained retailer. By formulating the retailer's and the supplier's objective functions respectively, we find that the preference of credit formats for the retailer and the supplier are different and it depends on the credit interest rate. We also do some sensitivity study on the preference of financial formats to demonstrate our conclusions.

Keywords Bank credit · Trade credit · Credit preference · Supply chain finance

1 Introduction

Capital constraint has become an important obstacle to the firms' operations in a supply chain. As we all know, if a firm in a supply chain encounters capital restriction, it may reduce its performance and even affect the performance of the whole supply chain [1]. Therefore, the firms with capital constraints will resort to some financial tools to support the operations. Among these tools, supply chain finance (SCF) is one of the most useful ways to cope with the capital difficulties. Compared with the traditional financing, SCF is less expensive and does not involve

---

F. Tao (✉) · Q. Jiang · Y. Cheng
Department of Management Science and Engineering, East China University of Science and Technology, Shanghai, China
e-mail: ftao@ecust.edu.cn; yancheng@ecust.edu.cn

Y.-Y. Wang
Dongwu Business School, Soochow University, Suzhou, Jiangsu, China
e-mail: wangyaoyu@suda.edu.cn

J. Bian
La Trobe Business School, La Trobe University, Melbourne, VIC, Australia

X. Li, X. Xu (eds.), *Proceedings of the Seventh International Forum on Decision Sciences*, Uncertainty and Operations Research,
https://doi.org/10.1007/978-981-15-5720-0_9

recourse [2]. There is also an experiment showing that employing supply chain finance practices can not only accelerate the collaboration within the supply chain but also enhance the competitive advantage [3]. Generally, the supply chain finance has two widely used financing formats in practice. The first one is external bank credit financing (BCF) which is used universally and extensively to release the capital pressure for the firms. The other one is trade credit financing (TCF) which is an internal financing support from the upstream supplier. Trade credit is a kind of delay in payment by downstream firms to upstream firms. Although these two above-mentioned financial formats are widely used in some developed countries such as the US and the other G7 countries [4], it is still not clear why a particular financial format is used in a firm while the other is not. Therefore, the main objective of this paper is to examine the performance difference between the two financial formats and identify how the preference of the retailer and the supplier for the financing format are affected by some system parameters (such as the bank or the trade interest rate).

2 Model and Analysis

In order to answer the above questions, we design a two-echelon supply chain consisting of one supplier (he) and one retailer (she). The unit production cost in supplier's side is c, the wholesale price charged by supplier is w, the retail price in retailer's side is p per unit. We assume that the market demand is deterministic and it takes the widely used form $D = a - \beta \cdot p$, where a represents the potential market demand for the product, and β indicates the price sensitivity of demand. This linear demand function is widely used in previous studies [5, 6]. The retailer's initial capital is B. Since the retailer's initial capital cannot cover all the capital of the order, e.g., $B < wD$, the retailer has to seek external financial support. In this paper, we consider bank credit case and trade credit case respectively to investigate the optimal decisions. In each case, we assume that the supplier is the Stackelberg leader and the retailer is the follower. We use backward induction approach to obtain the optimal solutions.

2.1 Bank Credit Case

In this subsection, we hypothesize that the retailer uses the bank credit to finance the operations. Due to lack of capital $B < wD$, the retailer borrows a loan $wD - B$ from a bank with an interest rate r_b. In the first step, the retailer determines the selling price p to maximize her own profit. Therefore, the retailer's objective function in bank credit case is:

$$\pi_{RB} = pD - (1 + r_b)(wD - B) \tag{1}$$

The subscript *RB* refers to the *R*etailer in *B*ank credit case. The first and second derivatives of π_{BR} with respect to p are $\frac{\partial \pi_{RB}}{\partial p} = a - 2\beta p + (1 + r_b)\,\beta w$ and $\frac{\partial^2 \pi_{RB}}{\partial p^2} = -2\beta < 0$. With the first order condition, we can obtain the retailer's best response selling price $p(w) = \frac{a+(1+r_b)\beta w}{2\beta}$.

In the second step, anticipating the pricing decision determined by the retailer, the supplier decides the wholesale price to maximize his own profit. Therefore, the supplier's objective function in Bank credit case is:

$$\pi_{SB} = (w - c)\,D \tag{2}$$

The subscript *SB* refers to the *S*upplier in *B*ank credit case. Substituting $p(w)$ into Eq. (2), we get $\pi_{SB} = (w - c)D = (w - c)(a - \beta \cdot p(w))$. The first and second derivatives of π_{SB} with respect to w are $\frac{\partial \pi_{SB}}{\partial w} = \frac{a}{2} - (1 + r_b)\,\beta w + \frac{(1+r_b)\beta c}{2}$ and $\frac{\partial^2 \pi_{SB}}{\partial w^2} = -(1 + r_b)\,\beta < 0$. Thus, with the first order condition, we know $w_B^* = \frac{a}{2\beta(1+r_b)} + \frac{c}{2}$ is the optimal wholesale price and it is also the unique maximizer of the profit π_{SB}. Substituting w_B^* back into $p(w)$, with some algebra, we can get the optimal selling price is $p_B^* = \frac{3a}{4\beta} + \frac{c(1+r_b)}{4}$. Finally, substituting w_B^* and p_B^* into Eqs. (1) and (2), we can obtain the retailer's optimal profit is $\pi_{RB}^* = (1 + r_b)\,B + \frac{(a-\beta c(1+r_b))^2}{16\beta}$, and the supplier's optimal profit is $\pi_{SB}^* = \frac{(a-\beta c(1+r_b))^2}{8\beta(1+r_b)}$.

2.2 *Trade Credit Case*

In this subsection, we investigate the optimal decisions when the retailer uses the trade credit to finance her operations. Due to lack of capital, the retailer gets trade credit $wD - B$ with an interest rate r_t from the supplier. Similarly, we use backward induction to derive the optimal solutions. In the first step, the retailer determines the selling price p to maximize her profit. Therefore, the objective function of the retailer in trade credit case is:

$$\pi_{RT} = pD - (1 + r_t)\,(wD - B) \tag{3}$$

The subscript *RT* represents the *R*etailer in *T*rade credit case. The first and second derivatives of π_{RT} with respect to p are $\frac{\partial \pi_{RT}}{\partial p} = a - 2\beta p + (1 + r_t)\,\beta w$ and $\frac{\partial^2 \pi_{RT}}{\partial p^2} = -2\beta < 0$. With the first order condition, we can obtain the retailer's best response selling price is $p(w) = \frac{a+(1+r_t)\beta w}{2\beta}$.

In the second step, anticipating the response pricing decided by the retailer, the supplier determines the wholesale price to maximize his own profit. Therefore, his objective function in Trade credit case is:

$$\pi_{ST} = (w - c)\,D + r_t\,(wD - B) \tag{4}$$

The subscript *ST* refers to the *S*upplier in *T*rade credit case. Substituting *p*(*w*) into Eq. (4), we get $\pi_{ST} = -r_t B + ((1+r_t)w - c)(a - \beta p^T)$. The first and second derivatives of π_{ST} with respect to w are $\frac{\partial \pi_{ST}}{\partial w} = \left(\frac{a}{2} - (1+r_t)\beta w\right)(1+r_t) + \frac{(1+r_t)\beta c}{2}$ and $\frac{\partial^2 \pi_{ST}}{\partial w^2} = -(1+r_t)^2\beta < 0$. Thus, with the first order condition, we know $w_T^* = \frac{a+\beta c}{2\beta(1+r_t)}$ is the optimal wholesale price and it is also the unique maximizer of the profit π_{ST}. Substituting w_T^* back into *p*(*w*), with some algebra, the equilibrium selling price is $p_T^* = \frac{3a}{4\beta} + \frac{c}{4}$. Finally, substituting w_T^* and p_T^* into Eqs. (3) and (4), we can obtain the optimal profit of retailer is $\pi_{RT}^* = (1+r_t)K + \frac{(a-\beta c)^2}{16\beta}$, and the optimal profit of supplier is $\pi_{ST}^* = -r_t B + \frac{(a-\beta c)^2}{8\beta}$.

2.3 Numerical Study

In this subsection, we focus on the retailer and the supplier's credit preference with respect to the bank credit interest rate and the trade credit interest rate. We use MATLAB R2016b to write the program codes and draw all the figures. We set $a = 100$, $\beta = 1$, $c = 5$, $B = 400$, the interest rate of bank credit and trade credit are taken values in the interval 0 ~ 0.3. The results are summarized in Fig. 1.

From Fig. 1, we can see that the retailer and the supplier's financing format preference jointly depend on the bank credit interest rate and the trade credit interest rate. Both credit formats could be the retailer's and the supplier's best choice. Figure 1a shows the retailer's preference for the credit format. Given the initial capital, the area where the retailer prefers to the trade credit is large than the bank credit area, which means the retailer would choose the trade credit to financing in the most cases. Especially, when the trade credit rate is larger than the bank credit interest rate, the trade credit is always the best choice for the retailer. Figure 1b demonstrates

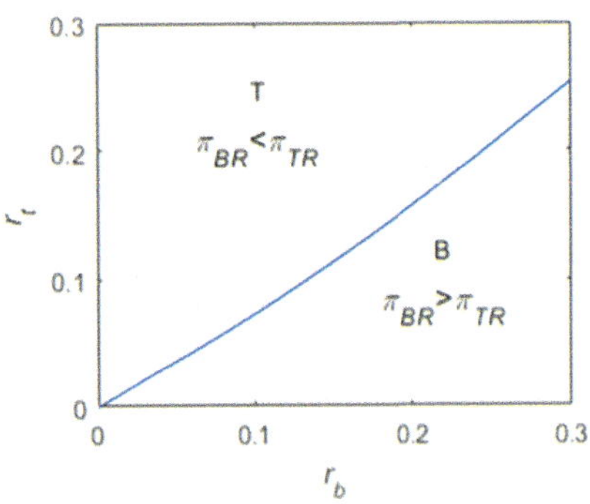

(a)

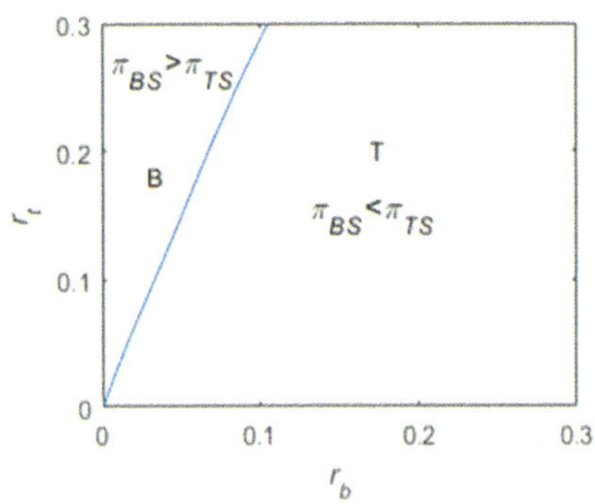

(b)

Fig. 1 Retailer's and supplier's credit preference. (**a**) Retailer's preference. (**b**) Supplier's preference

the supplier's credit preference. We can see that the supplier also prefers the trade credit in most cases. Particularly, when the bank credit interest rate is larger than the trade credit interest rate, the supplier would be better if the retailer chooses the trade credit.

3 Conclusions

This paper considers a two-echelon supply chain consisting of one dominant supplier and one capital constrained retailer. We investigate the optimal decisions in both the bank credit case and the trade credit case. The results indicate that the preference of credit formats for the retailer and the supplier are different and it jointly depends on the credit interest rate. Importantly, in the most cases, the retailer and the supplier both prefer the trade credit to the bank credit.

Acknowledgements The work described in this paper was supported by the National Natural Science Foundation of China [grant numbers 71872064, 71671119, 71772063, and 71471125]; in part by the Shanghai Pujiang Program [grant number 18PJC025]; in part by the Philosophy and Social Science Research Grand of Jiangsu Province [grant number 2016SJB630108]; in part by the China Postdoctoral Science Foundation [grant numbers 2016|T90500, 2015 |M580469, 2011M500745], and the Jiangsu Postdoctoral Science Research Foundation [grant number 1601249C].

References

1. Chen X, Wang A (2012) Trade credit contract with limited liability in the supply chain with budget constraints. Ann Oper Res 196(1):153–165
2. Wuttke DA, Blome C, Sebastian Heese H, Protopappa-Sieke M (2016) Supply chain finance: optimal introduction and adoption decisions. Int J Prod Econ 178:72–81
3. Chen X, Liu C, Li S (2019) The role of supply chain finance in improving the competitive advantage of online retailing enterprises. Electron Commer Res Appl 33:100821. https://doi.org/10.1016/j.elerap.2018.100821
4. Petersen MA, Rajan RG (1997) Trade credit: theories and evidence. Rev Financ Stud 10(3):661–691
5. Trivedi M (1998) Distribution channels: an extension of exclusive retailer-ship. Manag Sci 44(7):896–909
6. Wu CH, Chen CW, Hsieh CC (2012) Competitive pricing decisions in a two-echelon supply chain with horizontal and vertical competition. Int J Prod Econ 135(1):265–274

Increasing Pedestrian Safety and Security Management Using Internet of Things (IOT) Application

Ujjwal Khanna and Anjali Awasthi

Abstract Pedestrian safety has become an inherent problem all over the world. This work provides a unique framework for pedestrian safety using the Internet of Things. It aims to provide an IoT built motion-sensing system that ensures the safety of the pedestrians by providing smart notifications on their mobile devices of incoming vehicles as well as LED systems that notify vehicles of passing pedestrians. The system also includes location tracking, and other emergency security services (like emergency push buttons) that can be used by pedestrians as well as all other person in the vicinity. Various patterns were observed that helped identify the key elements to ensuring pedestrian safety that have been incorporated into this proposed solution. The proposed solution is highly efficient, cost effective and can be easily integrated into the current traffic management system. The key technologies used to build this component include the Internet of Things, Cloud Services, RESTful web services, and IFTTT web services. If incorporated into the current traffic management system, it can lead to enhancement in pedestrian safety, lower accident rates, and general safer traffic handling.

Keywords Internet of things · Cloud services · Motion sensor

1 Introduction

Pedestrian safety has become an important concern in every part of the world. With the increase in the number of vehicles on the roads, the rise in the number of accidents involving pedestrians has seen an exponential growth. The focus of this work is to reduce this problem by building a system that makes use of IoT, Cloud Services, RESTful web services, ThingSpeak and IFTTT web services. Nowadays,

---

U. Khanna (✉) · A. Awasthi
Concordia Institute of Information Systems Engineering (CIISE), Concordia University, Montreal, QC, Canada

X. Li, X. Xu (eds.), *Proceedings of the Seventh International Forum on Decision Sciences*, Uncertainty and Operations Research,
https://doi.org/10.1007/978-981-15-5720-0_10

every person on the street is usually looking into their smartphones while walking or is using their smartphone in some other way. The system aims to utilize this same smartphone to alert the pedestrians of their surroundings to prevent accidents.

The proposed system, in addition, makes use of hardware components such as ESP8266 NodeMCU WiFi Development Board, PIR motion sensor, and Push Button to achieve this task. This proposed solution aims to exploit the fact that every individual, today, owns a smartphone. Issuance of real-time alerts to prevent accidents is thus a key feature of the system. It also makes use of motion sensors that detect passing pedestrians on road intersections to ensure that the attached light systems remain on to notify incoming vehicles of the same. When implemented on a larger scale this system can prove to be extremely efficient in reducing the possibility of accidents.

Few works that have proposed solutions for pedestrian safety include "Smart Pedestrian Crossing Management at Traffic Light Junctions through a Fuzzy-Based Approach" by Giovanni Pau et al. [1]. This work provides a solution to dynamically control traffic lights through a Fuzzy Logic Controller (FLC). This solution provides easy adjustment of the traffic light phases depending upon the time of the day and the number of pedestrians about to cross the road. This can thus allow the pedestrian green light to be adjusted to a longer or shorter duration, depending upon the number of pedestrians that have accumulated. Another work proposed by Anubha Kumari et al. titled "Automatic Traffic Control for Pedestrian Safety" [2] proposes a solution that involves automatic control of the Traffic Lights such that as soon as a pedestrian crosses the road the traffic signal turns "red" alerting the vehicles to stop immediately. This would allow the traffic to stop only in the presence of pedestrians and thus be efficient. Yet another work titled "Pedestrian-safe Smart Crossing System based on IoT with Object Tracking" by Kwangeun An et al. [3] proposes a smart crossing system for pedestrians that makes use of a CCTV with object tracking to reduce the number of accidents involving pedestrians on the roads.

This work is organized as follows: Section 2 of the manuscript describes the materials and methodologies used to build the system. Section 3 provides the discussion which analyses the proposed solution in various situations. Section 4 concludes the paper followed by Acknowledgements and References.

2 Materials and Methodology

2.1 Materials

The system makes use of the following materials and technologies:

1. PIR Motion sensor: The PIR motion sensor is a readily available, low-cost, and efficient motion sensor. Its sensitivity can be easily adjusted to sense motions within a maximum range of 12 m from the sensor.

2. ESP8266 NodeMCU WiFi Development Board: The ESP8266 is a low-cost, and extremely efficient micro-controller. It has a full TCP/IP stack and a WiFi chip.
3. Digital Push Button, which can easily be connected to the ESP8266 micro-controller. The digital push button sends digital signals to the micro-controller, which acts accordingly.
4. IFTTT web services: IFTTT allow users to create custom applets that connect various web-based services meet the user's needs.
5. Cloud MQTT protocol: The sensed data is sent using MQTT protocol to the cloud where it is accessed and stored for analytical and other purposes.
6. Integrated Development Environment (ESPlorer IDE): The IDE is used to write the code in Lua language which can be further sent to the microcontroller with the NodeMCU Firmware installed on it.
7. Mobile device: Mobile device plays an important role in this system. The mobile devices of pedestrians are used to get alerts and notifications for safety and security purposes.
8. Breadboard, 220ohm resistors, male to male & male to female jumper wires.
9. LEDs and an active Internet Connection

2.2 *Methodology*

The proposed system works as follows:

1. The system is built using the components mentioned in the previous section (Fig. 1).
2. The motion detector connected to the system consistently checks for any movement within its vicinity. As soon as a motion is detected, the corresponding LEDs are turned on till the duration the motion exists, and this data is sent onto the cloud servers. This takes place as follows:
   (i) The motion sensor senses motion and sends data to the microcontroller, which in turn turns the LED on/off.
   (ii) The microcontroller then sends this (motion sensor and LED) data to the Cloud server.
3. These cloud servers can further be used to send notifications onto nearby mobile devices. This can be achieved my creating custom applets through IFTTT maker service. An applet is created which receives an alert trigger from the cloud server. This applet then sends the required alerts onto the mobile devices. The idea is to detect the passing pedestrians and turn on the LEDs embedded into the roads to alert incoming vehicles of passing pedestrians. Further the approaching vehicles are detected by another group of motion sensors which send this data onto the cloud. These cloud servers then send notifications onto mobile devices of nearby pedestrians (through IFTTT applets) to notify them of approaching vehicles.

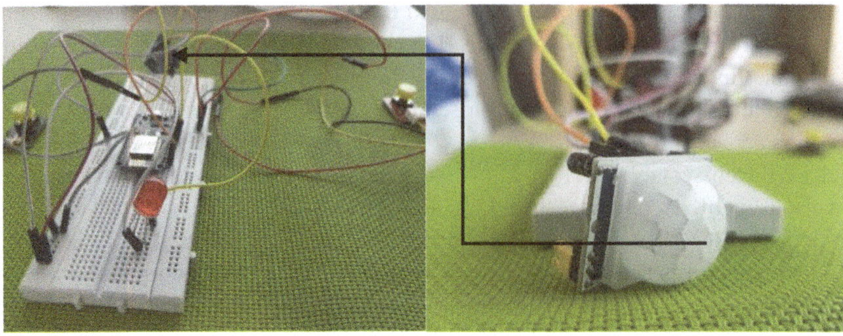

Fig. 1 System circuit with Motion sensor, LED

4. In addition, the roadsides would also be fitted with digital push buttons which can be used by pedestrians during emergency situations. Pushing the button would send notifications to nearby emergency authorities along with the roadside location to allow help to arrive as soon as possible. This would be achieved as follows:
   (i) On pressing the digital push button, the microcontroller (fitted with a GPS module) would fire a trigger.
   (ii) This would in turn trigger the respective IFTTT applet, which would send alerts to nearby emergency authorities.
   (iii) This data would then be sent onto the cloud server.
5. All this data is stored on the cloud servers and can be used later for analytical purposes as well.

Figure 2 shows how the proposed system can be used to manage the traffic on roads.

Figures 3 and 4 below show the sequence diagram of how the proposed system would work. The motion sensors would detect motion and accordingly the microcontroller would control the LEDs. In case of detection of vehicles or other obstructions alerts would be issues onto the mobile devices of the pedestrians. The sequence diagrams also show how the digital push button system would work.

Fig. 2 The system can be embedded in the roads to send data to the cloud servers and thus generate alerts on pedestrians' mobile devices. It also alerts approaching vehicles by making the LEDs glow

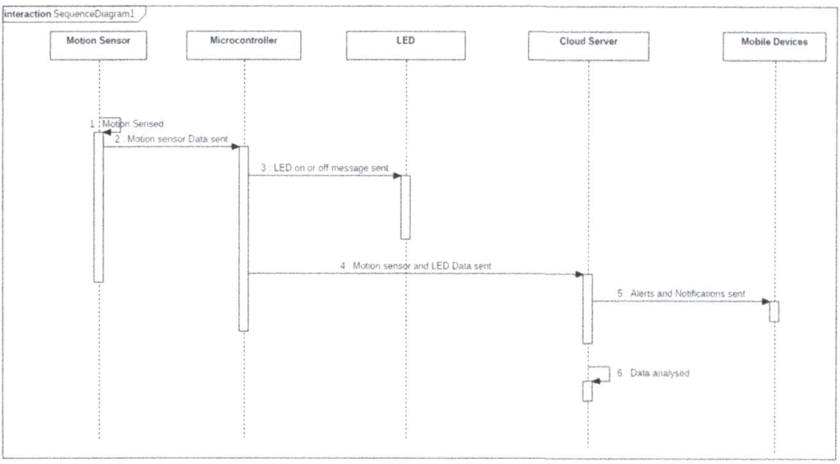

Fig. 3 Sequence diagram showing the working of the motion sensor and LEDs connected to the microcontroller, and the cloud

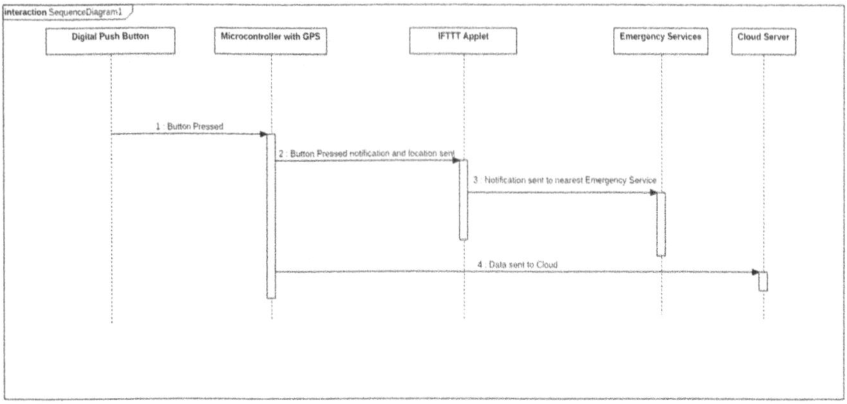

Fig. 4 Sequence diagram showing the working of the digital push button connected to the microcontroller, and the role of the cloud

3 Discussion

The proposed system, when compared with other existing technologies, provides a more promising solution due to its low-cost, efficiency, and reliability. The figures below highlight a few problems that are currently a major concern for pedestrians as well as overall traffic handling. Advanced sidewalks (Fig. 5) are built for the ease of pedestrians crossing the streets. They might be effective for small crossings but are dangerous for intersections, also psychologically it does not give pedestrians the feeling of being safe.

Speeding vehicles like the HMV's could cause harm to the pedestrians waiting to cross the streets on the advanced sidewalks. It creates a bottleneck for the approaching vehicles and thus is not an effective measure for the safety of pedestrians.

In Fig. 6, to enhance the visibility of the crossing, they are painted with bright colors. It might give an attractive path to the pedestrians to cross but for the consequent vehicles approaching it might be distracting, and not serve the purpose they are intended to serve, and accidents may still take place. Whereas, our proposed system will not only alert the pedestrians, but it will also be beneficial for the environment. Moreover, in case of emergency situations the push button system can easily be used to call for help.

Figures 7, 8, and 9 highlight more pressing issues that are a safety concern for pedestrians. These images highlight the problems currently observed in downtown Montreal, which need urgent attention. Our proposed system can be highly effective in solving these issues immediately by alerting pedestrians and calling for help. In Figs. 7 and 8, there is ongoing unenclosed construction taking place, and the sign board has fallen due to precipitation and wind flow. These have damaged the streets and people who are unaware of this can be in danger. In such scenarios the proposed

Fig. 5 Advanced sidewalks for pedestrians [4]

Fig. 6 Visible pedestrian crossing [4]

Fig. 7 Open, unattended construction site on pedestrian pathways

Fig. 8 Fallen sign boards

Fig. 9 Waste present on cycle track

system allows us to send alerts beforehand. Moreover, if any person notices it they can press the button and help can be called to handle the situation. Similarly, in Fig. 9 waste from restaurants is drawn towards the cycle track and can also be drawn towards the main road thus causing fatal accidents, using our system we can assure that the pedestrians, cyclists and drivers can be alerted of any approaching threat.

Figure 10 shows the ESPlorer IDE which was used to write and push the code onto the microcontroller. Figure 11 shows a snapshot of the system. In this, the motion sensor is sensing data and sending it onto the Cloud. Moreover, as the motion is being sensed, the LED is being turned on. This data is also being sent to the cloud.

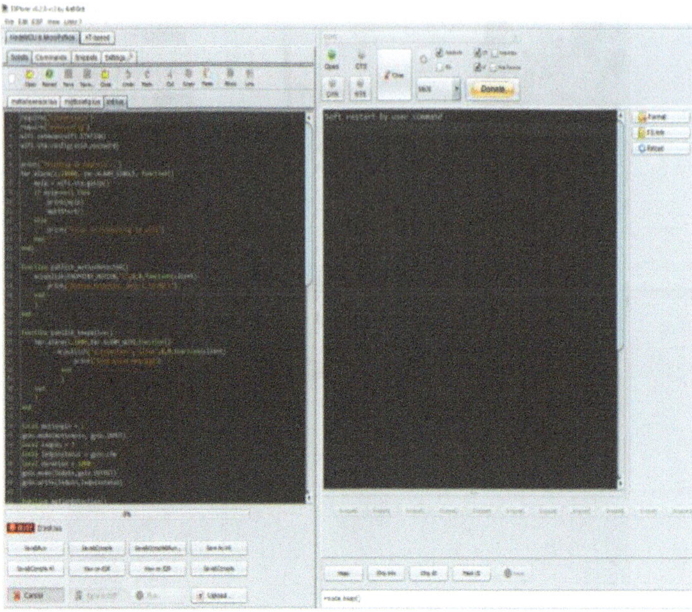

Fig. 10 Esplorer IDE with the code written in Lua language

Received messages

Topic	Message
motionsensor	Alive Motion
motionsensor	0
motionsensor	0
motionsensor	0
motionsensor	0
motionsensor	**Motion Detected*
motionsensor	*Turn on the LED*
motionsensor	0
motionsensor	1
motionsensor	1

Fig. 11 Data being received on the cloud

4 Conclusion

Pedestrian safety is an increasing concern all over the World, especially in areas which are densely populated. This work also analyses many patterns and risks to pedestrian safety that have recently been observed, and the solution proposed aims to handle these pressing concerns as well. Although many systems exist to enhance pedestrian safety, the system proposed in this work provides a solution that is not only low-cost and effective but is extremely reliable during emergencies. When implemented on a higher scale, this system can prove to be a boon to the traffic management system and prevent accidents that otherwise could not have been prevented.

Acknowledgements This work was performed under the guidance of Professor/Dr. Anjali Awasthi- Associate Professor and Graduate Program Director (M.Eng.), Concordia Institute for Information Systems Engineering *Education* Ph.D. (2004) Industrial Engineering and Automation, University of Metz, France.

Research interests: *City Logistics, Intelligent Transportation Systems, Quality assurance in supply chain management, IT & Decision making, Sustainable Supply Chain Management.*

Author Ujjwal Khanna is a Research Assistant at Concordia University pursuing Master of Science in Quality Systems and Engineering with Bachelors in Computer Science.

References

1. Pau G, Campisi T, Canale A, Severino A, Collotta M., Tesoriere G (2019) Smart pedestrian crossing management at traffic light junctions through a fuzzy-based approach. Semanticscholar.org. https://www.semanticscholar.org/paper/Smart-Pedestrian-Crossing-Management-at-Traffic-a-PauCampisi/ba898fa87af917316e7884e798971611bef69f0d. Accessed 10 June 2019
2. Kumari A, Satish B (2019) Automated traffic control for pedestrian safety - IEEE Conference Publication. Ieeexplore.ieee.org. https://ieeexplore.ieee.org/document/7975589. Accessed 10 June 2019
3. An K, Lee S, Jeong Y, Seo D (2019). https://www.researchgate.net/publication/321948233_Pedestrian-Safe_Smart_Crossing_System_Based_on_IoT_with_Object_Tracking. Accessed 10 June 2019
4. 6 aménagements pour accroître la mobilité et la sécurité des piétons | 100°, 100°, 2019. https://centdegres.ca/magazine/amenagement/6-amenagements-pour-accroitre-la-mobilite-et-lasecurite-des-pietons/. Accessed 10 June 2019

A Robust Optimization Model for a Last Mile Relief Network Design Problem

Pei-Yu Zhang, Yan-Kui Liu, Guo-Qing Yang, and Guo-Qing Zhang

Abstract In this paper, we present a robust model for the last relief network design problem. The last mile relief network can determine the locations of the points of distribution (PODs) and the locations of the demand nodes. Beside, there are many uncertainties after a disaster, we use the two uncertain sets to deal with the objective and chance constraints which obtain the uncertain parameters. In addition, we deduce the definite form of the relief network model under the uncertain sets. Finally, we verify the validity of the model by Wenchuan earthquake.

Keywords Last mile · Relief network design problem · Robust optimization · Uncertainty

1 Introduction

In recent years, frequent disasters have seriously affected the people lives and society property. relief organizations should respond quickly after a natural disaster, but they may face serious logistical challenges in actual relief operations during they transport relief supplies to victims in the affected areas. This stage of the relief operation called "last mile" in the relief network. Amiri [2] studied a distribution

P.-Y. Zhang · Y.-K. Liu
College of Mathematics and Information Science, Hebei University, Hebei, China

G.-Q. Yang (✉)
School of Management, Hebei University, Hebei, China

Department of Mechanical, Automotive & Materials Engineering, University of Windsor, Ontario, ON, Canada
e-mail: ygq@tju.edu.cn

G.-Q. Zhang
Department of Mechanical, Automotive & Materials Engineering, University of Windsor, Ontario, ON, Canada

X. Li, X. Xu (eds.), *Proceedings of the Seventh International Forum on Decision Sciences*, Uncertainty and Operations Research,
https://doi.org/10.1007/978-981-15-5720-0_11

relief network after a natural disaster, Ahmadi et al. [1] proposed a humanitarian logistics model which considering network failure in a real case study, Li et al. [8] proposed a mathematical model which considering the shelter locations and transportation planning. Li et al. [8] developed a bi-level optimization model to select the shelter locations and evacuation needs under the hurricane events. In this paper, we mainly study a last mile relief network design problem after a disaster. The last mile relief network design problem is the most difficult stage in the relief operation which directly affects the effectiveness of the total relief network. This is because there are many uncertain factors such as the traffic roads, the scarcity of resources and the demand of victims in the post-disaster environment.

This paper examines the last mile relief network design problem which provides relief organizations to transport relief supplies to victims as quickly as possible. It assumes that there has a large location distribution center (LDC), which is usually located nearby the airport. Relief organizations always deliver the relief supplies to the temporary distribution points (PODs). These PODs are the nodes located between the LDC and the demand nodes. Specifically, we need to determine the locations and capacities of the PODs. Finally, relief organizations delivered relief supplies from the PODs to demand nodes. Demand nodes are safe areas for displaced people. The 24 hours after a disaster is especially important for relief operations, thus the last mile relief network design problem must be determined in the uncertain environment after the disaster. Liu et al. [10] proposed a robust optimization model for relief distribution after disasters in an uncertain environment. Rahmani et al. [12] presented a humanitarian relief network structure to resist the risk of facility disruption after disasters. In their model, the uncertain parameters are the potential epicenters and the magnitudes of earthquakes. Shiva et al. [13] proposed a humanitarian relief chain in an uncertain environment. Liu et al. [9] designed a relief logistics planning in the relief network with uncertain demand and time. Usually, relief organizations can obtain information through the preliminary assessments, but these information of uncertain parameters are uncertain and crude. Therefore, we propose a robust last mile relief network under an uncertain environment.

In this paper, we propose a robust last mile network model with the objective which minimizing the transportation time. Chang et al. [5] studied a scenario planning method for the flood emergency logistics preparation problem in an uncertain environment, Garrido et al. [6] proposed a stochastic model for floods emergency logistics which considering the cost in the network. Noyan et al. [11] considered a stochastic model which considering the accessibility score of victims in demand nodes. In the supply chain network design problem, Yang and Liu [14] presented an equilibrium model under uncertain transportation costs and demand. Besides, they introduced a hybrid biogeography to deal with the model. Unlike these literature, we focus on the transportation time that victims can access relief supplies as quickly as possible. In addition, the disaster would destroy a lot of infrastructure that many road are not viable to transport the relief supplies in the relief network. Therefore, the demand and freight is uncertain in our last mile relief network model. Although relief organization can obtain the information through the preliminary assessments, but these information are uncertain and crude. We can not get exact probability distribution information for the uncertain parameters. In this way, we cannot deal with the objective and chance constraints with uncertain parameters. However, we can obtain the partial probability distribution information of the uncertain parameters after the disaster. Under this situation, we can use the robust optimization to deal the last mile network model [3, 4, 7]. For the objective, we deduce the exact tractable form by the Box uncertain set. For the chance constraints, we use the Box-Ball uncertain set to deduce the tractable forms. Finally, we have a manageable framework of the robust last mile relief network model.

2 Problem Statement of Last Mile Relief Network

Disasters not only cause a lot of casualties, but also damage a lot of infrastructures. Therefore, the relief organizations should make corresponding relief operations, and these rescue operations need to have a reasonable management system. Therefore this paper design a last mile relief network system for the distribution of relief supplies after a natural disaster. Next, we introduce structure of the last mile relief network. As shown in Fig. 1, the last mile network design problem includes a fixed LDC, a group of points of distributions (PODs) and a group of demand nodes. The LDC is a large warehouse for storing relief supplies. The temporary warehouse is the distribution point established temporarily in the network, and the demand node is the point where the disaster victims are located. The way of transport way between them is one-way, and relief organizations use the same means to transport relief supplies to victims.

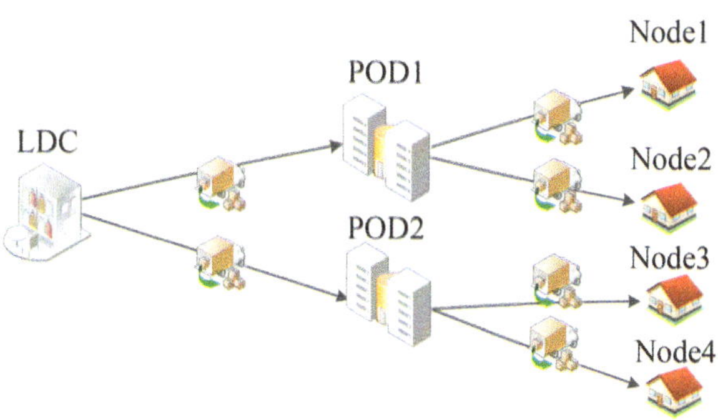

Fig. 1 The map of last mile network in TongHai country

3 The Robust Relief Network Model

In this section, we introduce the robust model for the last mile relief network.

$$\min_{p,z} \max_{p_1 \in P} E_{\mathbf{t} \sim Z_1} \left[\sum_{j \in A} p_j t_j + \sum_{j \in A} \sum_{i \in B} z_{ji} t_{ji} \right] \tag{1}$$

$$\text{s. t.} \sum_{j \in A} y_j \le N \tag{2}$$

$$\sum_{j \in A} p_j = Q \tag{3}$$

$$\sum_{j \in A} x_{ji} = 1 \qquad i \in B \tag{4}$$

$$x_{ji} \le y_j \qquad j \in A, i \in B \tag{5}$$

$$p_j \le M y_j \qquad j \in A \tag{6}$$

$$z_{ji} \le M x_{ji} \qquad j \in A, i \in B \tag{7}$$

$$r_j \le R_j \qquad j \in A \tag{8}$$

$$z_{ji} \ge d_i \qquad \forall \mathbf{d} \in Z_2,\ j \in A, i \in B \tag{9}$$

$$\sum_{i \in B} z_{ji} \le p_j \qquad j \in A \tag{10}$$

$$\sum_{j \in A} f_j r_j + \sum_{j \in J} \sum_{i \in I} f_{ji} z_{ji} \le C \qquad \forall \mathbf{f} \in Z_2 \tag{11}$$

In this model, the objective (1) we considered is to minimize the delivery time of the relief supplies in the entire relief network. Constraint (2) represents the limit of the PODs number. The constraint (3) means that the number of relief supplies transported to the PODs is equal to the available relief supplies. Constraint (4) and (5) represent the connection between the PODs and demand nodes. Each demand node can only connect to the one POD, and only if POD is open can the demand node be open. Constraint (6) means that only an open PODs can transport relief supplies. Similar to the constraint (7), only demand nodes can get relief supplies. Constraint (8) means that the relief supplies delivered to the POD cannot exceed its storage capacity. Constraint (9) means that the number of relief supplies transported to the demand node is greater than the demand of the victims. Constraint (10)means that the relief supplies delivered to the demand nodes are less than the POD capacity, and constraint (11) represents that the cost in the network is less than the budget level. Because of the existence of the uncertain parameters, the model is computationally unsolvable. The uncertain parameters in this model is transportation time, freight and the demand of victims in the demand nodes, and they are wave in different uncertain sets Z_1 and Z_2. The first uncertain set is Box uncertain set, and the second uncertain set is Box-Ball uncertain set. We transform the chance constraints with uncertain parameters into definite forms, and the final form of our robust model has the following form.

For the objective with uncertain parameters, we use the Box uncertain set to process. We assume that the uncertain parameter **t** has the following form: $t = t_o + t_l$. For the chance constraint (10) with uncertain parameters, we deduce the exact form under the Box-Ball uncertain set, and the uncertain parameter **d** has the following form: $d = d_o + d_l$. For the chance constraint (11) with the uncertain parameters **f**, we deduce the processable form under the Box-Ball uncertain set, and the uncertain parameter **f** has the following form: $f = f_o + f_l$. we can obtain the objective (12) is the equivalent form of (1), the constraint (21) and constrain (22) are the processable forms of the constraint (10), the constraint (23) and (24) are the processable forms of the constraint (10). Finally, we obtain the computationally processable form of the robust last mile relief network model.

$$\min_{p,z} \sum_{j\in J} p_j[t_j^0 + t_j^l] + \sum_{j\in J}\sum_{i\in I} z_{ji}[t_{ji}^0 + t_{ji}^l] \tag{12}$$

$$\text{s.t.} \sum_{j\in A} y_j \le N \tag{13}$$

$$\sum_{j\in A} p_j = Q \tag{14}$$

$$\sum_{j\in J} x_{ji} = 1 \qquad i \in B \tag{15}$$

$$x_{ji} \le y_j \qquad i \in B, j \in A \tag{16}$$

$$p_j \le M y_j \qquad j \in A \tag{17}$$

$$z_{ji} \le M x_{ji} \qquad j \in A, i \in B \tag{18}$$

$$p_j \le R_j \qquad j \in A \tag{19}$$

$$\sum_{i\in I} z_{ji} \le p_j \qquad j \in A \tag{20}$$

$$|w| + \Omega\sqrt{u^2} \le z_{ji} - d_i^0 \tag{21}$$

$$w + u = -d_i^l \tag{22}$$

$$|a| + \Omega\sqrt{b^2} + \le C - \sum_{j\in J} f_j^0 r_j - \sum_{j\in J}\sum_{i\in M_j} f_{ji}^0 z_{ji} \tag{23}$$

$$a + b = -\sum_{j\in J} f_j^l r_j - \sum_{j\in J}\sum_{i\in M_j} f_{ji}^l z_{ji} \tag{24}$$

4 Case Study in Wenchuan Earthquake

In this section, we apply our model to a real relief operations after Wenchuan earthquake. As we all know, the devastating of Wenchuan earthquake can not be estimated. A large number of victims are in urgent need of relief supplies. Therefore, in view of the Wenchuan earthquake relief operation, we propose a relief last mile relief network system. As shown in Fig. 2, we select a large warehouse near the airport as the LDC, and select three nodes as the candidate points for PODs. 10 nodes are selected as demand nodes in the entire last mile relief network.

4.1 Data in Model

Table 1 represents the distance from an opening LDC to the PODs. Table 2 stands for the distance from the PODs to the demand nodes. Table 3 implies the demand of the victims in a demand node, and the fluctuation term of demand is 50. The uncertain parameters **t** and **f** is related to the distance.

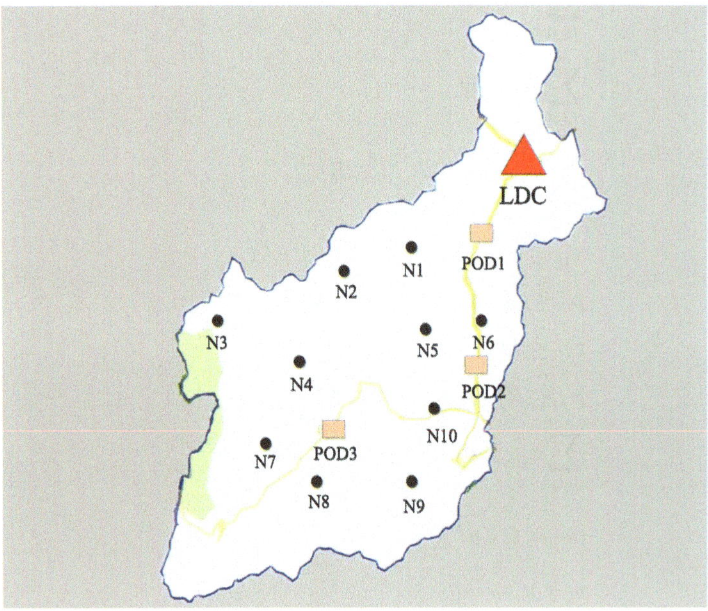

Fig. 2 The map of last mile network in WenChuan country

Table 1 The distance between LDC to PODs (in kilometer)

LDC	POD_1	POD_2	POD_3
	3.2	5.6	8.9

Table 2 The distance between the PODs and demand nodes (in kilometer)

	N1	N2	N3	N4	N5	N6	N7	N8	N9	N10
POD_1	3.2	3.6	4.9	4.9	5.6	8.0	8.2	11.2	10.5	13.5
POD_2	4.5	5.4	6.7	4.9	2.1	3.2	8.2	11.2	10.5	2.1
POD_3	14.5	10.4	9.7	8.9	10.1	7.2	3.6	4.2	3.2	2.7

Table 3 The demand of victim in demand nodes

	N1	N2	N3	N4	N5	N6	N7	N8	N9	N10
Demand	215	484	348	245	365	245	278	200	374	265

Table 4 The relief distribution in demand nodes

POD_1	POD_2	POD_3
N1(275)	N5(425)	N7(338)
N2(544)	N6(305)	N8(260)
N3(408)	N10(325)	N9(434)
N4(305)		

4.2 The Results

The number of relief supplies from the LDC to POD_1, POD_2 and POD_3 are 2000, 1968, and 1032. In addition, Table 4 represents the connections between the POD and the demand nodes, the number of relief supplies transported from the PODs to the demand nodes. The first column of the table represents that PON1 is connected with n1–n4, and the numbers in brackets represent the number of relief supplies that POD1 delivers to the demand nodes.

5 Conclusion

In this paper, we aimed to minimize the transportation time of relief supplies, and proposed a last relief network system to enable relief workers to make an effective last mile relief allocations decision. For the uncertain parameters in the last mile relief network, we use robust optimization to deal with the objective and chance constraints with uncertain parameters, and obtain a exact model which can be processed. We also provide an illustrative example and highlight the relationships between various decisions and the impact of different uncertain parameters on the model. The results show that the robust last mile relief network model proposed by this paper can well resist the uncertainty of the uncertain parameters.

Acknowledgments This work is supported by the National Natural Science Foundation of China (Grant No. 71801077 and Grant No. 61773150), the Top-notch talents of Heibei province (Grant No. 702800118009) the High-Level Innovative Talent Foundation of Hebei University and Natural Sciences and Engineering Research Council of Canada discovery grant (Grant No. RGPIN-2014-03594, RGPIN-2019-07115).

References

1. Ahmadi M, Seif A, Tootooni B (2015) A humanitarian logistics model for disaster relief operation considering network failure and standard relief time: A case study on San Francisco district. Transp Res E 75:145–163
2. Amiri A (2006) Designing a distribution network in a supply chain: Formulation and efficient solution procedure. Eur J Oper Res 171:567–576
3. Ben-Tal A, Nemirovski A (2008) Robust solutions of linear programming problems contaminated with uncertain data. Math Program 88:411–424
4. Ben-Tal AL, Ghaoui EL, Nemirovski A (2009) Robust optimization. Princeton University Press
5. Chang MS, Tseng YL, Chen JW (2007) A scenario planning approach for the flood emergency logistics preparation problem under uncertainty. Transp Res E Logist Transp Rev 43(6):737–754
6. Garrido RA, Lamas P, Pino FJ (2015) A stochastic programming approach for floods emergency logistics. Transp Res E 75:18–31
7. Goh J, Sim M (2010) Distributionally robust optimization and its tractable approximations. Oper Res 58(4):902–917
8. Li ACY, Nozick L, Xu N, et al. (2011) Shelter location and transportation planning under hurricane conditions. Transp Res E Logist Transp Rev 48(4):715–729
9. Liu YJ, Lei HT, Zhang DZ, Wu ZY (2018) Robust optimization for relief logistics planning under uncertainties in demand and transportation time. Appl Math Model 55:262–280
10. Liu YJ, Lei HT, Wu ZY, Zhang DZ (2018) A robust model predictive control approach for post-disaster relief distribution. Comput Ind Eng 135:1253–1270
11. Noyan N, Balcik B, Ataman S (2015) A stachastic optimization model for designing last mile relief networks. Transp Sci 50(3):1–22
12. Rahmani D, Zandi A, Peyghaleh E, Siamakmanesh N (2018) A robust model for a humanitarian relief network with backup covering under disruptions: a real world application. Int J Disaster Risk Reduct 28:56–68
13. Shiva Z, Ali BA, Sadjadi SJ (2016) Robust optimization model for humanitarian relief chain design under uncertainty. Appl Math Model 40:7996–8016
14. Yang G, Liu YK (2017) Optimizing an equilibrium supply chain network design problem by an improved hybrid biogeography based optimization algorithm. Appl Soft Comput 58:657–668

Optimal Pricing Policy Under Multi-Period Setting with Strategic Consumers

Haijiao Li, Kuan Yang, and Mohammed Almanaseer

Abstract Multi-period selling strategy is generally implemented by retailers to stimulate sales through better targeting different segments of the consumer population. In this study, we develop a multi-period model formwork to explore how the retailer could maximize the profit by determining and applying optimal prices in the three selling periods, including advance selling, regular selling, and clearance sales periods. Meanwhile, we find that the selling strategy that products are sold by three periods is beneficial for the retailer.

Keywords Advance selling · Clearance sales · Strategic consumers

1 Introduction

With innovation of information technologies and rapid development of economy, retailers are facilitated to promote selling of products by incorporating both the advance selling season and clearance sale season, in addition to regular selling season. The advance selling season has the characterization that the retailers offer customers to pre-order new products, such as books, electronics, and video games, from online distribution before their release dates [1]. According to Deloitte's survey, as of February 2014, up to 16% of online sales have made an advance selling strategy [2]. Meanwhile, clearance sale season has the typical feature that the retailers offer a steeper discount for consumers who strategically wait to purchase

H. Li · K. Yang (✉)
School of Business Administration, Hunan University, Changsha, China
e-mail: haijiaoli@hnu.edu.cn; yangkuan@hnu.edu.cn

M. Almanaseer
Supply Chain and Logistics Optimization Research Central, Department of Mechanical, Automotive & Materials Engineering, University of Windsor, Windsor, ON, Canada
e-mail: almanas@uwindsor.ca

X. Li, X. Xu (eds.), *Proceedings of the Seventh International Forum on Decision Sciences*, Uncertainty and Operations Research,
https://doi.org/10.1007/978-981-15-5720-0_12

at the end of the selling season [3]. BestBuy shows that an estimated 20% of customers strategically wait for their purchases due to a substantial price discount in the clearance sales [4].

Numerous research has been conducted over whether a retailer should sell products in advance [5, 6]. The effects of return police [7], capacity allocation [8], risk or loss aversion [9], and pricing schemes [10] on the benefit of the retailer have been systematically investigated. Similarly, clearance-sale and clearance pricing have also received sufficient attention [11], where fixed clearance price (salvage value) or a fixed discount at the end of selling period are assumed in most studies [12, 13]. However, the existing literature has been conducted by considering either advance selling or clearance sales individually. There exists a gap to explore both the advance selling and clearance sales in the multi-period setting.

In this paper, our research aims to fill this gap. We first portray the demand allocation among the various selling periods using utility theory. Using these demand portraits, we then establish a multi-period model formwork to study the determination of the retailer's optimal price to address strategic consumers who time their purchase in three selling periods: the "advance" selling period, the "regular" selling period, and the final "clearance" sales period. We finally carry on to analyze the effect on the profit of retailer and evaluate how the retailer choose the optimal selling strategy.

2 Model Description

Consider that a retailer sells one product to consumers through three different periods. Before the selling season, the retailer incurs a procurement cost c for every product sold and reveals all prices decisions p_1, p_2 and p_3, which are denoted as the advance price, the regular price, and the clearance price, respectively. It is intuitive that $p_1 \geq p_3$ is to be assumed, because the clearance sales is provided more generous discount for the wait-for-purchasing consumers than advance selling. All unsold products at the end of the selling season are normalized to zero.

Consumer utility is different for different selling periods. It is assumed that the consumers are heterogeneous in the production valuation v, which is uniformly distributed [0,1] [14]. All consumers are involved in advance selling period and each consumer desires no more than one unit product. In the first period, when the consumers order the products from the retailer in advance, the consumers could not inspect its valuation. Thus, the product may be returned to the retailer if the product valuation is lower than the actual valuation. Let β denote the probability that the consumers like the product is β, then the consumers expected utility U_a is $\beta(v - p_1)$. In the second period, since the consumers can know exactly about the product, they can choose to buy immediately at the regular price or wait for the sale at clearance price. If the price is attractive, the consumer may purchase the product immediately with the valuation v, where the consumer expected utility U_r is $v - p_2$. Otherwise, consumers may find it worthwhile to wait until clearance sale period even if the product may be sold out by then. Correspondingly, the consumers expected utility U_c is $q(v - p_3)$, where q denotes the probability that the product is in stock in the third period. Note that we assume $q < \beta$, otherwise there is no consumer purchasing product from the first period.

3 Equilibrium Analysis

In this section, we study the optimal equilibrium. Consumers make decisions to purchase via comparing their utilities among different selling periods. A consumer with a valuation of v may buy the products in period 1, in period 2, in period 3 if the utility functions are non-negative, namely, $U_a = \beta(v - p_1) \geq 0$, $U_r = v - p_2 \geq 0$ and $U_c = q(v - p_3) \geq 0$, respectively. Then, only one of the valuations attains the maximum in max $\{\beta(v - p_1), v - p_2, q(v - p_3)\}$, $v - p_2$, $q(v - p_3)$) for a product valuation of v, indicating that the consumers will purchase their desired product in one of the selling period with more consumer surplus. Therefore, the demand functions can be derived from the advance product Q_1, regular product Q_2, and clearance product Q_3 during different selling situations as follows.

Lemma 1 The demand functions are given by

$$(Q_1, Q_2, Q_3)\begin{cases} \left(\frac{p_2-\beta p_1}{1-\beta} - \frac{\beta p_1 - q p_3}{\beta - q}, 1 - \frac{p_2-\beta p_1}{1-\beta}, \frac{\beta p_1 - q p_3}{\beta - q} - p_3\right) & (p_1, p_2, p_3) \in R_1 \\ \left(0, 1 - \frac{p_2 - q p_3}{1-q}, \frac{p_2 - q p_3}{1-q} - p_3\right) & (p_1, p_2, p_3) \in R_2 \\ (0, 0, 1 - p_3) & (p_1, p_2, p_3) \in R_3 \\ \left(1 - \frac{\beta p_1 - q p_3}{\beta - q}, 0, \frac{\beta p_1 - \beta p_3}{\beta - q} - p_3\right) & (p_1, p_2, p_3) \in R_4 \end{cases}$$

where the regions R_i are defined as follows:

$$\begin{aligned} R_1 &= \left\{p_3 \leq p_1 \leq \frac{(\beta-q)p_2 + q(1-\beta)p_3}{\beta(1-q)}, p_2 \leq 1 - \beta + \beta p_1\right\} \\ R_2 &= \left\{\frac{(\beta-q)p_2 + q(1-\beta)p_3}{\beta(1-q)} \leq p_1 \leq 1, p_3 \leq p_2 \leq 1 - q + q p_3\right\} \\ R_3 &= \left\{\frac{\beta - q + q p_3}{\beta} \leq p_1 \leq 1, 1 - q + q p_3 \leq p_2 \leq 1\right\} \\ R_4 &= \left\{p_3 \leq p_1 \leq \frac{\beta - q + q p_3}{\beta}, 1 - \beta + \beta p_1 \leq p_2 \leq 1\right\} \end{aligned}$$

The proof is similar to Bernstein et al. [15], and thus is not presented here. According to the region of demand functions of Lemma 2, we can characterize the consumers' purchasing behavior in Fig. 1. In practice, there is always regular selling period which the retailers are highly focuses on. Thus, this study only pay attention to the regions that incur positive sales of the regular selling, i.e., the R_1 and R_2 Regions. Consequently, the profit of the retailer can be given by:

$$\Pi_r^i = \left(p_1^i - c\right) Q_1^i + \left(p_2^i - c\right) Q_2^i + \left(p_3^i - c\right) Q_3^i,$$

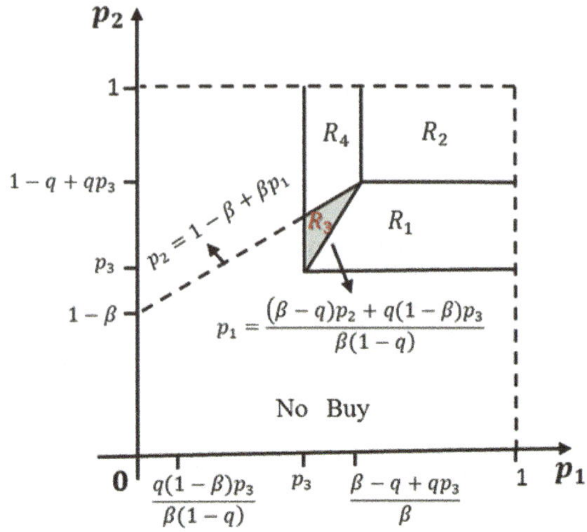

Fig. 1 The demand regions

where $i = 1, 2$.Then, we can characterize the corresponding equilibrium results, as shown below.

Theorem 1 The equilibria under Regions 1 ($i = 1$) and Regions 2 ($i = 2$) are as follows:

	p_1^i	p_2^i	p_3^i	Π_r^i
$i = 1$	$\frac{\beta^2+(c+1)\beta+cq}{\beta^2+2\beta+q}$	$\frac{(1+c)\beta^2+(cq+c-q+3)\beta+(1+c)q}{2(\beta^2+2\beta+q)}$	$\frac{(1+c)\beta^2+(3c-cq+q+1)\beta+(1+c)q}{2(\beta^2+2\beta+q)}$	$\frac{(1-c)^2(\beta^2-\beta q+3\beta+q)}{4(\beta^2+2\beta+q)}$
$i = 2$	n/a	$\frac{cq+c+2}{q+3}$	$\frac{2c+q+1}{q+3}$	$\frac{(1-c)^2}{q+3}$

According to Theorem 1, the retailer will charge the equilibrium price p_j^i, where $i \in \{1,2\}$ and $j \in \{1,2,3\}$, to extract the maximum consumer utility. In the basic model above, it is assumed that the consumers may purchase the product if the utility of buying is none negative, which implies that the consumers may buy product at a price p_j^i in period j even though they only get a zero utility. Similar assumption and results may be found in [16], where the consumers will buy the product when the reservation price is not less than the selling price, and the retailer can extract the maximum consumer utility by charging a price at the consumers' reservation price.

Theorem 1 shows that can be divided into two regions. The next will reveal that a Nash equilibrium can be sustained in Region 1 where the product is sold in three periods, that is, the retailer have no incentive to deviate from this solution.

Corollary 1 The global optimal decision is Region 1, that is, the optimal selling strategy of the retailer is that the product is sold in three periods.

This Corollary suggests that when sales of product occur in advance period, regular period, and clearance periods, the retailer can get the maximum profit. As a result, the selling way that the product is sold in three periods is more beneficial for the retailer than the other way that the product is sold in the last two period.

Early research has shown that the profit of retailer suffers from more sophisticated strategic consumers [17, 18]. Some scholars conclude that preannounced pricing, implying that the prices in the current and future market are determined and promised at the beginning of the selling season, is good tactic to discourage consumers from waiting for a markdown [19, 20]. However, we in this paper find that the introduction of the advance selling period can mitigate consumer's strategic waiting behavior to obtain high overall sales volume. It is significant for the retailer to offer managerial insights on some strategic selections.

4 Numerical Studies

From the above Corollary 1, we observe that the selling selection that the product are sold via three periods outperforms that that the product are sold via the last two periods. Consequently, we only center on the former selection discussed in the following. We first set the reasonable base parameter values for the numerical simulation. In practice, consumers who focus on advance period are loyal to per-order products. They will not return their desire products unless there is quality defect. As a result, the match probability that the product purchased in period 1 matches the consumer is set by $\beta = 0.8$. We know $q < \beta \leq 1$, so we set the availability probability that the product is in stock in the clearance period as $q = 0.3$.

We first study the effect of the match probability on the optimal results. From Fig. 2, we note that both the optimal prices, that is, the advance price, the regular price and the clearance price, increase in c, and the optimal profit decreases in c. It is intuitive for this finding. The increase procurement cost means that the retailer will spend more purchase cost to sell products to the final market, then correspondingly the retail prices increase. High retail prices has a negative on demand. As a result, the retailer's profit decreases in the product cost.

We then discuss the effect of the match probability on the optimal results. It follows from Fig. 3 that the optimal advance price and regular price increase in β, while the optimal clearance price decreases in β. This is straightforward because an increase in β intuitively means the consumers are more interested in pre-ordering products due to a better match, so the retailer sets a high advance price to capture this part profit. Based on information that is provided by the advance period, it is reasonable that the retailer sets high regular price to enhance own profit. At the end of the selling season, the retailer should decrease the clearance price to avoid inventory risk, which is accord with the real situation.

Finally, we explore the effect of the availability probability on the optimal results. In respond to Fig. 4, we test the reaction of the optimal results when q changes. The optimal advance and regular prices will decrease and the clearance price will increase as q increases, which is reasonable. When the increase of the availability probability leads more consumers to choose to wait for purchasing, which hurts retailer's profit. Consequently, the retailer should decrease the advance and regular prices so as to compensate for the decrease in revenue. On the other hand, the retailer

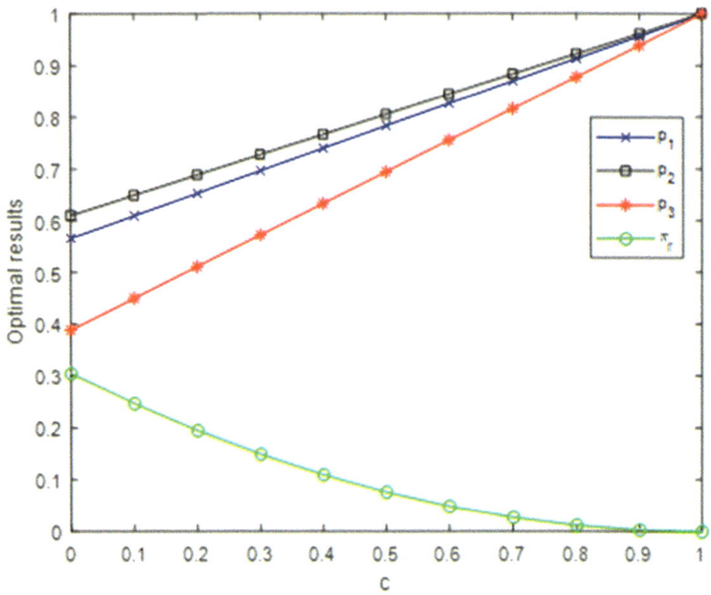

Fig. 2 Impact of the product cost

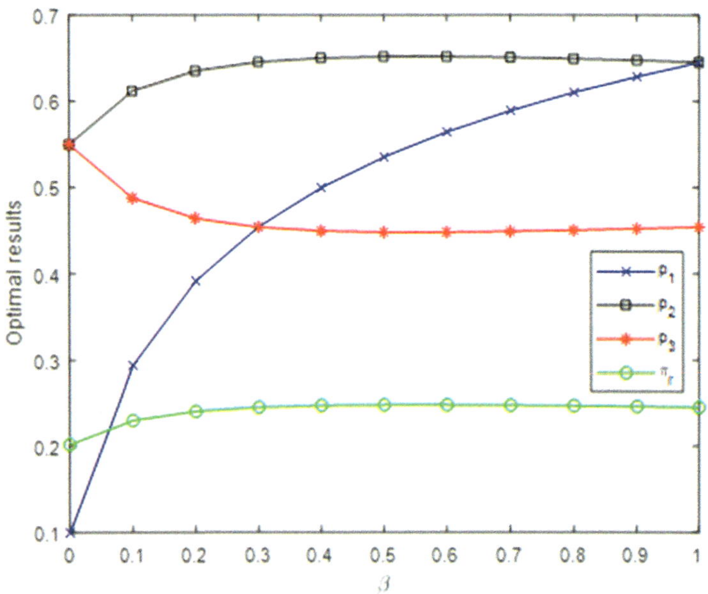

Fig. 3 Impact of the match probability

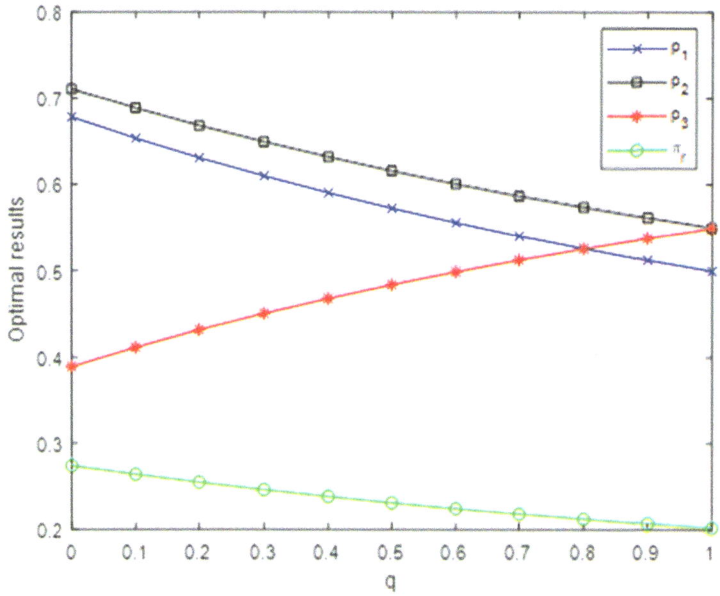

Fig. 4 Impact of the availability probability

is more central on regular seasons. As a result, the decrease of the regular price have an adverse effect on retailer's profit.

5 Conclusion

Many retailers have adopted advance selling period or clearance sales period to better target different consumer segment in order to increase profitability. This paper extends the two-period selling to the multi-period selling, and finds the optimal prices decisions in different selling periods, including the advance selling, the regular selling and the clearance sales periods to maximize the profitability of retailer. Moreover, we observe that the retailer can benefit from the selling strategy that the product is sold in three periods than that the product is sold in regular selling and clearance sales periods. Certainly, with the rise of the big data era, how social networks affect strategic consumers' valuations and purchasing decisions will be interesting areas to explore.

Acknowledgments This work was supported by Humanities and Social Science Program of Ministry of Education of China (Grant No. 17YJA630119), Natural Sciences and Engineering Research Council of Canada discovery grant (Grant No. RGPIN-2014-03594, RGPIN-2019-07115) and China Scholarship Council (No. 201806130044).

Appendix

Proof of Theorem 1. We first proof the region 2, and the other region 1 is similar. For the ease of notational convenience, we have omitted the superscript "2" in this proof. According to the profit of retailer

$$\Pi_r = (p_1 - c)\left(\frac{p_2 - \beta p_1}{1-\beta} - \frac{\beta p_1 - q p_3}{\beta - q}\right) + (p_2 - c)\left(1 - \frac{p_2 - \beta p_1}{1-\beta}\right) + (p_3 - c)\left(\frac{\beta p_1 - q p_3}{\beta - q} - p_3\right),$$

we can get the Hessian matrix H $= \begin{pmatrix} \frac{2(q-1)\beta}{(1-\beta)(\beta-q)} & \frac{1+\beta}{1-\beta} & \frac{q+\beta}{\beta-q} \\ \frac{1+\beta}{1-\beta} & -\frac{2}{1-\beta} & 0 \\ \frac{q+\beta}{\beta-q} & 0 & -\frac{2\beta}{\beta-q} \end{pmatrix}$ is negative-defined matrix, Hence, Π_r is joint concave in (p_1, p_2, p_3). Let $\frac{\partial \Pi_r}{\partial p_1} = 0$, $\frac{\partial \Pi_r}{\partial p_2} = 0$, $\frac{\partial \Pi_r}{\partial p_3} = 0$, and the following can be obtained

$$p_1 = \frac{\beta^2 + (c+1)\beta + cq}{\beta^2 + 2\beta + q},\ p_2 = \frac{(1+c)\beta^2 + (cq + c - q + 3)\beta + (1+c)q}{2(\beta^2 + 2\beta + q)},$$
$$p_3 = \frac{(1+c)\beta^2 + (3c - cq + q + 1)\beta + (1+c)q}{2(\beta^2 + 2\beta + q)}.$$

In the following, we verify that these prices lie in $R_1 = \left\{p_3 \le p_1 \le \frac{(\beta - q)p_2 + q(1-\beta)p_3}{\beta(1-q)},\ p_2 \le 1 - \beta + \beta p_1\right\}$. Clearly, $p_3 \le p_1$. Substituting p_1, p_2 and p_3 into R_1 yields

$$\frac{(\beta - q)p_2 + q(1-\beta)p_3}{\beta(1-q)} - p_1 = \frac{(\beta-1)(\beta-q)(c-1)}{2(\beta^2 + 2\beta + q)} \ge 0,$$

$$1 - \beta + \beta p_1 - p_2 = \frac{(\beta-1)(\beta+q)(c-1)}{2(\beta^2 + 2\beta + q)} \ge 0.$$

Hence, R_3 is not empty. Thus, the retailer's profit function is shown in Theorem 1.

Proof of Theorem 1: $\Pi_m^1 - \Pi_m^2 = \frac{(1-c)^2(q-1)(\beta-1)(\beta-q)}{4(q+3)(\beta^2+2\beta+q)} \ge 0$.

References

1. Shugan SM, Xie J (2000) Advance pricing of services and other implications of separating purchase and consumption. J Serv Res 2(3):227–239
2. Deloitte, the omnichannel opportunity: unlocking the power of the connected consumer. https://www2.deloitte.com/content/dam/Deloitte/uk/Documents/consumer-business/unlocking-the-power-of-the-connected-consumer.pdf
3. Su XM, Zhang FQ (2008) Strategic customer behavior, commitment, and supply chain performance. Manag Sci 54(10):1759–1773
4. McWilliams G (2004) Minding the store: analyzing customers, best buy decides not all are welcome. Wall Street J. http://www.wsj.com/articles/SB109986994931767086
5. Xie J, Shugan S (2009) Advance selling theory
6. Cheng Y, Li H, Thorstenson A (2018) Advance selling with double marketing efforts in a newsvendor framework. Comput Ind Eng 118:352–365
7. Wu M, Teunter RH, Zhu SX (2018) Online marketing: when to offer a refund for advanced sales. Int J Res Mark. https://doi.org/10.1016/j.ijresmar.2018.11.003
8. Oh J, Su X (2018) Reservation policies in queues: advance deposits, spot prices, and capacity allocation. Prod Oper Manag 27(4):680–695
9. Ma SS, Li G, Sethi SP, Zhao X (2019) Advance selling in the presence of market power and risk-averse consumers. Decis Sci 50(1):142–169
10. Xiao L, Xu M, Chen Z, Guan X (2019) Optimal pricing for advance selling with uncertain product quality and consumer fitness. J Oper Res Soc 9:1–18
11. Nocke V, Peitz M (2007) A theory of clearance sales. Econ J 117(522):964–990
12. Khanra A, Soman C, Bandyopadhyay T (2014) Sensitivity analysis of the newsvendor model. Eur J Oper Res 239(2):403–412
13. Aviv Y, Pazgal A (2008) Optimal pricing of seasonal products in the presence of forward-looking consumers. Manuf Serv Oper Manag 10(3):339–359
14. Zhou EF, Zhang JZ, Gou QL, Liang L (2015) A two period pricing model for new fashion style launching strategy. Int J Prod Econ 160:144–156
15. Bernstein F, Song JS, Zheng XN (2009) Free riding in a multi-channel supply chain. Nav Res Logist 56(8):745–765
16. Zhao X, Pang Z, Stecke KE (2016) When does a retailer's advance selling capability benefit manufacturer, retailer, or both? Prod Oper Manag 25(6):1073–1087
17. Cachon GP, Swinney R (2009) Purchasing, pricing, and quick response in the presence of strategic consumers. Manag Sci 55(3):497–511
18. Levin Y, McGill J, Nediak M (2010) Optimal dynamic pricing of perishable items by a monopolist facing strategic consumers. Prod Oper Manag 19(1):40–60
19. Cachon GP, Feldman P (2015) Price commitments with strategic consumers: why it can be optimal to discount more frequently … than optimal. Manuf Serv Oper Manag 17(3):399–410
20. Correa J, Montoya R, Thraves C (2016) Contingent preannounced pricing policies with strategic consumers. Oper Res 64(1):251–272

A Bi-objective Model for Last Mile Relief Network Design Problem Under Uncertain Demand

Pei-Yu Zhang, Yan-Kui Liu, Guo-Qing Yang, and Guo-Qing Zhang

Abstract In this study, we introduce a last mile relief network design problem, which determines the locations and capacities of distribution points under the uncertain environment. Also, we consider the uncertain demand in the relief network and deal with the chance constraint under the partial probability distribution information. Then, we build a model of the last mile relief network with uncertain demand. At the same time, we deduce the exact tractable form of the relief network model. Finally, we apply the mathematical model to the actual earthquake to verify the validity of the model.

Keywords Last mile relief network design problem · Bi-objective · Ambiguity set · Uncertainty

1 Introduction

The goal of the relief network is to deliver relief supplies quickly and safely to the affected areas after a natural disaster. After the disaster occurs, relief organization should distribute relief supplies to the victims in demand nodes quickly. First of all, the relief supplies arrive at the important hubs (airports) through different channels.

P.-Y. Zhang · Y.-K. Liu
College of Mathematics and Information Science, Hebei University, Hebei, China

G.-Q. Yang (✉)
School of Management, Hebei University, Hebei, China

Department of Mechanical, Automotive & Materials Engineering, University of Windsor, Ontario, ON, Canada
e-mail: ygq@tju.edu.cn

G.-Q. Zhang
Department of Mechanical, Automotive & Materials Engineering, University of Windsor, Windsor, ON, Canada

X. Li, X. Xu (eds.), *Proceedings of the Seventh International Forum on Decision Sciences*, Uncertainty and Operations Research,
https://doi.org/10.1007/978-981-15-5720-0_13

Next, the relief supplies are distributed to the large distribution center (LDC), and the supplies at the distribution centers are transferred to the points of distribution (PODs). At last, relief organizations transport relief supplies to the victims in the demand nodes. In the text, we are most concerned about the availability of effective supplies to victims. Therefore, we mainly consider the last mile phase in the relief network. In 2007, Kovcs et al. [6] discussed the humanitarian logistics after natural disasters. Sheu [10] considered the emergency logistics distribution approach to transport relief supplies for urgent demand. Yahyaei and Bozorgi-Amiri [12] studied the shelters and supply facility locations in the relief network. More research can be founded in Akbari and Salman [1], Najafi et al. [8], Noyan and Kahveci***ou*** [9].

Post-disaster relief operations often face many challenges such as the destroyed transport roads and resource constraint. It is a challenge for relief organizations to develop effective distribution plans in a complex post-disaster environment while maintaining coordinated action. In this paper, our goal is to design a last mile relief network to help decision makers make effective supplies distribution plans in the final stage. In this study, we study the last mile relief network design problem after a disaster. In this network, there is a large distribution center which the location is known, and the relief organizations deliver the relief supplies to the PODs. Finally, relief organizations transport relief supplies to the victims in the demand nodes. At the same time, the network determines the locations and capacities of distribution points, the locations of demand nodes and the number of relief supplies delivered between them.

For this relief network, we propose a bi-objective mathematical model. Noyan and Kahveci***ou*** [9] proposed a stochastic model to minimize the accessibility of the victims in the demand nodes. Liu et al. [7] presented a mathematical model which considering the unsatisfied demand in the relief network. Najafi et al. [8] studied multi-objective model to manage the logistics of the relief supplies and injured people after disaster. In this paper, we consider two objectives. The first objective is to minimize transportation time which aiming to deliver the relief supplies to the demand nodes quickly. The second objective is to minimize the cost of the entire relief network. The whole two-objective model is designed to transport relief supplies to the victims quickly and reasonably under a reasonable budget. The post-disaster environment is complex, and it is impossible for relief organization to obtain all the information in the first place. Therefore, many factors are uncertain. In this paper, we discuss the uncertain demand of victims in demand node. Due to the inadequacy of historical information and the lag of post-disaster information, we cannot obtain the accurate demand of the victims. Therefore, the demand of the victims in the last mile relief network are uncertain.

We deal with the chance constraint with uncertain parameters by distributionally robust optimization method Ben-Tal and Nemirovski [3], Wiesemann et al. [11]. If we know the distribution information of the uncertain parameters, maybe we can use the stochastic optimization method to deal with the chance constraint with uncertain demand [9]. However, the precise information of disaster victims are not available, and we can only obtain partial probability distribution information of them. Therefore, distributionally robust optimization is a method to deal with uncertain parameters [2, 4, 5]. In this paper, we derive the exact tractable form of the dual objective model. Besides, we use the constraint method to deal with the two objectives. Finally, the effectiveness of the model is verified by practical examples.

2 Problem Statement

In this section, we introduce the last mile relief network design problem. There be a relief network which obtaining a set of LDCs, a set of PODs, and a set of demand nodes. This last mile relief network design problem determines the location selection of LDCs, the locations and capacities of the PODs, and the number of relief supplies delivered between the PODs and the demand nodes. Whiling considers the time and cost of transportation over the relief network. Next, we describe the characteristics of this relief network.

As shown in Fig. 1, there is usually one or several LDCs close to the airport in the last relief network, and each LDC serves the demand nodes through several PODs. Specifically, there has a fixed LDC in the relief network, whose location is predetermined and has a certain capacity. After that relief organizations deliver relief supplies to the PODs which are temporary distribution points that can be located anywhere in the relief network. Finally, relief supplies are transported to the victims in the demand nodes supplies.

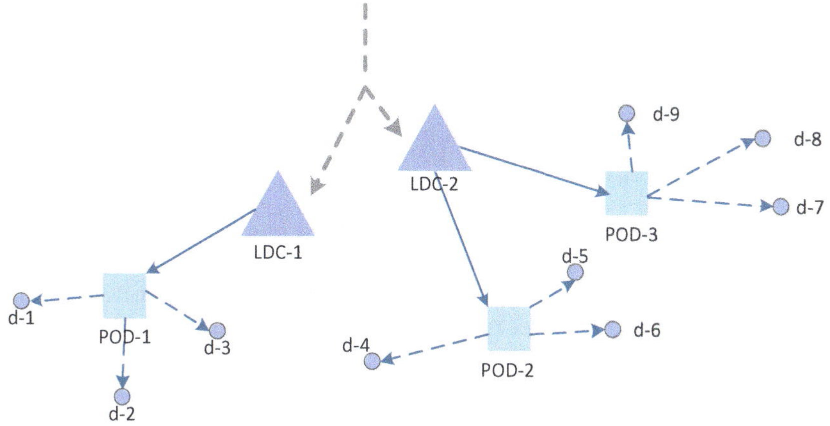

Fig. 1 An example of a last mile relief network

3 A Bi-objective Model for Last Mile Relief Network

The last mile relief network model of last mile relief network is written as following:

$$\min_{m,n} E\left[\sum_{j\in P} t_j m_j + \sum_{j\in P}\sum_{i\in N} t_{ji} n_{ji}\right] \tag{1}$$

$$\min_{y,m,n} E\left[\sum_{j\in P} f_j y_j + \sum_{j\in P} c_j m_j + \sum_{j\in P}\sum_{i\in M_j} c_{ji} n_{ji}\right] \tag{2}$$

$$\text{s.t. } z_1 \le \sum_{j\in P} y_j \le z_2 \tag{3}$$

$$\sum_{j\in P} x_{ji} = 1 \qquad i \in N \tag{4}$$

$$x_{ji} \le y_j \qquad j \in P, i \in N \tag{5}$$

$$n_{ji} \le G x_{ji} \qquad j \in P, i \in N \tag{6}$$

$$m_j \le G y_j \qquad j \in P \tag{7}$$

$$m_j \le R_j \qquad j \in P \tag{8}$$

$$\sum_{j\in P} m_j = \theta \tag{9}$$

$$\sum_{i\in N} n_{ji} \le m_j \qquad j \in P \tag{10}$$

$$\Pr_{\mathbf{o}\sim\mathbb{P}}\{n_{ji} \ge o_i\} \ge 1-\epsilon \qquad \mathbb{P}\in\mathcal{P}, i \in N, j \in P \tag{11}$$

In this model, we discuss two objectives. The first objective (1) is to minimize transport time, and the second objective (2) is to minimize the cost of the relief network. The two objectives can balance cost and time of the relief network, which help decision makers to deliver relief supplies to victims timely and reasonably. Constraint (3) limits the number of PODs, and z_1 and z_2 represent the upper bound and the lower bound of the number of PODs, respectively. Constraint (4) indicates that each demand node can only connect to one POD, which ensures that the decision maker can track the whereabouts of relief supplies. Constraint (5) means that the selection of demand node location is affected by the POD location. Constraint (6) represents the number of relief supplies delivered to the demand node depending on the location of the demand node. Constraint (7) implies that the number of relief supplies delivered to the POD is affected by the POD location. Constraint (8) represents the number of relief supplies for an open POD is limited by the capacity. Constraint (9) considers that the number of relief supplies in the network is equal to the available supplies. Constraint (10) means that the total relief supplies delivered to the demand nodes does not exceed the inventory of a POD. Constraint (11) implies the relief supplies are delivered to demand node must meet demand of victim with probability $1 - \eta$.

In our model, the demand of victim in demand nodes is uncertain. This is because the number of people affected after a disaster is not yet known, and the extent of the damage is impossible to estimate, thus the demand of the victims are uncertain. But we can use historical data and forecasting tools to get partly probability distribution information of uncertain demand, such as expectation and variance. Therefore, we will use these partial distribution information of uncertain demand to deal with chance constraint.

4 The Formulation of the Last Mile Relief Network Model

In this section, we discuss the processing of the last mile relief network model which discussed in last section. For the transportation time objective and cost objective, we use the ε-constraint method to balance the two objectives. For the chance constraint with uncertain demand, we use an ambiguous set $\mathcal{U}$ which obtaining the partly probability distribution information to deal with the chance constraint. Through the processing of objectives and constraints which contain uncertain parameters, we have a deterministic tractable model of the last mile relief network model:

$$\min_{m,n} \sum_{j \in P} u_{t_j} m_j + \sum_{j \in P} \sum_{i \in N} u_{t_{ji}} n_{ji} \tag{12}$$

$$\text{s.t.} \sum_{j \in P} f_j y_j + \sum_{j \in P} u_{c_j} m_j + \sum_{j \in P} \sum_{i \in M_j} u_{c_j} n_{ji} \leq \epsilon L \tag{13}$$

$$\sum_{j \in P} x_{ji} = 1 \qquad i \in N \tag{14}$$

$$x_{ji} \leq y_j \qquad j \in P, i \in N \tag{15}$$

$$n_{ji} \leq G x_{ji} \qquad j \in P, i \in N \tag{16}$$

$$m_j \leq G y_j \qquad j \in P \tag{17}$$

$$m_j \leq R_j \qquad j \in P \tag{18}$$

$$\sum_{j \in P} m_j = \theta \tag{19}$$

$$\sum_{i \in N} n_{ji} \leq m_j \qquad j \in P \tag{20}$$

$$-n_{ji} + o_i^0 + \beta \log\left(d_i^o \cosh(\frac{o_i^l}{\beta}) + 1 - d_i^0\right) + \beta \log(\frac{1}{\eta}) \leq 0 \tag{21}$$

Table 1 The expectation of distance between LDC to PODs (in kilometer)

LDC	XinFuXiang	JingXingXiang	SiNanJiangXiang
	[5, 6]	[3, 4]	[8, 9]

Table 2 The expectation of distance between the PODs and demand nodes (in kilometer)

	N1	N2	N3	N4	N5	N6	N7	N8	N9	N10
POD_1	[3, 4]	[5, 6]	[3, 4]	[7, 8]	[8, 9]	[9, 10]	[9, 10]	[12, 13]	[16, 17]	[17, 18]
POD_2	[9, 10]	[8, 9]	[6, 7]	[5, 6]	[4, 5]	[5, 6]	[9, 10]	[10, 11]	[11, 12]	[12, 13]
POD_3	[16, 17]	[17, 18]	[15, 16]	[10, 11]	[9, 10]	[8, 9]	[5, 6]	[4, 5]	[5, 6]	[3, 4]

Table 3 The demand in demand nodes

	N1	N2	N3	N4	N5	N6	N7	N8	N9	N10
Demand	318	275	412	348	298	302	207	385	274	319

5 Case Study

We present a practical example to verify the validity of the model. Mojiang county in Sichuan province was hit by a magnitude 5.6 earthquake in 2018, and 2,000 people were affected. Therefore, we propose the data required for the experiment of the earthquake in Mojiang county. Figure 1 shows each node in Mojiang county. There is a fixed LDC, three candidate PODs and 10 demand nodes. We will design a last mile relief network based on these nodes. Table 1 implies the expectation of distance between LDC to PODs, and the distance is a interval. Table 2 stands for the expectation of distance between the PODs and demand nodes. Table 3 expresses the demand of victims in a demand node (Fig. 2).

5.1 The Results

The number of relief supplies from the LDC to POD1, POD2 and POD3are 2000. In addition, Table 4 represents the connections between the POD and the demand nodes and the number of relief number. The first column of the table represents that PON1 is connected with N1–N3, and the numbers of relief supplies transported by POD1 represented in the brackets.

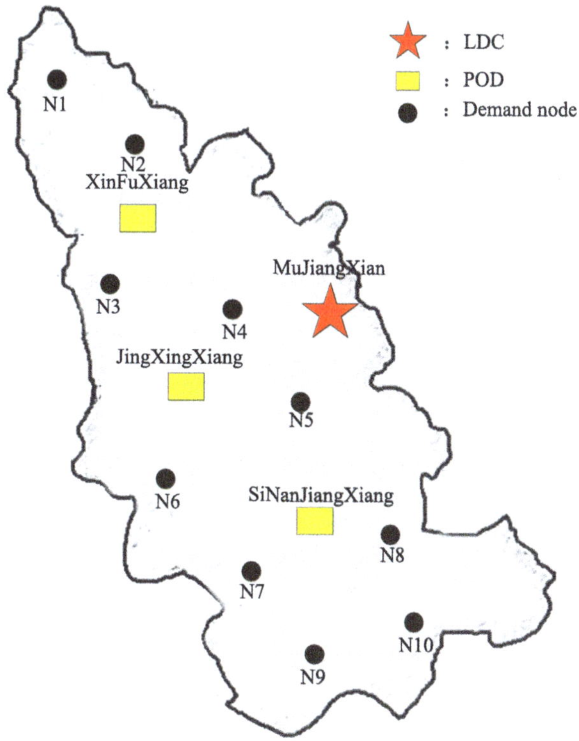

Fig. 2 An example of a last mile relief network

Table 4 The relief distribution in demand nodes

XinFuXiang	JingXingXiang	SiNanJiangXiang
N1(339.41)	N3(369.41)	N6(228.41)
N2(294.41)	N4(319.41)	N7(406.41)
N3(433.41)	N5(323.41)	N8(295.41)
		N8(340.41)

Acknowledgments This work is supported by the National Natural Science Foundation of China (Grant No. 71801077 and 61773150), the Top-notch talents of Heibei province (Grant No. 702800118009) the High-Level Innovative Talent Foundation of Hebei University and Natural Sciences and Engineering Research Council of Canada discovery grant (Grant No. RGPIN-2014-03594, RGPIN-2019-07115).

References

1. Akbari V, Salman FS (2017) Multi-vehicle synchronized arc routing problem to restore post-disaster network connectivity. Eur J Oper Res 257(2):625–640
2. Ben-Tal A, Hochman E (1972) More bounds on the expectation of a convex function of a random variable. J Appl Probab 9(4):803–812

3. Ben-Tal A, Nemirovski A (2008) Robust solutions of linear programming problems contaminated with uncertain data. Math Program 88:411–424
4. Bertsimas D, Sim D (2004) The price of robustness. Oper Res 52(1):1–22
5. Goh J, Sim M (2010) Distributionally robust optimization and its tractable approximations. Oper Res 58:902–917
6. Kovács G, Spens KM (2007) Humanitarian logistics in disaster relief operations. Int J Phys Distrib Logist Manag 37(2):99–114
7. Liu YJ, Lei HT, Zhang DZ, Wu ZY (2018) Robust optimization for relief logistics planning under uncertainties in demand and transportation time. Appl Math Model 55:262–280
8. Najafi M, Eshghi K, Dullaert W (2013) A multi-objective robust optimization model for logistics planning in the earthquake response phase. Transp Res E Logist Transp Rev 49(1):217–249
9. Noyan N, Kahveciou glu G (2018) Stochastic last mile relief network design with resource reallocation. Oper Res Spect 40(1):187–231
10. Shue JB (2007) An emergency logistics distribution approzch for quick response to urgent relief demand in disasters. Transp Res E Logist Transp Rev 43(6):687–709
11. Wiesemann W, Kuhn D, Sim M (2014) Distributionally robust convex optimization. Oper Res 62(6):1358–1376
12. Yahyaei M, Bozorgi-Amiri A (2018) Robust reliable humanitarian relief network design: An integration of shelter and supply facility location. Ann Oper Res, 1–20

Revenue-Sharing Versus Wholesale Price Contracts Under Chain-to-Chain Competition

Hai Shen, Jie Liu, Guoqing Zhang, Yelin Fu, and Kin Keung Lai

Abstract We consider price competition with a linear demand function and compare three scenarios. To compare the impact of revenue-sharing or wholesale price contracts on manufacturers, retailers and supply chains. In the three common cases, the maximum profit of retailers, manufacturers and supply chains was analyzed and compared. We consider the interaction between the various links of the supply chain, and through different strategies, achieve the optimal decision of wholesale price and order quantity. By comparing the profit trends between manufacturers, retailers and supply chains, and the difference in profits, we can get different strategies for the supply chain in the two competing supply chains. And the impact of the profits of retailers and manufacturers is significant.

Keywords Supply chain competition · Game theory · Revenue-sharing · Wholesale price contracts

1 Introduction

Inspired by the rapid development of information technology in recent years, firms that face more intense global competition are cooperating with one another as never before, to achieve successes in the market place. This paper offers a effectively

H. Shen (✉) · J. Liu
School of Business, Xi'an International Studies University, Xi'an, Shaanxi, China
e-mail: shenhai@xisu.edu.cn

G. Zhang
Mechanical, Automotive and Materials Engineering, University of Windsor, Windsor, Ontario, Canada
e-mail: gzhang@uwindsor.ca

Y. Fu · K. K. Lai
College of Economics, Shenzhen University, Shenzhen, China

X. Li, X. Xu (eds.), *Proceedings of the Seventh International Forum on Decision Sciences*, Uncertainty and Operations Research,
https://doi.org/10.1007/978-981-15-5720-0_14

examination of how to design and operate supply chains to effectively deal with supply chain competition. To compare the impact of revenue-sharing or wholesale price contracts on both manufacturers, retailers and supply chains.

2 Model

Consider two competing supply chains that distribute the homogeneous product in the market, where each supply chain consists of an exclusive manufacturer and a retailer. Each manufacturer can choose either a revenue-sharing contract or a wholesale price contract with the retailer. The retailers are engaged in contract competition by determining order quantities from their manufactures. Two supply chains, manufactures and retailers are indexed by i, and j, where $i, j \in \{1, 2\}$, $i \neq j$.

Several useful assumptions are proposed to derive the analytical solutions of this model and maintained throughout the forthcoming analysis:

1. All players are risk neutral.
2. The manufacturers can only contract with the retailers of their own supply chains [1].
3. The contract information is public to all manufactures and retailers [1].
4. The production costs associated with both manufactures are identical and have been normalized to zero [2].
5. The homogeneous product has a short life cycle and thus two supply chains only interact once.
6. Consumer demand for the product is represented by a linear, downward slopping, inverse demand function $p(q) = 1 - q$, where p and q are the price and the total amount of product in the market, respectively. This inverse demand function has been widely employed to depict quantity competition in extant literature [1–4]. Without loss of generality, the maximum market demand is assumed to 1.

3 Analysis

To compare the impact of revenue-sharing or wholesale price contracts on both manufacturers, retailers and supply chains, we investigate the following three scenarios:

3.1 *Scenario WW*

In this scenario, two competing retailers simultaneously choose their order quantities q_i, $i \in \{1, 2\}$ to maximize profits from retail sales, taking the wholesale prices

w_i, $i \in \{1, 2\}$ as given. The retailers' problem is:

$$\begin{cases} \max\limits_{q_1} \{(1 - q_1 - q_2 - w_1)\, q_1\}, \\ \max\limits_{q_2} \{(1 - q_1 - q_2 - w_2)\, q_2\}. \end{cases} \tag{1}$$

the retailers' profits $\prod_{r_i}^{WW}$, $i \in \{1, 2\}$, the manufacturers' profits $\prod_{m_i}^{WW}$, $i \in \{1, 2\}$ and both supply chains' profits $\prod_i^{WW}$, $i \in \{1, 2\}$, respectively:

$$\prod\nolimits_{r_i}^{WW} = \frac{4}{81}, \prod\nolimits_{m_i}^{WW} = \frac{5}{27}, \prod\nolimits_{i}^{WW} = \frac{19}{81}, i \in \{1, 2\}. \tag{2}$$

3.2 Scenario WR

This section considers the scenario WR in which manufacturer 1 offers wholesale price mechanism while manufacturer 2 provides revenue-sharing contract. More specifically, under the revenue-sharing contract, manufacturer 2 not only charges w_2 per product purchased, but also shares a percentage of the revenue of retailer 2. Let γ, $\gamma \in (0, 1)$ be the fraction of manufacturer 2 earns, so $1 - \gamma$ is the fraction of retailer 2 keeps. This mechanism (w_2, γ) extends the revenue-sharing contract provided by Cachon and Lariviere [5], and is in line with Yao et al. [6, 7]. The equilibrium outcomes in this scenario are also determined by backward induction. Given wholesale price contract w_1 offered by manufacturer 1 and revenue-sharing contract (w_2, γ) provided by manufacturer 2, both retailers choose profit-maximizing order quantities

$$\begin{cases} \max\limits_{q_1} \{(1 - q_1 - q_2 - w_1)\, q_1\}, \\ \max\limits_{q_2} \{(1 - \gamma)\,(1 - q_1 - q_2)\, q_2 - w_2 q_2\}. \end{cases} \tag{3}$$

The interaction between the wholesale price charged by manufacturer 2 and its kept fraction of the revenue earned by retailer 2 is demonstrated in the following Fig. 1. It is remarkable that the wholesale price is not always decreasing in γ, but increases when $\gamma > \frac{45-2\sqrt{102}}{28} \approx 0.8857$. This seems unreasonable but can be interpreted as a prevention mechanism that protects corresponding retailer from possible negative profit, and thus grants the implementations of revenue-sharing contract.

scenario *WR*, the optimal order quantity regarding retailer 1, 2

$$\begin{cases} q_{r_1}^{WR} = \frac{10-8\gamma}{45-28\gamma}, \\ q_{r_2}^{WR} = \frac{10}{45-28\gamma}. \end{cases} \tag{4}$$

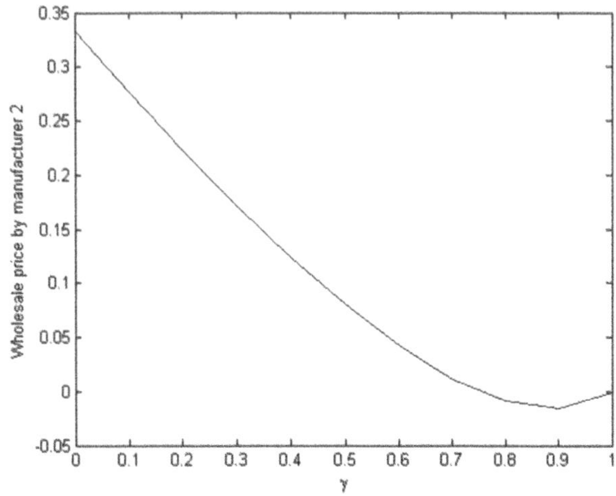

Fig. 1 The interaction between $w_{m_2}^{WR}$ and γ

Proposition 1 At the equilibrium of scenario WR, the optimal order quantity regarding retailer 1 is decreasing in $\prod_{r_i}^{WR}, i \in \{1,2\}$, while the optimal order quantity for retailer 2 is increasing in $\prod_{r_i}^{WR}, i \in \{1,2\}$. Furthermore, retailer 2 always orders more product than retailer 1.

The retailers' profits $\prod_{r_i}^{WR}, i \in \{1,2\}$, the manufacturers' profits $\prod_{m_i}^{WR}, i \in \{1,2\}$ and both supply chains' profits $\prod_{i}^{WR}, i \in \{1,2\}$, respectively:

$$\begin{cases} \prod_{r_1}^{WR} = \frac{4(5-4\gamma)^2}{(45-28\gamma)^2}, \\ \prod_{r_2}^{WR} = \frac{100(1-\gamma)}{(45-28\gamma)^2}, \end{cases} \tag{5}$$

$$\begin{cases} \prod_{m_1}^{WR} = \frac{6(5-4\gamma)^2}{(45-28\gamma)^2}, \\ \prod_{m_2}^{WR} = \frac{50(3-2\gamma)}{(45-28\gamma)^2}, \end{cases} \tag{6}$$

$$\begin{cases} \prod_{1}^{WR} = \frac{10(5-4\gamma)^2}{(45-28\gamma)^2}, \\ \prod_{2}^{WR} = \frac{50(5-4\gamma)}{(45-28\gamma)^2}. \end{cases} \tag{7}$$

Proposition 2 At the equilibrium of scenario WR.

The profit of supply chain 2 is always larger than that of supply chain 1, the difference between which is increasing in γ.

Proposition 2 is vividly demonstrated by the following Figs. 2, 3 and 4.

Fig. 2 Profits of retailers

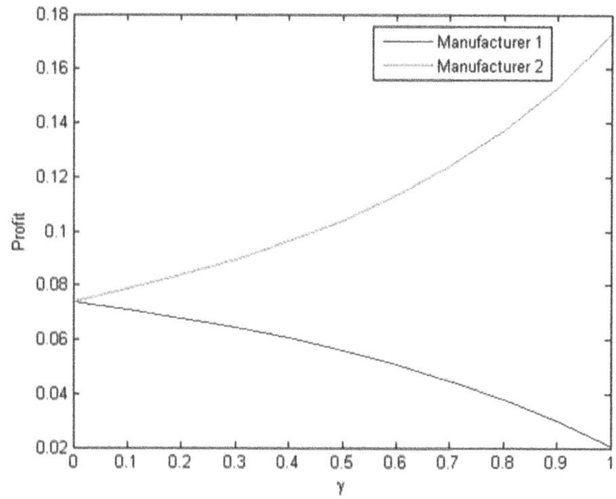

Fig. 3 Profits of manufacturers

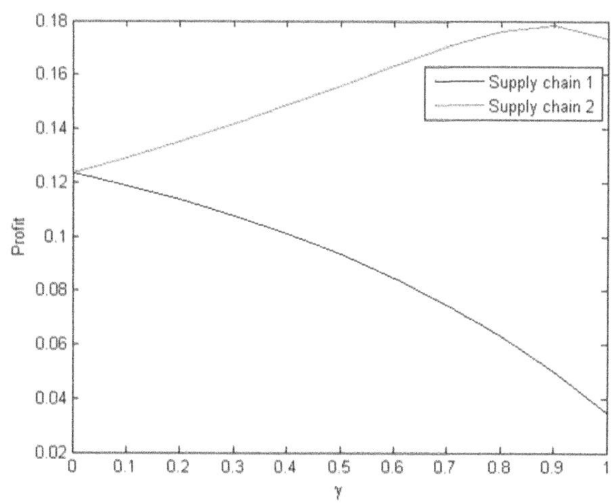

3.3 Scenario RR

In scenario RR, both manufactures offer revenue-sharing contracts. In details, manufacturer 1 provides revenue-sharing contract (w_1, α), $\alpha \in (0, 1)$, while manufacturer 2 offers revenue-sharing contract (w_2, γ), $\gamma \in (0, 1)$. These revenue-sharing contracts have been defined in scenario RW. The equilibrium outcomes in this scenario are determined by backward induction as well (Figs. 5, 6 and 7).

Proposition 3 At the equilibrium of scenario RR.

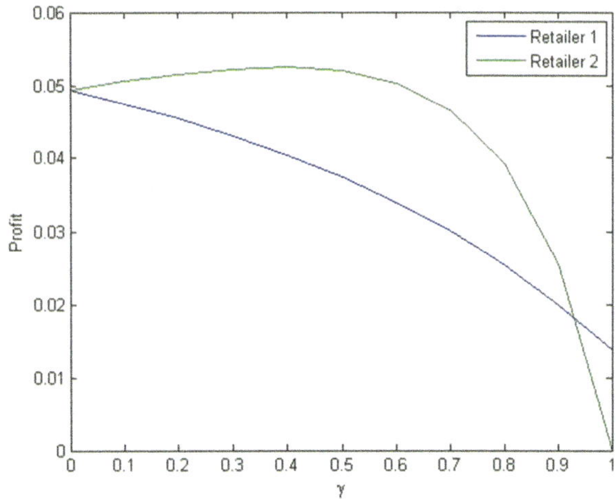

Fig. 4 Profits of supply chains

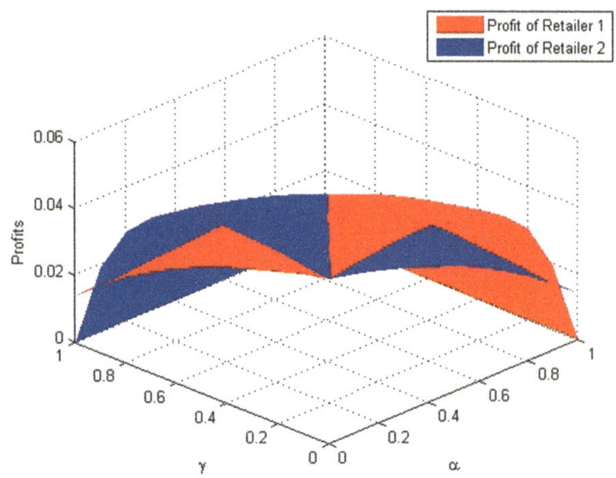

Fig. 5 Profits of retailers

4 Strategic Decisions

We first summarize and compare the profits of retailers in the presence of different contract mixtures, which are shown in the following Table 1. Hereafter, we denote supply chain 1 and 2 by S1 and S2, respectively.

Next, we also summarize and compare the profits of manufacturers in the presence of different contract mixtures, which are indicated in the Table 2.

Finally, we investigate the profits of both supply chains, which are demonstrated in Table 3.

In summary, when manufacturer i offers wholesale contract to retailer i, and the revenue fraction required by manufacturer j belongs to $\left(\frac{495}{784}, 1\right)$, the Nash equilibrium $\left(\underline{W}, \underline{W}\right)$ is valid for manufacturers, retailers and supply chains. In

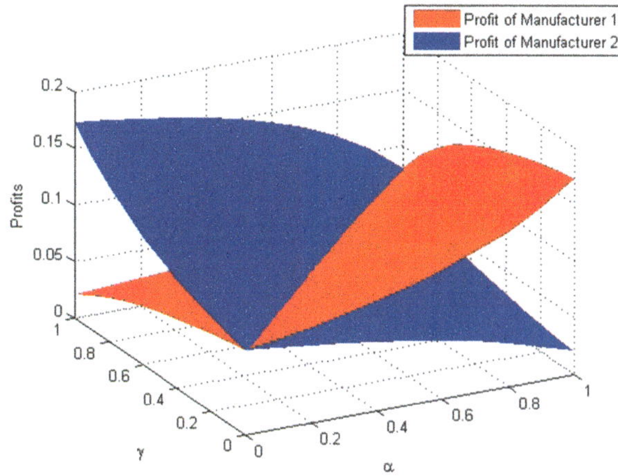

Fig. 6 Profits of manufacturers

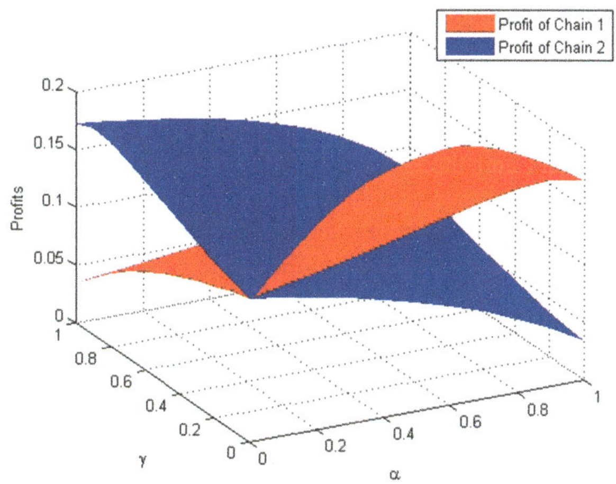

Fig. 7 Profits of supply chains

Table 1 Profits of retailers

		S2	
		W	R
S1	W	$\left(\frac{4}{81}, \frac{4}{81}\right)$	$\left(\frac{4(5-4\gamma)^2}{(45-28\gamma)^2}, \frac{100(1-\gamma)}{(45-28\gamma)^2}\right)$
	R	$\left(\frac{100(1-\alpha)}{(45-28\alpha)^2}, \frac{4(5-4\alpha)^2}{(45-28\alpha)^2}\right)$	$\left(\frac{4(1-\alpha)(5-4\gamma)^2}{[45-28(\alpha+\gamma)+16\alpha\gamma]^2}, \frac{4(1-\gamma)(5-4\alpha)^2}{[45-28(\alpha+\gamma)+16\alpha\gamma]^2}\right)$

addition, when manufacturer 1 offers revenue-sharing contract to retailer 1, and $(45-28\alpha)\sqrt{1-\gamma} - [45-28(\alpha+\gamma)+16\alpha\gamma] > 0$, the Nash equilibrium $(\underline{R}, \underline{R})$ is simultaneously accepted by manufacturers, retailers and supply chains. Symmetrically, when manufacturer 2 offers revenue-sharing contract to retailer 2, and $(45-28\gamma)\sqrt{1-\alpha} - [45-28(\alpha+\gamma)+16\alpha\gamma] > 0$, the Nash equilibrium $(\underline{R}, \underline{R})$ is also accepted by manufacturers, retailers and supply chains.

Table 2 Profits of manufacturers

		S2	
		W	R
S1	W	$\left(\frac{5}{27}, \frac{5}{27}\right)$	$\left(\frac{6(5-4\gamma)^2}{(45-28\gamma)^2}, \frac{50(3-2\gamma)}{(45-28\gamma)^2}\right)$
	R	$\left(\frac{50(3-2\alpha)}{(45-28\alpha)^2}, \frac{6(5-4\alpha)^2}{(45-28\alpha)^2}\right)$	$\left(\frac{2(3-2\alpha)(5-4\gamma)^2}{[45-28(\alpha+\gamma)+16\alpha\gamma]^2}, \frac{2(3-2\gamma)(5-4\alpha)^2}{[45-28(\alpha+\gamma)+16\alpha\gamma]^2}\right)$

Table 3 Profits of supply chains

		S2	
		W	R
S1	W	$\left(\frac{19}{81}, \frac{19}{81}\right)$	$\left(\frac{10(5-4\gamma)^2}{(45-28\gamma)^2}, \frac{50(5-4\gamma)}{(45-28\gamma)^2}\right)$
	R	$\left(\frac{50(5-4\alpha)}{(45-28\alpha)^2}, \frac{10(5-4\alpha)^2}{(45-28\alpha)^2}\right)$	$\left(\frac{2(5-4\alpha)(5-4\gamma)^2}{[45-28(\alpha+\gamma)+16\alpha\gamma]^2}, \frac{2(5-4\gamma)(5-4\alpha)^2}{[45-28(\alpha+\gamma)+16\alpha\gamma]^2}\right)$

5 Conclusion

First, when both manufacturers offer Different strategies contracts in the supply chain, the relationship between the order quantity selected by the two competing retailers and the maximum profit is obtained. At the same time, analysis of the wholesale price and order quantity optimization, how much each increase in retailers, manufacturers and supply chain revenue.

Second, we characterize the optimal terms for a wholesale price contract with linear penalty for any given level of supply chain competition intensity. We also show that, for such a linear contract there always exists a coordinating revenue-sharing contract which can make both supplier and retailer better off.

Finally, different strategies for manufacturing are different for manufacturers, retailers and supply chains. The Nash equilibrium is valid for manufacturers, retailers and supply chains. In addition, when manufacturer 1 offers revenue-sharing contract to retailer 1, and, the Nash equilibrium is simultaneously accepted by manufacturers, retailers and supply chains.

Acknowledgements This work was supported by China-Canada scholars' exchange program.

References

1. Ha AY, Tong S (2008) Contracting and information sharing under supply chain competition. Manag Sci 54(4):701–715
2. Shou B, Huang J, Li E (2009) Managing supply uncertainty under chain-to-chain competition. Working paper, College of Business, City University of Hong Kong, Hong Kong
3. Arya A, Mittendorf B, Sappington DEM (2008) The make-or-buy decision in the presence of a rival: strategic outsourcing to a common supplier. Manag Sci 54(10):1747–1758
4. David A, Adida E (2015) Competition and coordination in a two-channel supply chain. Prod Oper Manag 24(8):1358–1370

5. Cachon GP, Lariviere MA (2005) Supply chain coordination with revenue-sharing contracts: strengths and limitations. Manag Sci 51(1):30–44
6. Yao Z, Leung SCH, Lai KK (2008a) Manufacturer's revenue-sharing contract and retail competition. Eur J Oper Res 186(2):637–651
7. Yao Z, Leung SCH, Lai KK (2008b) The effectiveness of revenue-sharing contract to coordinate the price-setting newsvendor product's supply chain. Supply Chain Manag: Int J 13(4):263–271

A Clustering-Sequencing Approach for the Facility Layout Problem

Saeideh Salimpour, Sophie-Charlotte Viaux, Ahmed Azab, and Mohammed Fazle Baki

Abstract This paper presents a new approach that solves the unequal-area facility layout problem by conceptually clustering facilities into groups and then sequencing them. The objective is to minimize the total material handling cost by placing the facilities, which have more interactions (in terms of the flow of materials) with the rest of the facilities closer to the centroid of the production floor to the extent possible. The developed methodology provides promising results.

Keywords Clustering-sequencing approach · Optimization · Unequal-area facility layout problem

1 Introduction

The facility layout problem (FLP) is a vital issue that must be tackled in the early stages of the design of a manufacturing system [1]. About 20–50% of the total operating expenses and 15–70% of that of manufacturing-related costs are attributed to material handling cost [2]. Therefore, finding an efficient layout can reduce these costs by up to 30% in manufacturing [3, 4]; optimal arrangements of facilities within a shop will result in a dramatic cut of the total distance traveled by all units on the shop floor.

A multitude of algorithmic methods have been used to solve the FLP problem. FLP is categorized into two main classes geometrically, namely discrete and

S. Salimpour (✉) · S.-C. Viaux · A. Azab
Production and Operations Management Research Lab, University of Windsor, Windsor, ON, Canada
e-mail: salimpo@uwindsor.ca; sviaux@uwindsor.ca; azab@uwindsor.ca

M. F. Baki
Odette School of Business, University of Windsor, Windsor, ON, Canada
e-mail: fbaki@uwindsor.ca

X. Li, X. Xu (eds.), *Proceedings of the Seventh International Forum on Decision Sciences*, Uncertainty and Operations Research,
https://doi.org/10.1007/978-981-15-5720-0_15

continuous [1]. A continuous modeling approach was used by Allahyari and Azab [5] to solve the cellular manufacturing layout problem. Modeling FLP as a Quadratic Assignment Problem (QAP) is a discrete and NP-complete model; QAP is one of the most well-known models in the literature [5–7]. Modeling FLP with QAP requires two assumptions: (1) the equality in areas of the facilities; and (2) the fixed location of facilities, which are known in advance [8]. QAP was linearized; an integer linear programming was developed [9]; another linearized Mixed Integer Programming (MIP)-based QAP formulation was presented [10]. Other MIP formulations were introduced for the problem as well [11, 12]. A distance based-objective was formulated as MIP by Montreuil [13] in a continuous layout representation. Also, FLP was modeled using graph theory, where the desirable adjacency of each pair of facilities had been defined a priori [14–17]; however, there is no guarantee of optimality when it comes to solving unequal-area facility layout problems [8]. Branch and bound was also used to solve the problem [18, 19].

Due to the combinatorial nature of the optimization problem in FLP [20], the exact solution of the problem is complex and highly time-consuming [4] and is only successful for a very limited number of facilities (20 or fewer facilities) [21]. Therefore, near-optimal algorithms such as Simulated Annealing (SA) [1, 22], Genetic Algorithms (GAs) [23, 24], Tabu Search [25] and else have been employed as substitution of exact algorithms solving larger instances of FLP.

Wu et al. [26] developed a genetic algorithm to solve the cellular manufacturing layout problem. An integrated approach using the fuzzy set theory and GAs was developed by Karray et al. [24] to solve FLP. A pre-determined site layout was optimized by Yeh [27] using annealed neural network model. Taghavi and Murat [28] presented an iterative heuristic procedure for solving small to very large problem instances of the integrated layout design and product flow assignment. Their proposed procedure is based on the alternating heuristic of Cooper [29], perturbation algorithm and sequential location heuristic. For solving the layout problem modeled by QAP, an advanced approach based on SA was proposed by Wilhelm and Ward [30] and a robust meta-heuristic algorithm based on ant colonies optimization and guided local search was presented by Hani et al. [31].

Bhowmik [19] presented an iterative heuristic as well as a branch and bound algorithm for solving FLP. In this proposed approach, highly related departments are grouped using clustering methods into levels; the locations of the generated clusters at the different levels are obtained by solving a mathematical model using the branch and bound method; an iterative heuristic algorithm is used next to layout the different departments within each level. This approach has some weaknesses. Firstly, the maximum area permitted for each level is specified as input and the areas of the clusters of departments formed are not allowed to be more than that of this cap specified. Secondly, the author introduced some concept of cluster-level intervals to group departments into levels based on interactions between pairs of departments. However, the rules were not really specified for determining the cluster-level intervals and were left arbitrary; this is core to the algorithm. Moreover, the author specified a cap on areas of departments to be assigned at each level and did not really generate but one possible set of clusters with its intervals. Hence, the algorithm is very limited in terms of exploration of this combinatorial exponentially expanding solution space.

In this paper, a clustering-sequencing approach is presented to solve FLP. The outline of the paper is as follows: Sect. 2 presents the problem statement; Sect. 3 explains the four steps of this proposed approach to solve the problem; a comparative analysis versus one of the existing competing approaches from the literature is provided in Sect. 4, and finally, conclusions are provided in Sect. 5.

2 Problem Statement

One of the most popular applications of FLP is manufacturing systems and the arrangement of production facilities on shop floors. Hence, the facilities in context are ultimately machine tools in this case. For the purpose of the paper and from this point on, we are going to refer to the facilities simply as machines.

The problem is to arrange machines in a given shop to minimize the total distance traveled by all work in process, which is a good measure of the material handling (count per unit of time, volume, or weight multiplied by the distance traveled).

The assumptions that are taken for solving this problem are as follows:

(a) The shop floor has a rectangular shape with specified horizontal and vertical dimensions.
(b) Machines have rectangular shapes; they are not the same size and their sizes are given.
(c) The interaction (material handling flow) between each pair of machines is known in advance.
(d) Machines must be located within the given shop and should not overlap with each other.
(e) The workspace, which is required for the operator, material handling system, machinery maintenance workers and cleaning have been taken into account in determining machines' dimensions.

3 Methodology

Four steps to solve the problem are as follows:

3.1 Step 1: Grouping Machines in Different Clusters

For each cluster, machines are selected randomly and assigned vertically to a cluster at different levels. The horizontal dimension of a cluster is the maximum value of the horizontal dimensions of the machines within each level of that cluster. The vertical

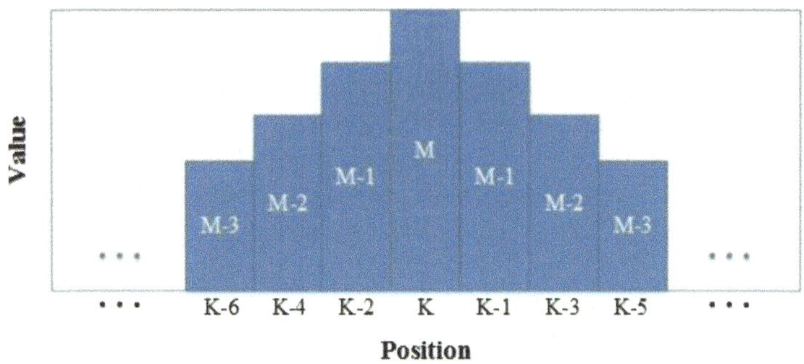

Fig. 1 Position of each location and the corresponding values

dimension of a level is equal to the vertical dimension of the shop floor. Next, at each level, it is checked whether another machine can be assigned horizontally near the already assigned machine.

3.2 *Step 2: Selecting Between Clusters and Sequencing Them*

In this step, appropriate clusters are selected and sequenced horizontally, keeping in consideration the fact that when a cluster is selected, other clusters that have the same machines as the selected cluster cannot be chosen. Moreover, each machine should be present in one and only one cluster and the sum of the horizontal dimensions of the selected clusters should not exceed the horizontal dimension of the given shop. In addition, the first cluster is selected randomly to have different solutions.

The configuration of the selected clusters is optimized by allocating the clusters with more interactions to the most valuable locations on the shop floor. The centroid of the shop has the maximum value (M) and this value will decrease when the location is going to be closer to the sides of the shop as it is shown in Fig. 1.

3.3 *Step 3: Sequencing Machines in Each Cluster*

Now, each machine is in one selected cluster and the location of that cluster is known. Also, the machines that are together horizontally in a cluster are determined. In this step, the machines inside each cluster are sequenced vertically. The basic idea is the same as sequencing the clusters. The centroid of each cluster has more value and is assigned for the machine which has more interactions with other machines. If a machine is placed beside another machine horizontally within a cluster, then

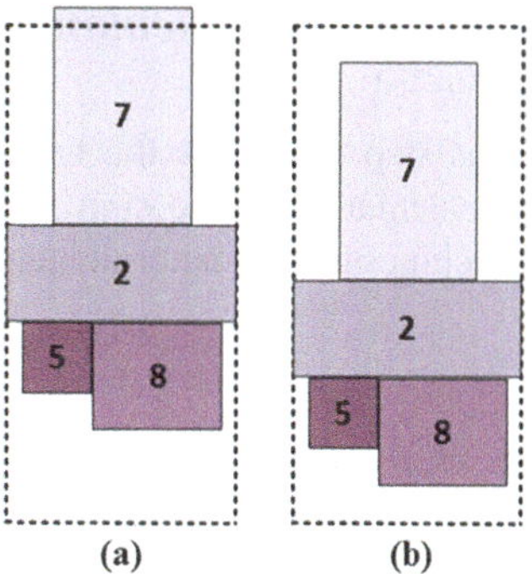

Fig. 2 A sample cluster (**a**) Machine 2 is centralized and the configuration of the machines exceeds the dimension of the cluster. (**b**) All the machines inside the cluster are behaved like a batch and placed in the centroid of the cluster

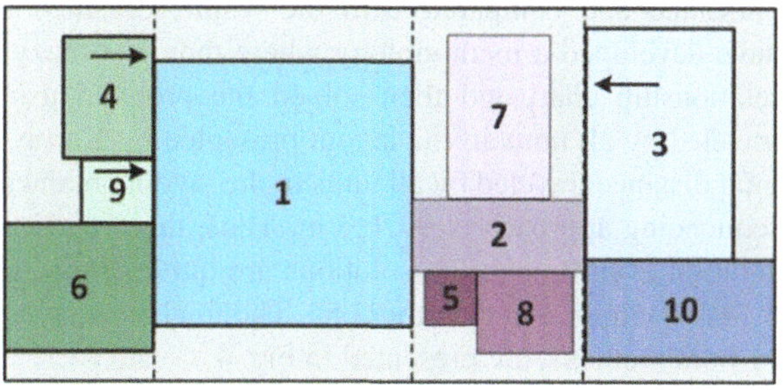

Fig. 3 Decentralizing machines which are in the endpoint clusters

the sum of interactions of both machines is considered when comparing with the other machines in the same cluster for positioning. Machines should not exceed the dimensions of their cluster and they are not allowed to overlap with each other.

Centering a machine here does not mean that it has to be exactly in the middle of the cluster; it means that it is in the centroid of the group of the machines, which are in the given cluster. Sometimes after placing the machine with the most of the interactions in the centroid and applying the same for other machines allocating them to the closest available location to the centroid, it does not fit the cluster as it is shown in Fig. 2 (a). To fix this issue, all the machines inside any cluster are behaved like a batch and placed in the centroid of the cluster Fig. 2 (b).

To improve the configuration and reduce the travel distance between machines, machines that are in the endpoint clusters are not horizontally centralized. Because for instance, machines that are in the first left-hand-side cluster of the shop do not have any interaction with their left-hand side and all their interactions are between each other (vertically) and with their right-hand side, they are better to be positioned in the right side of their cluster. The same applies to the last cluster in the shop. Figure 3 depicts these movements.

3.4 Step 4: Calculation of Total Distance Traveled by All Units

This step calculates the total distance traveled by all units in the system, which is calculated by the sum of the multiplication of the distance between pairs of machines by the material handling flow between them.

4 Computational Experiment

The computational results of the proposed clustering-sequencing approach are presented and compared with the results obtained by Karray et al. [24], who have developed a methodology where they use fuzzy sets to generate the facility relationship chart and then solved the problem using GAs. The total distance traveled by all units in the layout presented by Karray et al. [24] is 9990.5 m. The total distance traveled by all units in the layout obtained by the proposed clustering-sequencing approach is 9976.3 m. Thus, the proposed approach obtained a better solution even though the solutions are quite similar and the improvement is only 0.14% compared to the other one. The final layouts, results of solving the problem by both methods, are presented in Fig. 4.

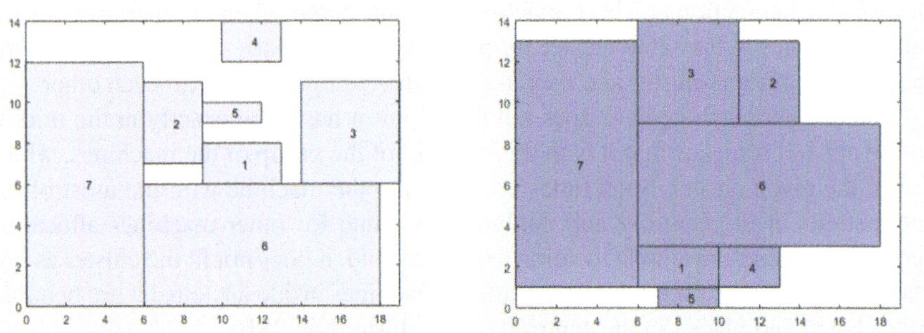

(a) (b)

Fig. 4 (**a**) The best layout obtained by Karray et al. [24] using GAs (**b**) The layout result of solving by the proposed clustering-sequencing approach

5 Conclusions

This paper presents a technique that divides the problem conceptually into those of clustering and sequencing. At first, the clusters of vertically aligned facilities are formed and then, these clusters are sequenced horizontally. Although the goal is to minimize the total distance traveled by all units in the shop floor, the objective function is alternatively defined in such a way to maximize interactions between machines. By maximizing the objective function, clusters that have more interactions with other clusters are assigned closer to the centroid of the shop. Hence, the inter-distances between facilities that have more interactions among each other are minimized and subsequently, the total distance traveled by all units in the shop floor is minimized.

One of the prominent features of this method is the randomness by which assignment of the different machines to the different clusters. Also, the selection of the first cluster in the final layout is random, which improve the exploration capabilities of the overall developed search method in comparison to counterpart heuristics from the literature. A benchmark problem has been used to justify the merit of the developed heuristic; the results demonstrate the advantage of using the developed algorithms.

Acknowledgments The authors are thankful for the Natural Science and Research Council of Canada. This research was funded by NSERC Discovery grant 811008 awarded to the third author.

References

1. Chwif L, Barretto MRP, Moscato LA (1998) A solution to the facility layout problem using simulated annealing. Comput Ind 36(1–2):125–132
2. Pourvaziri H, Azimi P (2014) A tunned-parameter hybrid algorithm for dynamic facility layout problem with budget constraint using GA and SAA. J Optim Ind Eng 7(15):65–75
3. Tompkins JA, White JA, Bozer YA, Tanchoco JMA (2010) Facilities planning. Wiley, Hoboken
4. Ghassemi Tari F, Neghabi H (2015) A new linear adjacency approach for facility layout problem with unequal area departments. J Manuf Syst 37(Part 1):93–103
5. Allahyari MZ, Azab A (2015) A novel bi-level continuous formulation for the cellular manufacturing system facility layout problem. Procedia CIRP 33:87–92
6. Kusiak A, Heragu SS (1987) The facility layout problem. Eur J Oper Res 29(3):229–251
7. Laursen PS (1993) Simulated annealing for the QAP—optimal tradeoff between simulation time and solution quality. Eur J Oper Res 69(2):238–243
8. Meller RD, Gau K-Y (1996) The facility layout problem: recent and emerging trends and perspectives. J Manuf Syst 15(5):351–366
9. Lawler EL (1963) The quadratic assignment problem. Manag Sci 9(4):586–599
10. Burkard RE, Bönniger T (1983) A heuristic for quadratic Boolean programs with applications to quadratic assignment problems. Eur J Oper Res 13(4):374–386
11. Love R, Wong J (1976) On solving a one-dimensional space allocation problem with integer programming. Inf Syst Oper Res 14(2):139–143
12. Heragu SS, Kusiak A (1991) Efficient models for the facility layout problem. Eur J Oper Res 53(1):1–13

13. Montreuil B (1991) A modelling framework for integrating layout design and flow network design. In: Material handling '90. Springer, Berlin, pp 95–115
14. Goetschalckx M (1992) An interactive layout heuristic based on hexagonal adjacency graphs. Eur J Oper Res 63(2):304–321
15. Leung J (1992) A new graph-theoretic heuristic for facility layout. Manag Sci 38(4):594–605
16. Hassan MMD, Hogg GL (1987) A review of graph theory application to the facilities layout problem. Omega 15(4):291–300
17. Foulds LR (2012) Graph theory applications. Springer Science & Business Media, Berlin
18. Solimanpur M, Jafari A (2008) Optimal solution for the two-dimensional facility layout problem using a branch-and-bound algorithm. Comput Ind Eng 55(3):606–619
19. Bhowmik R (2008) An approach to the facility layout design optimization. Int J Comput Sci Netw Secur 8(4):212–220
20. Said GAE-NA, Mahmoud AM, El-Horbaty E-SM (2014) A comparative study of meta-heuristic algorithms for solving quadratic assignment problem. arXiv preprint arXiv:14074863
21. Heragu SS (2008) Facilities design. CRC, New York
22. Ariafar S, Ismail N (2009) An improved algorithm for layout design in cellular manufacturing systems. J Manuf Syst 28(4):132–139
23. Kochhar JS, Foster BT, Heragu SS (1998) HOPE: a genetic algorithm for the unequal area facility layout problem. Comput Oper Res 25(7–8):583–594
24. Karray F, Zaneldin E, Hegazy T, Shabeeb A, Elbeltagi E (eds) (2000) Computational intelligence tools for solving the facilities layout planning problem. American Control Conference, 2000 Proceedings of the 2000
25. Samarghandi H, Eshghi K (2010) An efficient tabu algorithm for the single row facility layout problem. Eur J Oper Res 205(1):98–105
26. Wu X, Chu C-H, Wang Y, Yan W (2007) A genetic algorithm for cellular manufacturing design and layout. Eur J Oper Res 181(1):156–167
27. Yeh I-C (1995) Construction-site layout using annealed neural network. J Comput Civ Eng 9(3):201–208
28. Taghavi A, Murat A (2011) A heuristic procedure for the integrated facility layout design and flow assignment problem. Comput Ind Eng 61(1):55–63
29. Cooper L (1963) Location-allocation problems. Oper Res 11(3):331–343
30. Wilhelm MR, Ward TL (1987) Solving quadratic assignment problems by 'simulated annealing'. IIE Trans 19(1):107–119
31. Hani Y, Amodeo L, Yalaoui F, Chen H (2007) Ant colony optimization for solving an industrial layout problem. Eur J Oper Res 183(2):633–642

Difficulties in the Supply Chain in Post-conflict Zones in Colombia

Oscar Eduardo Sarmiento Saavedra, William Eduardo Mosquera Laverde, Carlos Hernan Cruz Castro, and Juan Camilo Bohorquez Rodriguez

Abstract The efficient supply chains in the regions of Colombia affected by the armed conflict are complex and difficult. This is thanks to the fact that they have a problem since they no longer contribute to the fulfillment of the organizational objectives of the units of tourism business in the areas of study (Uribe, Lejanía, and Mesetas). Due to the informal behavior of the companies and the breach of the technical regulations of the Ministry of Tourism and the Ministry of Labor, there is no strengthened supply chain, therefore, research shows a way to integrate tour operators of the mentioned populations to improve the economic development of the country. For this purpose, the categories to be studied were defined and six instruments were designed to diagnose the hotel logistics operation. This revealed flaws in terms of organizational management and the supply chain. To improve them, protocols and guides for easy web applications were designed to help improve the income, logistics, and business management of these tour companies.

Keywords Logistics · Tourism · Post-conflict · Supply chain

1 Introduction

In the investigation, a study of the basic organizational and logistics management was carried out in order to know how the supply chains of the hotel companies are in the department of Meta, Colombia, mainly in the municipalities of Lejanías, Uribe, and Mesetas. In this way, the logistic structure was explored and it was possible to identify why it is necessary to apply the basic organizational management models,

O. E. S. Saavedra · W. E. M. Laverde (✉) · C. H. C. Castro · J. C. B. Rodriguez
Servicio Nacional de Aprendizaje SENA, Universidad Cooperativa de Colombia, Bogotá, D.C., Colombia
e-mail: oesarmiento682@misena.edu.co; williame.mosquera@campusucc.edu.co; ccruzc@misena.edu.co; juancamilo.b@misena.edu.co

X. Li, X. Xu (eds.), *Proceedings of the Seventh International Forum on Decision Sciences*, Uncertainty and Operations Research,
https://doi.org/10.1007/978-981-15-5720-0_16

as well as the way in which they are implemented in the big companies, in the SMEs and in the hotels registered in the Ministry of Tourism. Taking this into account, companies should not be understood only as a productive entity, but also as the scenario where decisions are made. This is why logistics is a fundamental part of the correct development of these. When an organizational technology is accompanied such as balanced scorecards in Excel, social media management and online shopping, among others. For this reason, and because there is a need to convert the region into a competitive sector given the current needs, it is important to determine the difficulties in the implementation of efficient supply chains in post-conflict municipalities of Meta, specifically in the areas of Mesetas, Lejanías and Uribe, located in the center of the country in order to generate economic and business inclusion.

It is necessary to understand that Colombia is one of the countries affected by the armed conflict and, as a result, various economic, social and cultural factors are adversely affected. Since the term of Virgilio Barco, in 1986, until that of César Gaviria, in 1994, it was impossible to achieve any negotiation with the guerrilla groups. However, a light of hope has emerged thanks to the peace agreement reached during the government of Juan Manuel Santos, when the establishment of a specific negotiation began. However, this is just a sample since there are several armed groups against the law in Colombia. One of the largest and most recognized is the FARC, which after more than 50 years of struggle and failed agreements, finally decided to leave their differences behind and on November 24, 2016, at the Colon Theater in Bogotá signed the Peace Agreement. A new stage then arises, full of political, social, humanitarian and economic challenges that the country must assume. In this context, the department of Meta has been affected by the armed conflict since its appearance, preventing cultural and educational advances, and contributing to having vague and scarce levels of administrative and logistical knowledge [1].

For this, qualitative research was conducted, where a diagnosis was made according to some variables collected in fieldwork carried out in the area under investigation and schemes and models of logistics management were identified. Additionally, the requirements of the technical standards that are implemented in the Colombian tourism sector are listed, such as the Sectoral Technical Standard (NTS 002), which is used to promote ecotourism in Colombia currently [2].

The study has the contribution of the Cooperative University of Colombia, the research group Organizations and Strategy 4.0, in conjunction with the National Learning Service. SENA, and its SENNOVA group. The study analyzed factors such as the environment, safety, ecotourism, quality of tourist services and characteristics of the places where it is expected to provide excellent quality service, bearing in mind that not only the needs of tourists, but also that contribution to the society of these areas must be achieved.

When the program was implemented and socialized with the population, there were many skeptics and many others very enthusiastic. Nevertheless, the process of consolidating local tour operators began, but other factors of competitiveness were not taken into account, such as the infrastructure that many of the municipalities have, which directly affects the supply chain of tour operators and discourages visitors to reach these municipalities.

2 Issues Discovered

The research identified different problems in the activities of tour operators in the municipalities of Lejanías, Mesetas, and Uribe, in the department of Meta, Colombia. These municipalities were directly affected by the armed conflict in the country, but they have unique tourist attractions such as waterfalls, rivers, endemic flora and fauna species, their geography, among others. These municipalities are distant from the capital of the country, Bogotá, and other cities from where the main products or supplies for this region of the country are distributed, not to mention the multiple road infrastructure problems. This clearly generates delays in the logistic processes, in addition to increasing transportation costs or cause the use of more means of transport. This phenomenon is due to the lack of a supply chain between the operators and the producers or suppliers of inputs [3].

In this context, it becomes essential for the study to know the tourism environment in the municipalities studied, but taking into account the external tourist supply chain, from which is essential to highlight the type of information required, as well as its management and control. This information corresponds to the personal data of the ecotourists (management, payments, security), the processes and operations of the travel agencies, the information and routes of the issuing tourist operator—who is the one that connects the ecotourist with the destination zone, the logistics of the receiving tour operator—which is responsible for knowing the area to visit and needs that it has in order to cover them and provide a pleasant stay to the ecotourist, service providers, and protected areas—which are the object of study. This last aspect presents the biggest drawbacks in the operation because they are completely empirical businesses and are just beginning in this activity [4]. That said, the following question was posed: Do the municipalities of Lejanías, Mesetas and Uribe have adequate supply chains to provide quality tourist services?

3 Post-conflict Process in the Department of Meta

As a result of the signing of the peace agreement, the security conditions in the areas of Colombia where armed groups existed were improved, which is why a program of tourism incentives was structured in those regions. For this reason, it is so important to know the state of security in the area of study.

3.1 Tourism in Colombia

Tourism began with the creation of the Colombian Association of Hotels (ACOTEL) in Barranquilla in 1954, during the development of violence in the country. This association later led to the creation of the Association of International Airlines in Colombia (ALAICO). In 1959, the Institute of Culture and Commerce was created, which, despite the consternation that Colombia faced thanks to the violence, started and controlled Colombian tourism. However, between 1946 and 1958, certain events occurred, marking the country as a violent territory with little social order [5].

A clear example of the above mentioned was the "Bogotazo", which happened after the assassination of Jorge Eliécer Gaitán. Such an event triggered an undeclared civil war based on political expediency. Furthermore, this caused the formation of liberal guerrillas, made up of over 10,000 armed men in the Eastern Plains, western Cundinamarca, southern Tolima, Sumapaz, Santander Middle Magdalena, southern Cordoba, and Antioquia. Guerrillas had as main objective fighting the injustice and authoritarianism of the conservative party. For this reason, rural areas started experiencing environmental impacts due to pacification measures and campaigns. Guerrillas also practiced the tactic of "scorched earth", a method that consists of abandoning and destroying towns, cities, infrastructure, killing animals, burning crops; in other words, destroying everything that could serve the enemy to supply itself. Which became a problem that marked the country in its economy and economic behavior [6].

3.2 Tourism in Meta

Meta is a department in the center of Colombia affected by the armed conflict. However, thanks to the peace agreement, the government decided to provide this department with resources in order to foster its development. Currently, there are several tourist projects in the region that seek to offer greater guarantees to the sector, helping to leave behind problems of public order. Such factors strengthen the idea that visiting Colombia is an adventure and a risk for many foreign tourists who do not have references other than violence and the armed conflict [7].

As pointed out by the former Minister of Industry and Commerce, María Claudia Lacouture, what is sought is to generate tourist circuits with the aim of integrating 311 municipalities of 32 departments to boost the development of the regions and create multiple jobs, thus creating a wide offer in cultural matters (religious and archaeological destinations, and national celebrations), nautical practices, adventure (diving and extreme sports), wellness (thermals and spas), health, and business (congresses and conventions), among others. Despite this, Meta shows a notable disadvantage in terms of logistics management thanks to the armed conflict [8].

3.2.1 Tour Operators in Post-conflict Zones

Finally, the Tourism and Peace program is presented. Considering this, three (3) stages of the implementation process were created. Only 132 out of the 344 Zones of integration of ex-fighters were selected and distributed in three categories: I. Pilot Destinations (42 municipalities), II. Emerging Destinations (34 municipalities) and III. Post-conflict Destinations—Post-agreement (56 municipalities). As for the pilot destinations, they were divided into five (5) tourist routes. The advantage of these destinations was their minimum investment cost to start the tourism operation. To do this, the Vice Ministry of Tourism began the intervention of these regions through the territorial entities, municipal mayors, and the Ministry of Tourism of the department in order to advance quickly in the implementation of the program. This work was carried out through working groups agreed with the community. Once the working groups were established, those interested in participating were identified and the process of characterization of the possible tour operators was done by the researchers [9].

The characterization began by determining the tourist attractions of each operator and the possible services that they could offer. This was done based on the infrastructure and the possibility of investment of the interested parties. The advantage of starting from the tourism sector, from the perspective of the national government, is the little or no investment in contrast with other economic sectors, in addition to being able to take advantage of the natural resources available, many of which are in the properties of the logistics operators.

4 Deficiencies in Tourist Logistics in Meta

Tour operators do not have the necessary elements to carry out a good service, to identify the competitiveness factors, three (3) instruments were applied to identify weaknesses in the supply chain (Protocol characterization of attractiveness, general observation guidance and organizational management in the tourism and hotel sector), the information collected it was analyzed through the Likert Scale, in this process several factors were identified that affect the logistics process in the development of the supply chain, factors such as road infrastructure, ignorance or inexperience that allows them to sustain their businesses [10], but knowledge and experience are the first risks of the operators, are not clear about the process of supplying the necessary elements for their operation, in these municipalities there is a deficiency in the road infrastructure, poor reception of the mobile phone signal, in addition they do not have access to all drinking water supplies, sewerage, electric power, natural gas, among other services, this is due to the little interest that the state had for many years, many of these municipalities had constant confrontations with groups raised in arms, little or no presence of state institutions, low budget to execute the works of impact in the community, all this led to a poor development of these municipalities, who were not made visible by the war they had, but with

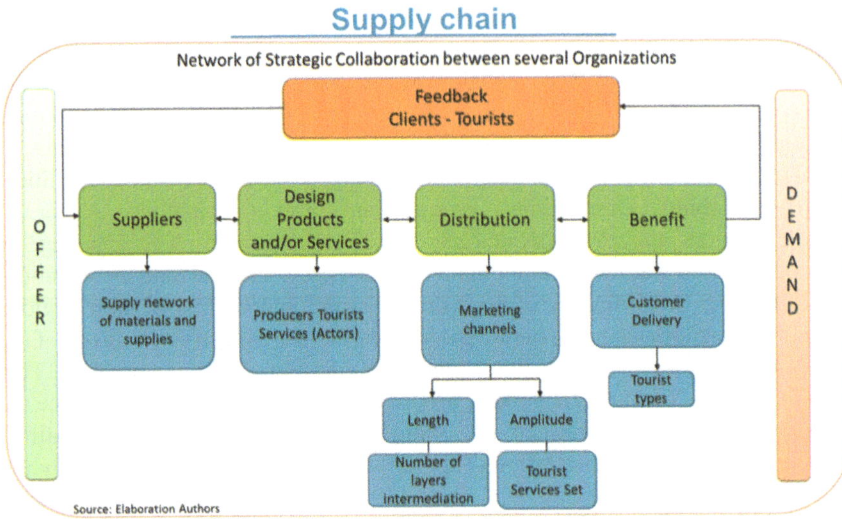

Fig. 1 Red de Colaboración Estrategica entre Varias Organizaciones. Own source

the reduction of the intensity of the armed conflict they saw how they had a great backlog. This leads to the non-compliance with the minimum standards of tourism sustainability.

El Espectador [11], the sustainability standard is mandatory for all tour operators, which include hotels, restaurants, travel agencies, tour guides, transport companies, tourist inns, resorts, for this they must accredit the sustainability standard through the National Registry of Tourism (RNT), but the implementation of this norm requires a series of commitments, investments and procedures that guarantee the entities territorial services quality, this is where the logistics process is of great importance, because they should standardize storage processes, inventory valuation systems, establish minimum criteria to avoid shortages, define delivery times and receipt, establish direct relationship with suppliers, these difficulties generate complications in the general operation of all the companies that are part of this supply chain.

The supply chain requires a continuous feedback process, Fig. 1, which is not being carried out, it is also necessary to integrate the actors that allow streamlining the deliveries and reduce the costs of the operation, this would lead the operators to generate greater efficiency in the process and obtain, as a direct result, greater profits in your investment.

Acknowledgements This work was carried out thanks to the support of Servio Nacional De Aprendizaje, (SENA), Universidad Cooperativa de Colombia, the Vice Ministry of Tourism of Colombia, The Municipal Mayors of Lejanías, Mesetas and Uribe, The tour operators of the intervened municipalities.

References

1. Barbero A (2006) Construyendo paz en medio de la guerra: Colombia. Universidad Autónoma de Barcelona, Barcelona
2. Mosquera-Laverde WE, Vásquez-Bernal OA, Gómez-Espinosa CP (2018) Green engineering that focuses on ecotourism as an environmental strategy. Global J Eng Edu 20(2)
3. Guarín Salinas C, Martínez Sánchez ML (2018) Estado del arte de la historia y patrimonio cultural de Vichada. Doctoral dissertation, Corporación Universitaria Minuto de Dios
4. Schulte S (2003) Guía conceptual y metodológica para el desarrollo y la planificación del sector turismo, vol 25. United Nations Publications
5. Rengifo Russi EY (2017) Estudio para la Viabilidad de la Creación del Parque Ecoturístico "las Lajas", Vereda Subia Pedregal Municipio de Silvania-Cundinamarca. Doctoral dissertation
6. Cantor RV (2015) La dimensión internacional del conflicto social y armado en colombia injerencia de Los estados Unidos, contrainsurgencia y terrorismo de estado
7. Beltran Siachoque MA, Romero Moreno CF, Socha Montejo E (2018) Propuesta turística para la población del posconflicto en el municipio de Restrepo-Meta
8. Cabrera-Rodríguez Y (2014) Análisis del proceso de paz con las FARC: comparación de los desarrollados en 1998 y el actualmente en curso
9. Ministerio de Comercio, Industria y Turismo (2018) Turismo y Paz MINCIT – Ministerio de Comercio, Industria y Turismo [Institucional], mayo 3. Recuperado 28 de mayo de 2019, de Ministerio de Comercio, Industria y Turismo website: http://www.mincit.gov.co/minturismo/analisis-sectorial-y-promocion/turismo-y-paz
10. Dinero MA (2018) Sostenibilidad es rentabilidad, febrero 23. Recuperado 26 de febrero de 2018, de Sostenibilidad es rentabilidad por Adriana Molano. http://www.dinero.com/opinion/columnistas/articulo/sostenibilidad-es-rentabilidad-por-adriana-molano/255694
11. El Espectador P (2018) Turismo Sostenible, la clave para el futuro de las regiones, julio 31. Recuperado 17 de agosto de 2018, de ELESPECTADOR.COM. https://www.elespectador.com/noticias/

Benefits of Big Data in Supply Chain Management

M. Indralingam, M. I. M. Wahab, and L. Fang

Abstract Big data has the potential to become a key driver in revolutionizing the functioning of a supply chain. Data storage, data access, and data visibility have widened, allowing for the innovation of new processes to extract latent information about the key entities: customers, products, and markets within a supply chain. A comprehensive overview of how big data is utilized for enhancing the performance of stages within a supply chain is presented. This overview provides a foundation for describing the benefits of adopting big data for firms to gain a competitive advantage.

Keywords Big data analytics · Supply chain management · Big data benefits · Machine learning applications

1 Introduction

The big data revolution has been underway for the better part of the last decade in several industries [1, 2]. Supply chains have historically known to produce large amounts of data [2]. Hence, big data techniques can be applied in supply chain management, and the solutions will be valuable to improve the supply chain performance [3, 4]. Big data solutions expand the scope of analysis beyond that of traditional Enterprise Resource Planning (ERP) systems and apply modern machine learning and/or statistical techniques to derive relationships and insights, which will aid in decision making across the whole chain [5, 6].

Technological advances have allowed for faster retrieval and storage of data. Supply chains with their excessive data generation have the potential to generate value. Sensors and Internet of Things (IoT) devices have allowed for data generation

---

M. Indralingam · M. I. M. Wahab (✉) · L. Fang
Department of Mechanical and Industrial Engineering, Ryerson University, Toronto, ON, Canada
e-mail: wahab@ryerson.ca

X. Li, X. Xu (eds.), *Proceedings of the Seventh International Forum on Decision Sciences*, Uncertainty and Operations Research,
https://doi.org/10.1007/978-981-15-5720-0_17

and acute monitoring of processes within the chain. Internet data, including social media data, trends data, clinical data, and weather data, are very useful for gathering insights into business processes within the supply chain [7–10]. Potential for big data has been identified and accepted by subject matter experts and supply chain specialists. Models and methodologies on incorporating big data analytics (BDA) solutions have been discussed. These solutions have the potential to transform the performance of supply chains, but such approaches have not become a norm. This is due to the lack of appreciation of the benefits of these BDA solutions, as such these benefits have been overlooked and have not been discussed.

This paper attempts to motivate the need to introduce BDA solutions by exploring the benefits. Although there are challenges, these solutions will deliver benefits, which can be easily measured. This paper provides a simple framework identifying opportunities to derive value within each functional area in a supply chain and explores in detail the various benefits that BDA solutions could provide. Section 2 briefly summarizes the literature review. Section 3 presents a framework, which identifies the functional areas of the supply chain and possible applications of the BDA in each functional area. Section 4 concludes the paper.

2 Literature Review

Current research has focused primarily on unique applications of big data. Studies have identified a process improvement within the supply chain, applied a big data solution, and discussed the results. These solutions have typically fallen into two categories: descriptive and predictive analysis [4]. The majority of the studies have focused on predictive analysis, where non-traditional data was used to create better forecasts, and feature analysis on social media data was used to predict aggregate sales [11]. Forecast accuracy was measured often using Google Trends Data [11, 18] and, on a related note, sentiment analysis in conjunction with sales data was used to quantify demand for product categories [12]. Descriptive analysis has been primarily used for visibility of performance across processes within the supply chain and, to some extent, the whole supply chain. In Lau et al. [12] and Foster et al. [13], key performance indicators (KPIs) were analyzed via aggregating several data elements, both internal and external to the supply chain. Mukherjee and Sinha [14] estimated error rates and probabilities of product recall decisions. As seen, the existing literature does not provide common themes that can be captured as part of the detailed analysis of benefits observed within each functional area of the supply chain.

3 A Framework to Identify Big Data Analytics (BDA) Benefits in Supply Chain Management

BDA solutions are localized and usually applicable within a functional area within a supply chain, but the benefits of the process improvement or innovation are seen across the supply chain as a whole. In this paper, the benefits observed within each functional area of the supply chain are discussed. Such functional areas are (a) Inventory and Operations Planning; (b) Sourcing and Production; (c) Logistics and Transportation; and (d) Retail.

3.1 Inventory and Operations Planning

Planning is the most data-intensive process within the supply chain, with multiple inputs and outputs. Analysis of these data elements can improve the agility and responsiveness of the supply chain by making it more real-time [3]. Managing inventory has prone to be quite costly, but with the availability and visibility of point of sales (POS) data, data generated through IoT devices, and traditional inventory data, the production key performance indicators (KPIs) can be analyzed and verified real-time to identify mismatches. This innovation has the potential to drive actions, including price changes, the addition of new products within lines, and even the creation of new lines altogether [17]. Moreover, retailers can also use other data sources for acute demand sensing [15] and better planning. The IBM Watson technology, for example, aided a bakery supply chain to increase sales amongst its customers by accurately predicting the demand for product categories based on consumer preferences [6]. Amazon has proven the benefits of big data processing, being a pioneer in using and creating new innovative processes to shape demand in consumer analytics on the web.

3.2 Sourcing and Production

Sourcing has traditionally dealt only with supply data and reviews on supplier performance. However, with the advent of trend analysis, similar to Google trends, data can be gathered to identify any major disruptions, including strikes and bankruptcies. This predictive risk management technique provides an edge to the chain against its competitors. Data visualization and analysis will provide an understanding of the costs of the various suppliers and their services. Frequent information on commodities and utilization can be added to the model to identify the best suppliers for the projects at hand [16]. Manufacturing processes can benefit significantly from data and analytics, especially during the scheduling of resources as well as fluctuating prices of commodities and electricity. Gathering and storing data on manufacturing parameters can be used in defect analysis and more through quality assessments. IoT devices are key in capturing this data. Furthermore, they provide information on indicators, including the current state, efficiency of the machines, and potential improvements. This will potentially allow for a comprehensive and real-time view of the manufacturing process.

3.3 Logistics and Transportation

Logistics has traditionally focused on minimizing cost where companies are continually looking for technology capable of providing distinct advantages. Recent focus has been on the efficiency of space utilization within the facility and minimization of travel costs and required personnel. Big data provides improvements across the board with a collection of real-time information to identify waste, and this information typically involves video images, sensor inputs including shelf weight, temperature, type of material, which can be used for warehouse efficiency, productivity, and inventory accuracy. The information derived from such devices is pushed to the cloud and can be accessed and dissected globally increasing the convenience. Transportation uses fuel consumption analytics and GPS data to identify driver efficiencies and wait times. Unsuccessful delivery attempts are the ones big data is capable of reducing. Logistics providers are now capable of delivering with fewer attempts by accurate prediction of when a customer or client is likely to be home. On an overall strategy point of view, the chain is able to cut costs and even carbon emissions by selecting the best routes, and also identify modes of transport for different goods. For example, some goods might require faster shipping by truck, but for some goods, slower train delivery might be sufficient.

3.4 Retail

At the tail end of a supply chain, at point of sale, BDA solutions have been heavily used for space optimization and mark-down pricing. The velocity feature of big data allows retailers to decide which items to be placed in high-traffic locations, also to understand if it is worthwhile to group or cluster products at specific locations. Challenge has always been to proactively identify out-of-stock scenarios, where manual inspection and recurrent checking from the personnel is a viable option but is costly. BDA solutions can monitor out-of-stock indicators that can trigger alerts, for example, if an item, which is usually sold at a given interval, is not being bought by customers. The alert will notify the personnel in store to check the availability of the item on the shelf [7]. In-store cameras and weight sensors can be used in tandem to monitor stock levels and analyze stock levels. Ultimately, data gathered in relation to all consumer activities can be utilized to better shape consumer demand.

4 Conclusion

BDA benefits are plentiful, but the lack of motivation and vision have been factors preventing key personnel in firms adopting BDA solutions. This paper provides a strong motivation for adopting such solutions to enhance the performance of a supply chain as a whole. This paper identifies the key functional areas and potential solutions with their corresponding benefits and examples of existing implementations of such solutions. These solutions have the capacity to understand demand and provide visibility by merging the analytical and operational capabilities of firms allowing for an adaptive and agile supply chain, which is more flexible for customer needs. Based on the current trends within the supply chain, these benefits will in time motivate the adoption of BDA solutions, which will create innovations and changes within the supply chain workflow allowing for improved supply chains.

Acknowledgements This work was supported by the NSERC discovery grant.

References

1. Singhal K, Feng Q, Ganeshan R, Sanders NR, Shanthikumar JG (2018) Introduction to the special issue on perspectives on big data. Prod Oper Manag 27:1639–1641
2. Swaminathan JM (2018) Big data analytics for rapid, impactful, sustained, and efficient (RISE) humanitarian operations. Prod Oper Manag 27:1696–1700
3. Lee HL (2018) Big data and the innovation cycle. Prod Oper Manag 27:1642–1646
4. Sanders NR, Ganeshan R (2018) Big data in supply chain management. Prod Oper Manag 27:1745–1748
5. Harrison N (2018) Supply chain big data series Part 1. https://Assets.kpmg.com. assets.kpmg.com/content/dam/kpmg/au/pdf/2017/big-data-analytics-supply-chain-performance.pdf. Accessed 2 May 2018
6. Knut A, Christoph G, Per-Magnus K, Kai H (2018) Big data and the supply chain: the big-supply-chain analytics landscape. https://www.mckinsey.com/business-functions/operations/our-insights/big-data-and-the-supply-chain-the-big-supply-chain-analytics-landscape-part-1. Accessed 25 May 2018
7. Fisher M, Raman A (2018) Using data and big data in retailing. Prod Oper Manag 27:1665–1669
8. Cohen MC (2018) Big data and service operations. Prod Oper Manag 27:1709–1723
9. Guha S, Kumar S (2018) Emergence of big data research in operations management, information systems, and healthcare: past contributions and future roadmap. Prod Oper Manag 27:1724–1173
10. Feng Q, Shanthikumar JG (2018) How research in production and operations management may evolve in the era of big data. Prod Oper Manag 27:1670–1684
11. Cui R, Gallino S, Moreno A, Zhang DJ (2018) The operational value of social media information. Prod Oper Manag 27:1749–1769
12. Lau RY, Zhang W, Xu W (2018) Parallel aspect-oriented sentiment analysis for sales forecasting with big data. Prod Oper Manag 27:1775–1794
13. Foster K, Penninti P, Shang J, Kekre S, Hegde GG, Venkat A (2018) Leveraging big data to balance new key performance indicators in emergency physician management networks. Prod Oper Manag 27:1795–1815

14. Mukherjee UK, Sinha KK (2018) Product recall decisions in medical device supply chains: a big data analytic approach to evaluating judgment bias. Prod Oper Manag 27:1816–1833
15. Li L, Chi T, Hao T, Yu T (2016) Customer demand analysis of the electronic commerce supply chain using big data. Ann Oper Res 268:113–128
16. Zhong RY, Newman ST, Huang GQ, Lan S (2016) Big data for supply chain management in the service and manufacturing sectors: challenges, opportunities, and future perspectives. Comput Ind Eng 101:572–591
17. Hopp WJ, Li J, Wang G (2018) Big data and the precision medicine revolution. Prod Oper Manag 27:1647–1664
18. Boone T, Ganeshan R, Hicks RL, Sanders NR (2018) Can Google trends improve your sales forecast? Prod Oper Manag 27:1770–1774

Knowledge-Guided Neighborhood Search Algorithm for Close-Open Vehicle Routing Problem

Gao-Ji Sun

Abstract A realistic variant of conventional vehicle routing problems, which simultaneously considers the open and close routes in the solution of the problem, is introduced in this paper. The objective is to obtain the optimal routing planning and minimize the total costs for operating the open and close routes. A knowledge-guided neighborhood search (KGNS) algorithm is designed to handle this vehicle routing problem, and the results of experiments show that the proposed KGNS algorithm can effectively produce the satisfied solutions.

Keywords Vehicle routing problem · Close-open vehicle routing · Knowledge-guided neighborhood search algorithm

1 Introduction

With the development of Internet economy, logistics and distribution companies can easily hire vehicles from the online platform. Therefore, these companies will no longer to keep a large number of private vehicles, which leads to that the companies often uses private vehicles and hired vehicles to complete the distribution task together. Under normal circumstances, the private vehicles need to return to the depot after completing their tasks, but the hired vehicles are not required, i.e. the coexistence of close and open vehicle routing problems has emerged.

Since the vehicle routing problem (VRP) was introduced sixty years ago by Dantzig and Ramser [1], both close vehicle routing problems (Close-VRP) and open vehicle routing problems (Open-VRP) have been widely studied, the recent researches on VRP can be referred to the literature reviews [2–4]. However, the combined considerations of Close-VRP and Open-VRP are not common. To the

G.-J. Sun (✉)
College of Economic and Management, Zhejiang Normal University, Jinhua, China
e-mail: gsun@zjnu.edu.cn

X. Li, X. Xu (eds.), *Proceedings of the Seventh International Forum on Decision Sciences*, Uncertainty and Operations Research,
https://doi.org/10.1007/978-981-15-5720-0_18

best of our knowledge, the close-open mixed vehicle routing problem (COMVRP) was put forward by Liu and Zhang [5] for the first time, the objective of their COMVRP model is to minimize the fixed and variable costs for operating the open and close routes, and designed an effective memetic algorithm to solve their COMVRP model. Brito et al. [6] improved and extended the formulation COMVRP model proposed by Liu and Zhang [5] via considering precise time windows, and introduced a variable neighbourhood search procedures to solve their proposed VRP model. Meanwhile, Brito et al. [7] also proposed a close-open vehicle routing model with imprecise factors, in which the capacity and time windows constraints are considered flexible and modelled as fuzzy constraints. Alinaghian et al. [8] developed a close-open vehicle routing model with delivery section which adopting close route and pickup section which using open route, and they assumed that the nodes can be visited by more than one vehicle. Azadeh and Farrokhi-Asl [9] combined the multi-depot vehicle routing problem (MDVRP) and close-open mixed vehicle routing problem to propose a new kind of VRP model.

Compared with the extensive research of Close-VRP and Open-VRP, the research of close-open vehicle routing problem (COVRP) is just in its infancy. However, COVRP has significant applications in transportation system, especially after the advent of a great many of online rental platforms. Therefore, we construct a simple COVRP model, in which the distribution company has a limited private vehicles, when faced with the following delivery mission and a fixed contract fee for one external vehicle, the company needs to plan the delivery route. Since the Close-VRP and the Open-VRP have been proved to be NP-hard [2, 10], the COVRP is also NP-hard since it reduces to the Close-VRP when the number of the vehicles which perform the open routes is zero, and reduces to the Open-VRP when all the routes are open. In fact, the COVRP is even harder to be tackled than the Close-VRP and the Open-VRP. To handle the proposed model, we design a knowledge-guided neighborhood search algorithm.

The remainder of this paper is organized as follows. Section 2 formulates a mathematical programming formulation of the COVRP. Section 3 proposes a knowledge-guided neighborhood search algorithm for solving the COVRP model, and computational results on one given instances are reported. Finally, conclusions are included in the last section.

2 Problem Description and Formulation

The proposed COVRP model is applied to solve the route planning problems of distribution companies that have a number of private vehicles and can hire external vehicles which must serve specified and dispersed demand points, satisfying a finite set of constraints and minimizing total operating costs. The objective consists in finding a set of routes that minimize the total operating costs. Each route starts at the depot and ends either at the depot (private vehicles) or at a customer (hired vehicles). Each customer is visited once and only once by exactly one vehicle and the demand of each customer must be completely fulfilled by a single vehicle, and the total demand served by each vehicle must not exceed vehicle capacity.

The COVRP includes one single depot, N customers, P private vehicles and K hired vehicles. The customers are identified by the index i or j, and the index 0 denotes the depot. For the private vehicles, the cost of travelling between nodes i and j, where $i, j = 0, 1, 2, \cdots, N$ represent nodes, is denoted by c_{ij}, but for each hired vehicle, the distribution company should pay an one-off hiring cost C for working no more than a pregiven T hours. In our model, the private vehicles and hired vehicles are homogeneous, they have the same restrictions on work timing T and maximum allowable capacity Q. The customer j has its own demand amount q_j which it must be served. All vehicles must leave from the depot to carry out the deliveries, and t_{ij} denotes travel time from node i to node j. Each self-owned vehicle or leased vehicles is uniformly represented by index k, where $k = 1, 2, \cdots, P+K$, and the first P indices correspond to the private vehicles that are required to return to the depot, while the rest are hired vehicles and they end their routes at the last visited customers. The decision variables contain x_{ij}^k and the routing strategy of each vehicle. For each arc, two indices i and j, and each vehicle k, we define $x_{ij}^k = 1$ if and only if vehicle k travels from i and j, otherwise $x_{ij}^k = 0$.

The COVRP can be formulated as a linear integer programming problem as follows:

Minimize

$$\sum_{k=1}^{P}\sum_{i=0}^{N}\sum_{j=0}^{N} c_{ij}x_{ij}^k + C * K \tag{1}$$

Subject to:

$$\sum_{k=1}^{P+K}\sum_{i=0}^{N} x_{ij}^k = 1 \quad j = 1, 2, \cdots, N \tag{2}$$

$$\sum_{j=1}^{N} x_{0j}^k = 1 \quad k = 1, 2, \cdots, P+K \tag{3}$$

$$\sum_{i=1}^{N} x_{i0}^k = 1 \quad k = 1, 2, \cdots, P \tag{4}$$

$$\sum_{i=0}^{N} x_{ij}^k - \sum_{i=0}^{N} x_{ji}^k \geq 0 \quad k = 1, 2, \cdots, P+K; \; j = 1, 2, \cdots, N \tag{5}$$

$$\sum_{i=0}^{N}\sum_{j=1}^{N} q_j x_{ij}^k \leq Q \quad k = 1, 2, \cdots, P+K \tag{6}$$

$$\sum_{i=0}^{N}\sum_{j=0}^{N} t_{ij}x_{ij}^{k} \leq T \quad k = 1, 2, \cdots, P + K \tag{7}$$

$$x_{ij}^{k} \in \{0, 1\} \quad k = 1, 2, \cdots, P + K; \; i, j = 0, 1, 2, \cdots, N \tag{8}$$

The whole objective (1) is to minimize the sum of delivery costs of private vehicles and the lease costs of hired vehicles. Constraint (2) guarantees that exactly only one vehicle visits each customer. Constraints (3) and (4) ensure that each vehicle leaves the depot and each private vehicle returns to it. Constraint (5) ensures that if a vehicle depart from a customer, it must arrives at the customer. Constraint (6) establishes that the total of customer demand in any route does not exceed the vehicle capacity Q. Constraint (7) guarantees the total traveling time for each route cannot exceed the restrictive work timing T.

3 Optimization Approach and Computational Experiments

Many different algorithms have been proposed to deal with the VRP problems, such as branch-and-cut algorithm [11], branch-and-price algorithm [12], exact algorithms [13, 14], heuristic algorithms [15, 16], neighborhood/local search algorithms [17, 18] and so on. Furthermore, owing to the prior knowledges have important effect on the algorithm's efficiency, some researcher committed to propose new algorithms based on the guidance with problem-knowledge. For instance, Arnold and Sörensen [19] conducted a series of experiments to determine how local search can be effectively combined with perturbation and pruning, and applied problem-specific knowledge to guide the search to promising solutions more effectively, whereafter Arnold et al. [20] outlined the challenges of very large-scale VRPs, and proposed corresponding solutions based on their previous knowledge-guided local search algorithm.

3.1 Optimization Approach

In consideration of neighborhood/local search has proven to be the cornerstone of many solution techniques for various combinatorial optimisation problems, and problem-specific knowledge indeed can enhance the effectiveness of algorithm. We design a knowledge-guided neighborhood search (KGNS) algorithm to tackle the COVRP model. The core idea and its steps are summarized in the following frame construction (**Algorithm 1**).

Algorithm 1 Knowledge-guided neighborhood search algorithm

Step 1. *Initial partition: Convert the customer's existing location information into polar coordinates, and connect the depot and the nearest node to depot as the initial line, then clockwise rotate the initial line and inspect the total demand amounts of the nodes that have been swept, when the total demand amounts is close to the maximum allowable capacity, then allocates these nodes to the first vehicle. Continue with the rotation until all nodes have been assigned. In addition, randomly generate an angle as the starting line for the distribution of other individuals, then dividing the customers according to the above-mentioned method, until the initial population is generated.*

Step 2. *Plan the initial route of each vehicle: For the private vehicles, owing to the closed-loop characteristics, the nodes are divided into two groups according to their locations, and the initial route is arranged to go from near nodes to far nodes, and back from far nodes to near nodes; for the hired vehicles, since these vehicles are not required to return, a rational route is orderly go from the nearest nodes to farthest nodes.*

Step 3. *Internal adjustment based on neighborhood: For each route, randomly select a node and swap the order with the adjacent node, and compare the fitness values of the two routes before and after modification and reserve the better one. Continue the operation until it has no change for a given number of times in a row.*

Step 4. *External adjustment based on neighborhood: Randomly select a route and swap some nodes (the closer to the common boundary, the greater probability that the node will be selected) with the adjacent route. Moreover, the probability of route selection depends on its total distance and total demand amounts.*

Step 5. *Repeat step 3 and step 4 until the triggering condition are met, then return the best solution.*

According to the above **Algorithm 1**, it is easy to see that problem-specific knowledge are used in the initial partition, initial route planning, the selection of nodes and route in the optimization process, and the core operation is neighborhood search.

3.2 Computational Experiments

To verify the effectiveness of the proposed KGNS algorithm, we provide a numerical example which contain one depot and 30 nodes (their locations and demand amounts are randomly generated from a given scope, and collected in Table 1). Moreover, both the traveling cost and traveling time between code i and j $(i, j = 0, 1, 2, \cdots, N)$ are set to their Euclidean distance. There are 2 private vehicles and 1 hired vehicle, and their working time limit and stowage limit are set to be 150 and 120, respectively. The rental fee of one hired vehicle is 120 one day.

Table 1 The data information related to the VRP problem

Customer ID	1	2	3	4	5	6	7	8	9	10	11	12	13	14	15
x coordinate	93	15	23	53	13	29	47	23	67	21	93	67	69	53	25
y coordinate	57	67	43	5	75	73	40	71	45	49	43	13	25	35	39
Demand	4	13	8	17	14	12	10	18	17	16	8	18	15	13	10
Customer ID	16	17	18	19	20	21	22	23	24	25	26	27	28	29	30
x coordinate	85	81	77	45	31	49	63	44	33	39	49	49	87	37	19
y coordinate	69	27	79	43	75	92	9	37	47	69	3	81	39	91	33
Demand	5	6	10	7	8	20	12	7	5	8	11	13	14	10	12

Table 2 The result information related to the VRP problem

Vehicle ID	Distribution arrangement	Loading capacity	Working time
Private vehicle 1	(0,24,10,3,30,15,19,7,23,14,9,0)	105	123.26
Private vehicle 2	(0,25,20,6,8,2,5,29,21,27,0)	116	141.20
Rental vehicle	(0,18,16,1,11,28,17,13,12,22,4,26)	120	146.71

Solved by the proposed KGNS algorithm, we apply a population of 50 individuals and 10000 generations to obtain the final decision, the result is summarized in Table 2.

4 Conclusions

Renting vehicles using online platform has become an important way for modern logistics and distribution companies to operating costs, which leads to that the close-open vehicle routing problem (COVRP) becomes more and more important. Therefore, we build a COVRP model based on the practical rental market and distribution problem. In addition, a knowledge-guided neighborhood search algorithm is proposed to tackle that complicated model, and the results based one numerical example has shown the effectiveness of proposed algorithm.

Acknowledgments This work was supported by the National Natural Science Foundation of China under Grant Nos.71701187.

References

1. Dantzig GB, Ramser JH (1959) The truck dispatching problem. Manag Sci 6:80–91
2. Laporte G (2009) Fifty years of vehicle routing. Transp Sci 43:408–416
3. Braekers K, Ramaekers K, Nieuwenhuyse IV (2016) The vehicle routing problem: State of the art classification and review. Comput Ind Eng 99:300–313
4. Gansterer M, Hartl RF (2018) Collaborative vehicle routing: A survey. Eur J Oper Res 268: 1–12

5. Liu R, Jiang ZB (2012) The close-open mixed vehicle routing problem. Eur J Oper Res 220:349–360
6. Brito J, Expósito A, Moreno JA (2016) Variable neighbourhood search for close-open vehicle routing problem with time windows. IMA J Manag Math 27:25–38
7. Brito J, Martínez FJ, Moreno JA, Verdegay JL (2015) An ACO hybrid metaheuristic for close-open vehicle routing problemswith time windows and fuzzy constraints. Appl Soft Comput 32:154–163
8. Alinaghian M, Kalantari MR, Bozorgi-Amiri A, Raad NG (2016) A novel mathematical model for cross dock open-close vehicle routing problem with splitting. Int J Math Sci Comput 3:21–31
9. Azadeh A, Farrokhi-Asl H (2019) The close-open mixed multi depot vehicle routing problem considering internal and external fleet of vehicles. Transp Lett 11:78–92
10. Brandão J (2004) A tabu search algorithm for the open vehicle routing problem. Eur J Oper Res 157:552–564
11. Liu T, Luo ZX, Qin H, Lim A (2018) A branch-and-cut algorithm for the two-echelon capacitated vehicle routing problem with grouping constraints. Eur J Oper Res 266:487–497
12. Yu Y, Wang SH, Wang JW, Huang M (2019) A branch-and-price algorithm for the heterogeneous fleet green vehicle routing problem with time windows. Transp Res B 122:511–527
13. Louveaux FV, Salazar-González J (2018) Exact approach for the vehicle routing problem with stochastic demands and preventive returns. Transp Sci 52:1463–1478
14. Dinh T, Fukasawa R, Luedtke J (2018) Exact algorithms for the chance-constrained vehicle routing problem. Math Program 172:105–138
15. Zhang S, Gajpal Y, Appadoo SS (2018) A meta-heuristic for capacitated green vehicle routing problem. Ann Oper Res 269:753–771
16. Marinakis Y, Marinaki M, Migdalas A (2019) A multi-adaptive particle swarm optimization for the vehicle routing problem with time windows. Inf Sci 481:311–329
17. Subramanian A, Uchoa E, Ochi LS (2013) A hybrid algorithm for a class of vehicle routing problems. Comput Oper Res 40:2519–2531
18. Liu R, Tao YY, Xie XL (2019) An adaptive large neighborhood search heuristic for the vehicle routing problem with time windows and synchronized visits. Comput Oper Res 101:250–262
19. Arnold F, Sörensen K (2019) Knowledge-guided local search for the vehicle routing problem. Comput Oper Res 105:32–46
20. Arnold F, Gendreau M, Sörensen K (2019) Efficiently solving very large-scale routing problems. Comput Oper Res 107:32–42

Research on Order Batching Problem of Intelligent Warehouse Picking System

Jun Tao Li, Kai Liu, and Ke Qin

Abstract Because of its high efficiency and flexibility, the intelligent warehousing picking system has gradually become the development trend of order picking system of the e-commerce logistics distribution center. The intelligent warehousing picking system is a kind of "parts-to-picker" operation mode, in which the logistics robot carries the shelf to the designated picking station for picking operation. In order to improve the efficiency of order picking, this paper studies the order batching problem under this new picking mode, establishes a mathematical model, and proposes an improved dynamic clustering algorithm.

Keywords Intelligent warehouse picking system · Order batching; similarity · Load balancing · Clustering algorithm

1 Introduction

With the rapid development of e-commerce and the rising labor costs, traditional warehousing logistics technology has become more and more difficult to adapt to the needs of e-commerce development. An intelligent warehousing picking system, which is suistations for multiple varieties, high frequency and small batch characteristics of e-commerce logistics, emerges as the times require. It is an automated "parts-to-picker" mode, such as Amazon purchased the Kiva system in 2012 [1]. In the intelligent warehousing picking system, the picking workstation is located at the boundary of the system. After the order arrives, the order is assigned to the corresponding picking workstation after the order batch strategy is processed. Then the handling task is sent to the logistics robot, which carries the target shelf to the workstation for the staff to pick. This "goods to people" picking mode greatly improves the efficiency of the warehouse. At the same time, there are

J. T. Li (✉) · K. Liu · K. Qin
School of Information, Beijing Wuzi University, Beijing, China

X. Li, X. Xu (eds.), *Proceedings of the Seventh International Forum on Decision Sciences*, Uncertainty and Operations Research,
https://doi.org/10.1007/978-981-15-5720-0_19

many problems that need to be studied urgently in intelligent warehousing picking system, including road network layout [2], storage allocation [3], order batching, task scheduling [4] and path optimization [5].Order batching is an important part of intelligent warehousing picking system. A reasonable order batching strategy can improve the picking efficiency of the system.

In intelligent warehousing picking system, order batching problem is considered as NP hard problem. There are many research methods about order batching at present. Xuanguo Xu [6] studied how to realize the batch processing of orders to reduce the diversification of products to a certain extent. Füßler [7] proposed simultaneous processing of orders after batching can reduce the number of shelves moving, and designed a heuristic algorithm. Zhenping Li [8] established the order batch model according to the similarity of items between orders, and designed a heuristic clustering algorithm to solve the problem; Caixia Zhang [9] proposed a saving algorithm to solve the order batch problem, and proposed the target function of the least number of times for logistics robots to carry shelves; Boysen N [10] pointed out that optimizing the order processing process and sorting orders can effectively reduce the shelf movement. Zeyi Shao [11] proposed an order batch model based on order similarity, and used improved genetic K-means algorithm to solve the model.

Aiming at the operation mode of intelligent warehouse picking system, the selection of the order picking operation is carried out by means of wave picking. The wave picking [12] refers to determining the number of picking orders in a certain period of time according to the efficiency of order picking and other factors, and picking these orders at a certain time is conducive to improving the efficiency of order picking. In this paper, we define the similarity between orders based on the number of the same shelves of any two orders, maximize the average similarity of orders on each picking station and load balancing of each picking station, establish a bi-objective order batching model, and design a dynamic clustering algorithm to solve the problem of order batching.

2 Problem Description

The order batching problem studied in this paper can be described as: for a certain wave of N orders $O1$, $O2$, ..., ON, there are many goods on different shelves on each order. Assuming that each goods is only on one shelf, the picking operation order which moves the same shelf is divided into batches and placed on a picking stations as far as possible. Considering the balance of picking time of the picking stations, the running cost of the robot is reduced. Based on how to reduce the number of shelf handling, maximize the average similarity of orders on each picking stations and make the picking time of the picking stations balanced, this paper establishes a bi-objective order batching model. Next, a small example is given to illustrate how to improve the picking efficiency by simultaneously reducing the number of shelf handling and balancing the picking time of the picking stations.

3 The Construction of Mathematical Model for Order Batch Problem

3.1 Model Construction

3.1.1 Phase I Model

In the first stage model, the parameters and variables needed are as follows:

n: Order, $n = 1, 2, \ldots, N$
q: Shelf, $q = 1, 2, \ldots, Q$
s: Picking stations, $s = 1, 2, \ldots, k$
W: The maximum capacity of the picking desk to process orders, the specific value is to divide the number of orders by the number of picking desks multiplied by 150%, that is: $W = \frac{N}{k} \times 150\%$

$$bnq = \begin{cases} 1, & Complete\ order\ n\ to\ move\ the\ shelf\ q \\ 0, & Otherwise \end{cases}$$

$$xns = \begin{cases} 1, & Order\ n\ is\ waiting\ for\ picking\ on\ the\ picking\ station\ s \\ 0, & Otherwise \end{cases}$$

γ: Similarity matrix

$$\gamma = \begin{bmatrix} \gamma 11 & \gamma 21 & \cdots & \gamma N1 \\ \gamma 21 & \gamma 22 & \cdots & \gamma N2 \\ \vdots & \vdots & \ddots & \vdots \\ \gamma N1 & \gamma N2 & \cdots & \gamma NN \end{bmatrix} \tag{1}$$

According to the number of the same shelf q transported by two orders n and m, the similarity γmn between the two orders is calculated. The formula of similarity γmn is as follows:

$$\gamma nm = \begin{cases} \dfrac{\sum_{q=1}^{Q} bnqbmq}{\sum_{q=1}^{Q} bnq + \sum_{q=1}^{Q} bmq - \sum_{q=1}^{Q} bnqbmq} & n \neq m \\ 0 & n = m \end{cases} \tag{2}$$

When $i = j$, γmn is the correlation degree of the same order. Since the correlation degree is only for two different orders, it is not meaningful to calculate the correlation degree of the same order. Let $\gamma mn = 0$ in this case.

Among them, the greater the similarity between orders, the more the number of the same shelves to be moved to complete two orders. Placing the similar orders on the same picking stations for picking can shorten the total picking time and reduce the running cost of the robot. Therefore, for the same batch of orders, the similarity between orders on the same picking stations should be as large as possible.

The objective function is as follows:

$$\text{Max } Z = \sum_{s=1}^{k}\left(\frac{\sum_{n=1}^{N}\sum_{m=1}^{N} \gamma nmxnsxms}{\left(\sum_{n=1}^{N} xns\right)\left(\sum_{n=1}^{N} xns - 1\right)}\right) \tag{3}$$

Constraints:

$$\sum_{s=1}^{k} xns = 1 \quad n = 1, 2, \ldots, N \tag{4}$$

$$\sum_{q=1}^{Q} bnq \geq 1 \quad n = 1, 2, \ldots, N \tag{5}$$

$$2 \leq \sum_{n=1}^{N} xns \leq W \quad s = 1, 2, \ldots, k \tag{6}$$

$$xns \in \{0, 1\} \quad n = 1, 2, \ldots, N; s = 1, 2, \ldots, k \tag{7}$$

$$bnq \in \{0, 1\} \quad n = 1, 2, \ldots, N; q = 1, 2, \ldots, Q \tag{8}$$

3.1.2 Phase II Model

In the second stage model, based on the previous stage model, the parameters and variables needed are as follows:

$$\text{Goods}: \quad i = 1, 2, \ldots, l$$

$tpick$: Time for staff to pick up a cargo;

$$\alpha in = \begin{cases} 1, & C\arg o\ i\ on\ the\ order\ n \\ 0, & Otherwise \end{cases}$$

$$\beta iq = \begin{cases} 1, & Goods\ i\ on\ the\ shelf\ q \\ 0, & Otherwise \end{cases}$$

Based on the analysis of the process flow and the establishment of the above model, the picking time to complete the order on the picking stations s can be expressed as follows:

$$ts = \left(\sum_{n=1}^{N}\sum_{i=1}^{I} xns \times \alpha in\right) \times tpick \tag{9}$$

The objective function is as follows:

$$\text{Min Max } ts \qquad s = 1, 2, 3 \ldots, k \tag{10}$$

Constraints:

$$\sum_{q=1}^{Q} \beta iq = 1 \quad i = 1, 2, \ldots, I \tag{11}$$

$$\sum_{i=1}^{I} \alpha in \geq 1 \quad n = 1, 2, \ldots, N; \tag{12}$$

$$\sum_{q=1}^{Q} \beta iq \times bnq \geq \alpha in \quad i = 1, 2, \ldots I; n = 1, 2, \ldots, N \tag{13}$$

$$\beta iq \in \{0, 1\} \quad i = 1, 2, \ldots, I; q = 1, 2, \ldots, Q \tag{14}$$

$$\alpha in \in \{0, 1\} \quad i = 1, 2, \ldots, I; n = 1, 2, \ldots, N \tag{15}$$

4 Experimental Verification

4.1 Experimental Description

In order to verify the effectiveness of the intelligent warehouse picking system order batch model and algorithm, the simulation was carried out in a 200 m^2 warehouse with 120 shelves, a total of 300 kinds of goods, 4–8 kinds of goods per shelf, 5 picking Workstation, 8 logistics robots, now assumes that the order number of a wave is 100, the maximum capacity of each picking station is 30 orders, and the time for picking each item is 10 s/piece.

4.2 Simulation Experiment

In the matlab2015b environment, the clustering algorithm proposed in this paper is used to solve the order batching problem simulation program. The experiment is carried out under the WIN10 64Bit operating system and 8GB memory environment. The layout structure of the warehouse is shown in the figure.

4.3 Analysis of Calculation Results

(1) Complete 100 order picking results analysis (Table 1)

(2) Analysis of batch policy results of different orders under different quantities.

1. Shelf handling times

   Figure 1 is a comparison of the number of pallets handled by different orders in batches under different order quantities. As the number of orders increases, the similarity between orders will become larger and larger, and the number of shipments of shelves will increase steadily. However, it can be seen that the order batching strategy proposed in this paper and the order batching strategy considering only the similarity of orders. The number of moving shelves is lower than the random order batching strategy, so the order

Table 1 Order batch result

Batch	Order number	Carrying shelves	Picking time
1	1 8 10 12 13 37 40 43 45 47 53 64 73 75 82 89 92 93 96	34	710
2	17 21 22 23 24 29 39 44 54 57 61 62 66 72 86 88 91 99	30	630
3	2 3 4 5 6 7 14 25 26 28 31 32 35 36 42 52 59 67 81 87	33	680
4	9 11 15 18 30 34 38 41 51 55 68 71 74 76 77 78 80 94 95 100	28	650
5	16 19 20 27 33 46 48 49 50 56 58 60 63 65 69 70 79 83 84 85 90 97 98	34	740

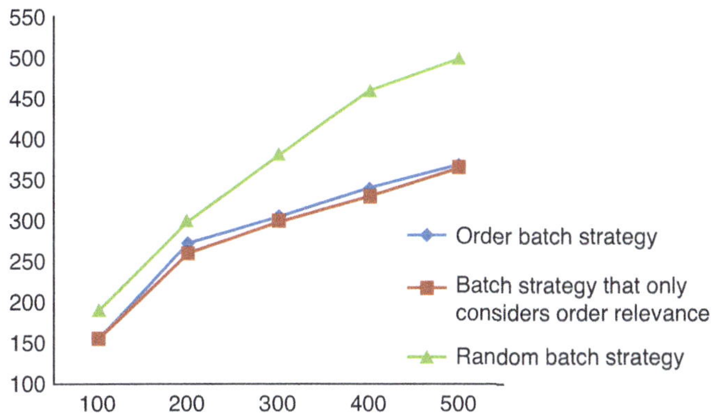

Fig. 1 Comparison of the number of handling shelves under three order batch strategies

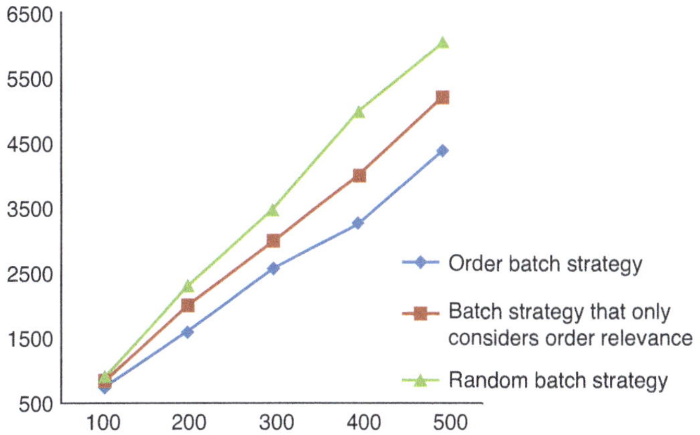

Fig. 2 Comparison of the number of handling shelves under three order batch strategies

batching strategy proposed in this paper can effectively reduce the number of shelves.

2. Picking time

   Figure 2 is a comparison of batching time selection times for different orders under different order quantities. With the increase of the number of orders, the picking time is getting bigger and bigger. Through the comparative analysis of the three methods, the order batching strategy proposed in this paper has the smallest picking time of the picking station, which can ensure the load balancing of the picking station and avoid the robot. Congestion during handling can effectively improve the efficiency of system picking.

5 Conclusion

In the intelligent warehouse picking system, in order to speed up the picking efficiency of the system, this paper optimizes the order batching problem in the system. A mathematical model is established considering the reduction of the number of rack handling and the sorting time of the picking station, and the model is solved by an improved clustering algorithm. The specific work is as follows:

1. Define a similarity between orders based on the number of times the same shelf is shipped for any two orders, establish a mathematical model that maximizes the average similarity of each picking order; mathematics for picking station load balancing to minimize picking time for the largest picking station The model constitutes the two-objective mathematical model proposed in this paper.
2. An improved clustering algorithm is proposed to solve the order batch model.
3. According to the method of wave picking, in the parallel operation mode of multiple picking stations, according to different order quantities, the order batching strategy proposed in this paper is simulated and verified. The experimental results show that the model and method of order batching proposed in this paper can effectively reduce the number of rack handling and ensure the balance of picking time of each picking station to ensure the load balancing of the picking station, effectively reduce the congestion of the system, and thus improve the order picking efficiency.

Acknowledgements This work was supported by Young top-notch talent project of high level teacher team construction in Beijing municipal universities (CIT&TCD201704059); Funding Project for Beijing Intelligent Logistics System Collaborative Innovation Center; Funding Project for Beijing Key Laboratory of intelligent logistics systems; Beijing excellent talents support project (2017000020124G063); The logistics robot system scheduling research team of Beijing Wuzi University support.

References

1. Enright JJ, Wurman PR (2011) Optimization and coordinated autonomy in mobile fulfillment systems. In: AAAI conference on automated action planning for autonomous mobile robots. AAAI Press, 2011
2. Zou B, Gong Y, Xu X et al (2017) Assignment rules in robotic mobile fulfilment systems for online retailers. Int J Prod Res 1–18
3. Roy D, Nigam S, Adan I et al (2019) Robot-storage zone assignment strategies in mobile fulfillment systems. Transp Res E 122:119–142
4. Ruiping Y, Huiling W, Lirui S, Juntao L (2018) Research on task scheduling of "goods to goods" order picking system based on logistics AGV. Oper Res Manag 27(10):133–138
5. Ma H, Koenig S, Ayanian N et al (2017) Overview: generalizations of multi-agent path finding to real-world scenarios
6. Xuanguo X, Zhongmei L, Wenmin H (2012) Cluster analysis of customer order under mass customization. China Mech Eng 23(14):1678–1681

7. Füßler D, Boysen N (2017) High-performance order processing in picking workstations. EURO J Transp Logist
8. Li W (2016) Research on multi-robot task assignment in intelligent warehouse system. Beijing Materials College
9. Zhang C (2016) Research on e-commerce order picking optimization based on "goods to people" mode. Zhejiang University of Science and Technology
10. Boysen N, Briskorn D, Emde S (2017) Parts-to-picker based order processing in a rack-moving mobile robots environment. Eur J Oper Res:S0377221717302758
11. Zeyi S, Dong B (2018) Multi-variety and small-volume order batching method based on improved genetic K-means algorithm. J Zhejiang Sci-Tech Univ (Nat Sci) 39(06):732–738
12. Yingde L (2013) Model and algorithm for collaborative optimization of picking fashion box and location assignment problem in wave sub-area. Syst Eng Theor Pract 33(5):1269–1276

Customized Passenger Transport Service Innovation for Intelligent Time: Evidence from Empirical Data in Siping

Jiawei Gui and Qunqi Wu

Abstract Road transportation market gradually shrank since high-speed rail network in China has achieved rapid development in recent years. Along with the social progressing and economy soaring, passengers have generated more and more personalized travel demands that traditional fixed schedule or conventional existing routes are unsustainable. These various challenges have led to sluggish business at many road passenger transport companies, especially small and medium size ones. To seek a way, it was necessary for them to reform management principles and improve business modes as well. In this study, customized passenger transport service was proposed as a feasible management innovation. First, several similar problems and some related works till date were reviewed. Second, an analysis framework of customized passenger transport service was built to calculate financial results based on Cost-Volume-Profit analysis method. Third, empirical data of SPT Company was adopted to verify the validity of the analysis framework. Results showed that SPT Company got benefits from customized business mode and turned profit in the next year. It indicated that customized passenger transport service gained positive awareness within the vast majority of passengers and it had a bright future in the field of road transportation markets. Future directions could be improving analysis framework and expanding data.

Keywords Road transportation market · Travel demand · Customized service · CVP analysis

J. Gui (✉)
School of Economics and Management, Chang'an University, Xi'an, Shanxi, China
e-mail: gjw@chd.edu.cn

Q. Wu
Center of Comprehensive Transportation Economic Management, Chang'an University, Xi'an, Shanxi, China
e-mail: wqq@chd.edu.cn

X. Li, X. Xu (eds.), *Proceedings of the Seventh International Forum on Decision Sciences*, Uncertainty and Operations Research,
https://doi.org/10.1007/978-981-15-5720-0_20

1 Introduction

Road transportation market gradually shrank since high-speed rail network in China has achieved rapid development in recent years. Along with the social progressing and economy soaring, passengers have generated more and more personalized travel demands that traditional fixed schedule or conventional existing routes could not satisfy any longer. These various challenges have led to sluggish business at many road passenger transport companies, especially small and medium size ones. To seek a way, it was necessary for them to reform management principles and improve business modes as well.

1.1 Road Transportation Market Shrank

Passenger traffic volume is one of the main indicators reflecting the transportation market scale. During 2014–2018, the passenger traffic volume of railway, waterway and civil aviation were on upward trends, however, the road passenger traffic volume decreased year by year (see Table 1). It indicated that road transportation market in China gradually shrank in recent years.

1.2 Transportation in Intelligent Time

Twenty-First century is an intelligent time and transportation in twenty-first century tends to comprehensive, intelligent and automation. Dumbaugh et al. indicated that value capture and livability were two objectives of urban transportation development for the twenty-first century [1]. People pursue the quality of transportation service rather than transportation itself. Fargnoli et al. proposed a Quality Function Deployment (QFD) method and indicated the validity of such an approach in enhancing customer satisfaction, while reducing environmental concerns and costs [2]. In other words, passengers in twenty-first century have more options and preferences than before. Sun et al. investigated air travel demand and incumbents' strategic responses in three Jeju Island routes and indicated that air passengers favored frequent flights

Table 1 Passenger traffic volume in Mainland China (unit: million persons)

Year	Road	Railway	Waterway	Civil Aviation	Total
2014	17, 362.70	2304.60	262.93	391.95	20, 322.18
2015	16, 190.97	2534.84	270.72	436.18	19, 432.71
2016	15, 427.59	2814.05	272.34	487.96	19, 001.94
2017	14, 567.84	3083.79	283.00	551.56	18, 486.20
2018	13, 671.70	3374.95	279.81	611.74	17, 938.20

and larger aircraft [3]. Song et al. proposed a planning concept from the perspective of economic equilibrium with the aim of optimizing a supply structure for transport passenger transportation corridors [4]. Gui et al. proposed several models for vehicle movement analyses [5, 6]. As a result, traditional transportation services could not satisfy all the passengers any longer. To solve this problem, it is vital for road passenger transport companies to ensure that supply meets the real demand of passengers. Customized service can be regarded as an innovation to practice.

1.3 Customized Service Innovation

In recent years, customized service has received growing concerns by researchers and practitioner. Lin et al. indicated that familial-type logistic supply chains may choose more efficient customized production level than public-type logistic supply chains [7]. Crudden et al. proposed a customized transportation intervention for people with visual impairments and indicated that it had a positive effect on social problem-solving skills [8]. During the China's National Day and Mid-Autumn festival, Xi'an Railway Bureau drove two crowdfunding trains between Xi'an and Yulin for the first attempt in China from October 7th to October 8th in 2017 as introduced by Gui et al. [9].

In recent years, quite a few researchers proposed group purchasing and pricing strategies for customized services. Ke et al. investigated a group-buying mechanism that considers strategic consumer behavior and indicated that the behavior of the strategic consumers influences the group-buying success rate and the seller's profit [10]. Ahmadi et al. indicated that group purchasing organizations play a strategic role in the purchasing process, and also it is turned out that they behave in a way which results in satisfying all members of the supply chain [11]. Rubel investigated the optimal competitive pricing strategies and indicated that long term profits of competing firms can increase with intensities of the jump processes governing product harm crises [12]. Zhang et al. investigated the interplay between buyer search behavior and firm pricing strategy in a commodity market and indicated that high-low pricing strategy can be an optimal strategy for firms when buyers search for price information sequentially [13]. However, few of them focused on customized passenger transport service or financial analysis for customized services.

2 Customized Passenger Transport Service

Compared with traditional services, customized services meet the demands of consumers better. Customized services are conducive to expand the market (see Fig. 1).

In Fig. 1, shaded areas in Fig. 1a, b represent the volume between the supply and the demand. The red area in Fig. 1b represents customized service. It indicated that

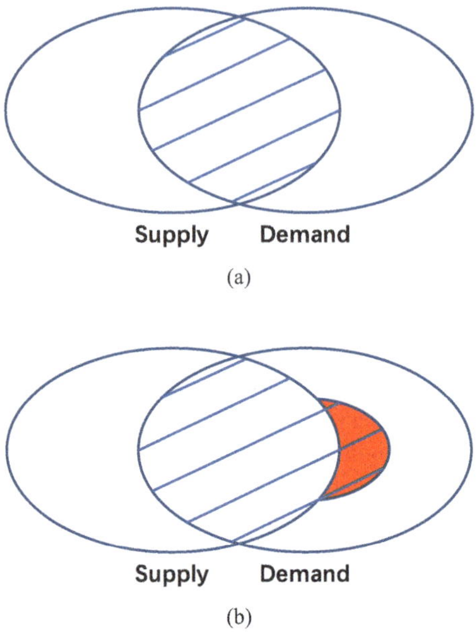

Fig. 1 The schematic diagram of customized service innovation

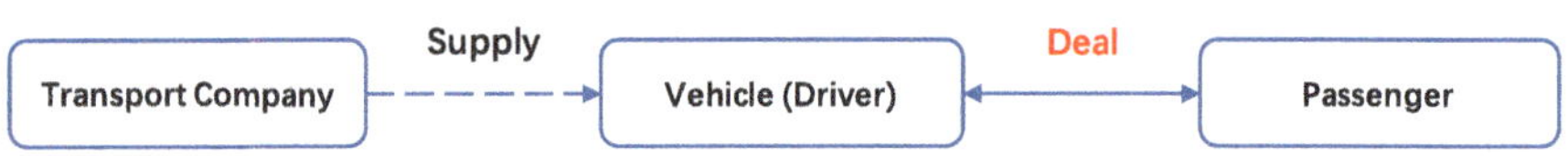

Fig. 2 The schematic diagram of traditional passenger transport service

customized service is an innovation based on traditional supply and it caters for a part of demands of consumers.

Traditional passenger transport services begin with transport companies (see Fig. 2). Transport companies supply vehicles at specific routes according to fixed timetables based on their experiences and then passengers choose to participate. However, it could not meet all the demands of passengers.

As road transportation market gradually shrank, more and more road passenger transport companies in China, especially small and medium size ones, planned to launch new services in recent years. Unlike the traditional, customized passenger transport services begin with passengers (see Fig. 3). Passengers come up with their requirements about customized service and pass on to transport companies. And then transport companies make a decision whether they supply vehicles at customized routes according to variable timetables. If the answer is yes, they make a deal as a result.

There are two steps in the customized passenger transport service framework (see Fig. 4).

Fig. 3 The schematic diagram of customized passenger transport service

In Fig. 4, the dashed lines in Fig. 4a represent information flow while the solid lines in Fig. 4b represent feedbacks. First, the big data platform collects all kinds of information, including real-time locations, vehicle conditions, the availability of drivers and the customized demand of passengers. Second, the administration of transport company makes a decision deal or not. Third, transport company dispatches appropriate drivers and vehicles to provide customized services for relevant passengers.

Customized services are feasible because they meet customized demands of passengers. However, customized services have higher costs than traditional services. Thus, it is necessary to make economic simulations for passenger transport companies before providing customized services.

3 Financial Analysis

3.1 Notations for Formulas

P: The total profit of passenger transport service, unit: yuan.
I: The total income of passenger transport service, unit: yuan.
C: The total cost of passenger transport service, unit: yuan.
p: The sales price of passenger transport service, unit: yuan per passenger.
v: The volume of deal, unit: passengers.
c_v: The variable cost of passenger transport service, unit: yuan.
c_f: The fixed cost of passenger transport service, unit: yuan.
BE: The Break-Even point, unit: passengers.

3.2 Cost-Volume-Profit Analysis

Cost-Volume-Profit (CVP) analysis is a method of cost accounting that looks at the impact that varying levels of costs and volume have on operating profit as introduced by Drury [14]. The variable P represents the total profit. The variable I represents the

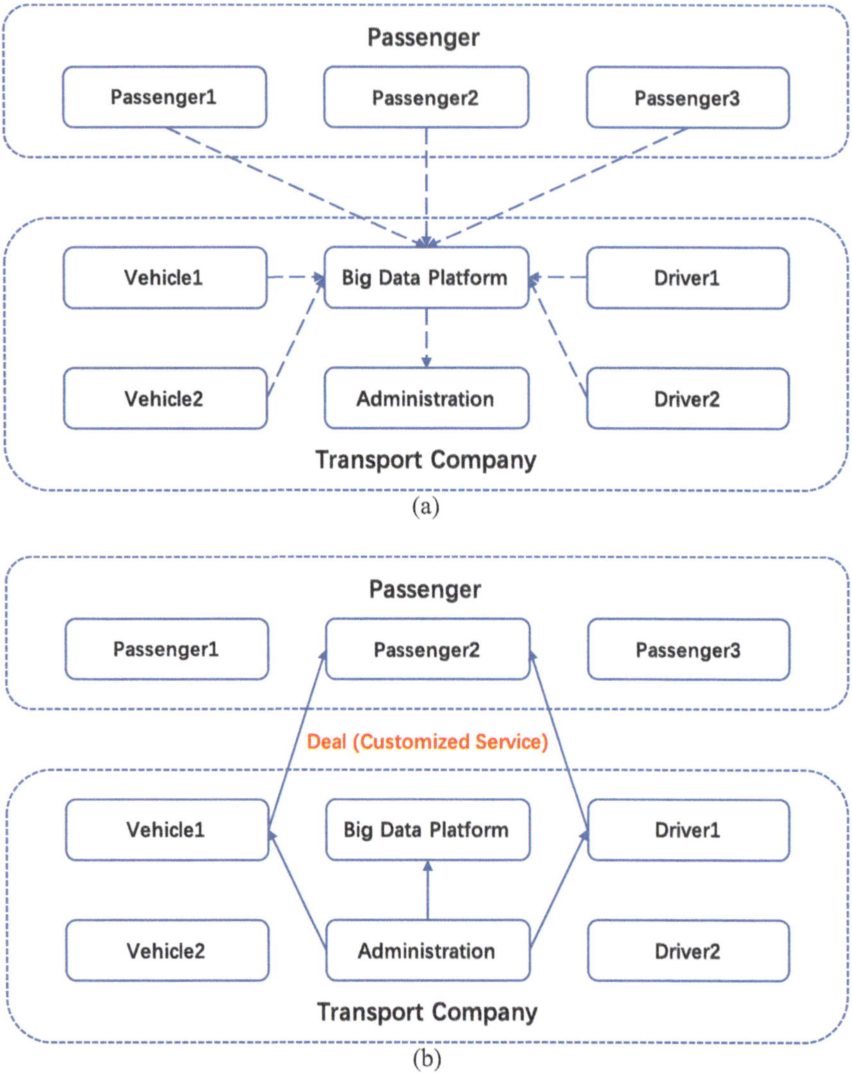

Fig. 4 The schematic diagram of customized passenger transport service based on big data platform

total income. The variable C represents the total cost. And then P can be computed, as is shown in Formula (1).

$$P = I - C \tag{1}$$

The variable p represents the sales price. The variable v represents the volume of deal. And then I can be computed, as is shown in Formula (2).

$$I = p \times v \tag{2}$$

The variable c_v represents the variable cost. The variable c_f represents the fixed cost. And then C can be computed, as is shown in Formula (3).

$$C = c_v \times v + c_f \tag{3}$$

Based on Formulas (2) and (3), Formula (1) can be converted into Formula (4).

$$P = (p - c_v) \times v - c_f \tag{4}$$

CVP analysis is also commonly known as Break-Even (BE) analysis, looks to determine the BE point for different sales volumes and cost structures, which can be useful for managers making short-term economic decisions. Based on Formulas (4), BE can be calculated by Formula (5).

$$BE = \frac{c_f}{p - c_v} \tag{5}$$

Furthermore, different value of v result in different situations, which are described as follows:

(i) When $v < BE$, total income is less than total cost and total profit is a negative number.
(ii) When $v = BE$, total income is equivalent to total cost and total profit is zero.
(iii) When $v > BE$, total income is more than total cost and total profit is a positive number.

Besides, CVP analysis makes several assumptions, which are described as follows:

(i) All costs can be categorized as variable or fixed.
(ii) All revenues and cost have a linear relationship with volume.
(iii) The variables p, c_v and c_f are constant.
(iv) The sales mix of a company remains constant.

3.3 Case Analysis

The case analysis takes SPT Company as an example. However, some values of income in this paper were hidden because of the privacy requirements of data source. SPT Company is a road passenger transport company in Lishu, Siping,

Jilin Province of China. During the period of 2014–2016, it lost passengers year by year because of long interval timetables, dilapidated vehicles and poor quality of service. Many passengers chose to ride illegal taxis or even reduce travel frequency. At the end of 2016, the average seat occupancy rate was less than 30%. For instance, one vehicle run three round trips per day, and its monthly CVP analysis can be as follows: $I = 7000(yuan)$, $C = 14,000(yuan)$, $P = -7000(yuan) < 0$. As a result, SPT Company had serious losses and several routes were cancelled.

Traditional services were not sustainable any more for SPT Company. Thus, it reformed its management principles and improved its business modes as well from March in 2017. It bought new vehicles and launched customized services among Lishu, Guojiadian and Wanfa. At the end of 2017, SPT Company already had 66 specific routes, 154 vehicles and 275 employees. During 2017, its volume added up to 877,000 passengers and 24.45 million kilometers. As a result, it turned a loss into a profit.

4 Conclusion

This article describes customized passenger transport service as a feasible management innovation in the field of road transportation market and proposed an analysis framework of customized passenger transport service to calculate financial results based on Cost-Volume-Profit analysis method. The case analysis based on SPT Company results in success. It indicated that road passenger transport companies need to reform management principles and improve business modes, and they could benefit from launching customized services. Future directions could be improving the analysis framework of customized passenger transport service and expanding data.

Acknowledgments The authors are indebted to the anonymous referees for their thoughtful comments and anonymous editors for their editing services. In particular, Jiawei Gui is indebted to Anjali Awasthi from Concordia University and Shervin Espahbod from Wilfrid Laurier University for their thoughtful suggestions during the parallel session at CEI 2101 in University of Windsor on July 27th, 2019. Jiawei Gui is also indebted to Guoqing Zhang, Guoqing Yang, Haijiao Li and anonymous volunteers for their organizing services during the conference, ICITL 2019. Besides, Jiawei Gui was rewarded by the National Scholarship of China for doctoral students and appreciated that. The work described in this article was supported in part by the National Social Science Fund of China [17BJY139], in part by the Strategic Planning Research Project of Ministry of Transport of China [2018-7-9] and [2018-16-9], in part by the Science Technology Project of Jilin Transportation Department [2019-1-15], in part by Chang'an University Excellent Doctoral Dissertation Cultivation Project of Chinese Universities Scientific Fund of China [300102239718].

Authors' Contributions Jiawei Gui contributed to investigation, methodology, software, validation, formal analysis, data curation, funding acquisition in part and manuscript preparation for all versions. Qunqi Wu contributed to conceptualization, funding acquisition in part and project administration. In particular, the concept of customized passenger transport was proposed by Qunqi Wu while Jiawei Gui built up the model.

References

1. Dumbaugh E, Marshall W (2018) Cities and the future of urban transportation: a roadmap for the 21st century. Res Transp Bus Manag 29:4–13
2. Fargnoli M, Costantino F, Di Gravio G et al (2018) Product service-systems implementation: a customized framework to enhance sustainability and customer satisfaction. J Clean Prod 188:387–401
3. Sun JY (2017) Airline deregulation and its impacts on air travel demand and airline competition: evidence from Korea. Rev Ind Organ 51(3):343–380
4. Song JN, Chen F, Wu QQ et al (2019) Optimization of passenger transportation corridor mode supply structure in regional comprehensive transport considering economic equilibrium. Sustainability 11(4):1–18
5. Gui J, Wu Q (2018) Taxi efficiency measurements based on motorcade-sharing model: evidence from GPS-equipped taxi data in Sanya. J Adv Transp 4360516:1–10
6. Gui J, Wu Q (2020) Vehicle movement analyses considering altitude based on modified digital elevation model and spherical bilinear interpolation model: evidence from GPS-equipped taxi data in Sanya, Zhengzhou, and Liaoyang. J Adv Transp 6301703:1–21
7. Lin XD, Ma LJ, Zheng ZX (2015) Customized transportation, equity participation, and cooperation performance within logistics supply chains. Math Probl Eng 792792:1–9
8. Crudden A, Antonelli K, O'Mally J (2017) A customized transportation intervention for persons with visual impairments. J Vis Impair Blind 111(4):341–353
9. Gui J, Wu Q (2019) An advanced simulation and optimization for railway transportation of passengers: crowdfunding train. In: Proceedings of the sixth international forum on decision sciences, Jinan, pp 283–304
10. Ke CX, Yan B, Xu RF (2017) A group-buying mechanism for considering strategic consumer behavior. Electron Commer Res 17(4):721–752
11. Ahmadi A, Pishvaee MS, Heydari M (2019) How group purchasing organisations influence healthcare-product supply chains? An analytical approach. J Oper Res Soc 70(2):280–293
12. Rubel O (2018) Profiting from product-harm crises in competitive markets. Eur J Oper Res 265(1):219–227
13. Zhang X, Chan TY, Xie Y (2018) Price search and periodic price discounts. Manag Sci 64(2):495–510
14. Drury CM (1992) Cost-volume-profit analysis. Management and cost accounting. Springer, New York, pp 205–235

Optimization of Closed-Loop Supply Chain with Changes of External Environment

Kuan Yang, Lin Tong, and Wei-Jin Xu

Abstract In the closed-loop supply chain where the manufacturer as a recycler, the cost of recycling is inversely related to the cost of remanufacturing. When the external environment changes (the establishment of government carbon tax and the interruption of raw material supply), the manufacturer can reduce its total cost through the game between the number of remanufactures and the number of manufactures. Therefore, we can study the relationship between carbon tax and supply disruption on the total cost of manufacturers, in order to minimize the loss of manufacturers caused by changes in the external environment. In this paper, the average total cost function of the manufacturer is established. The feasibility of the algorithm and the effectiveness of the model are verified by lingo, particle swarm optimization and genetic algorithm, and the optimal strategies are given by numerical analysis.

Keywords Optimal strategies · Carbon tax · Supply disruption

1 Introduction

With the advent of economic globalization, the whole supply chain system presents more and more complex links, so today's supply chain is threatened by complex environment than ever before. For the manufacturing industry, the changes of the external environment have a great impact on the profits of enterprises, focusing on the environment and supply disruption problems. Remanufacturing can relieve environmental pressure to some extent [1], thus more and more researchers pay attention to carbon dioxide emissions and carbon tax policies in supply chains [2–4]. Haddadsisakht and Ryan [5] provide a three-stage hybrid robust model, which

K. Yang (✉) · L. Tong · W.-J. Xu
School of Business Administration, Hunan University, Changsha, China
e-mail: yangkuan@hnu.edu.cn

X. Li, X. Xu (eds.), *Proceedings of the Seventh International Forum on Decision Sciences*, Uncertainty and Operations Research,
https://doi.org/10.1007/978-981-15-5720-0_21

considers the carbon tax with tax rate uncertainty. Wang and Guo [6] studied the optimal operation strategy of multi-cycle hybrid manufacturing/remanufacturing system considering carbon tax. Supply disruption as a major research area has achieved a lot [7–10]. However, these studies focus on one aspect of environmental or supply disruption, which often coexists in reality. Considering the limitations of existing research, this paper considers the environment and supply disruption as factors, establishes the total cost function model of the manufacturer, and gives the manufacturer's positive coping strategies through numerical analysis.

2 Format of Function

In the closed-loop supply chain the manufacturing and remanufacturing process is shown in Fig. 1:

2.1 Notations

Consider a closed-loop supply chain where the manufacturer as the recycler that defines the parameters used as follows, as shown in Table 1.

T, m, n, q are decision variables, where T means length of a manufacturing and remanufacturing cycle; m presents for number of remanufacturing lots, while n is number of manufacturing lots, and q is the required minimum quality level of returned products.

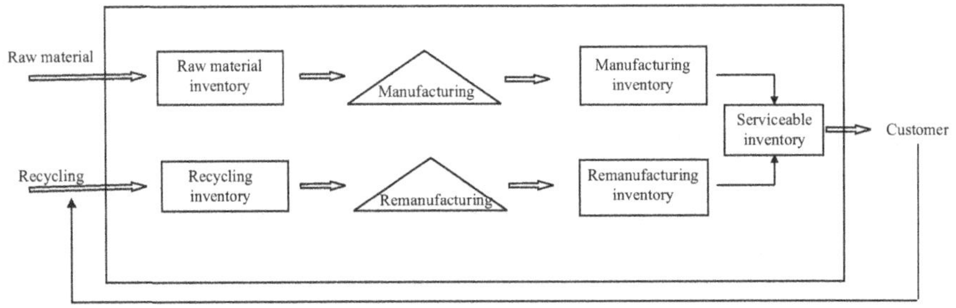

Fig. 1 The manufacturing and remanufacturing process

Table 1 Parameter definition

Symbol	Meaning	Symbol	Meaning
a, θ	Parameter of the buyback cost function	p	Buyback cost ratio
b, ψ	Parameter of the recycling rate function	d	Return rate
c, δ	Parameter of the remanufacturing cost function	ω	Probability of supply disruption for the raw materials from the primary supplier
D	Demand rate	α	Marginal recycling rate
$(1\text{-}\beta)$ D	Manufacturing rate	S_m	Remanufacturing installation cost
$(1\text{-}\gamma)$ D	Remanufacturing rate	S_n	Manufacturing installation cost
$d_1(d_2)$	Purchasing cost per unit of raw materials charged by major (secondary) suppliers	$e_m\ (e_n)$	The amount of carbon emissions from unit remanufactured (manufactured) goods
$h_s\ (h_r, h_{raw})$	Holding cost per unit time of serviceable (returned, raw materials) stock	$H_m\ (H_n, H_r, H_{raw})$	The average inventory cost of remanufactured (manufactured, returned, raw materials) products
C_{raw}	Purchasing cost for raw material per unit	$T_m\ (T_n)$	Time interval of a remanufacturing (manufacturing) lot
C_n	Manufacturing cost per unit	C_l	Cost of carbon tax per unit emission
C_0	Ordering cost		

2.2 *Functions*

In common closed-loop supply chain, the manufacturer's total cost consists of buyback cost V_1, remanufacturing cost V_2, manufacturing cost V_3, inventory holding cost V_4-which is the sum of H_m, H_n, H_r and H_{raw}, raw material cost V_5, ordering cost V_6 and setup cost V_7 (as in [11]). Note that in this article we assume that the quality of returned products q obeys the standard normal distribution, $q \sim N(0,1)$. In addition to the above costs, this paper takes environmental and supply disruption into account, so carbon tax cost V_8 and supply disruption cost V_9 are contained as follows:

$$V_8 = C_l\,[\alpha De_m + (1-\alpha)\ De_n]\,/T \tag{1}$$

$$V_9 = (1-\omega)\ (1-\alpha)\ Dd_1 + \omega\,(1-\alpha)\ Dd_2 \tag{2}$$

To sum up, the average total cost function ATC is as follows:

$$\begin{aligned}
ATC &= V_1 + V_2 + V_3 + V_4 + V_5 + V_6 + V_7 + V_8 + V_9 \\
&= aD\left(C_n + C_{raw}\right)be^{-\varphi q + \frac{\theta^2 - 2\theta}{2}}\left[\phi\left(1-\theta\right) - \phi\left(q-\theta\right)\right] \\
&+ cDC_n be^{-\varphi q + \frac{\delta^2 + 2\delta}{2}}\left[\phi\left(1+\delta\right) - \phi\left(q+\delta\right)\right] + \left(1-\alpha\right)DC_n \\
&+ \frac{1}{2m^2}h_s\left(1-\gamma\right)\alpha^2 DT + \frac{1}{2n^2}h_s\left(1-\beta\right)\left(1-\alpha\right)^2 DT \\
&+ \frac{1}{2}h_r\left[\alpha\left(1-\alpha\right) + \frac{\alpha^2}{m}\left(1-\gamma\right)\right]DT + \frac{1}{2}h_{raw}(1-\alpha)^2\frac{\beta+n-1}{n}DT \\
&+ \left(1-\alpha\right)DC_{raw} + C_0/T + \left(mS_m + nS_n\right)/T + \frac{C_1}{T}\left[\alpha De_m + \left(1-\alpha\right)De_n\right] \\
&+ \left(1-\omega\right)\left(1-\alpha\right)Dd_1 + \omega\left(1-\alpha\right)Dd_2
\end{aligned}$$

3 Optimization Algorithm

In this paper, particle swarm optimization algorithm and genetic algorithm are used to calculate the optimal value—avoiding limitation each other (Flows of these algorithms are shown in Figs. 2 and 3). Meanwhile to confirm our calculated result to verify the model of the recycled products in closed-loop supply chain, we achieve the computational results by particle swarm optimization algorithm, genetic algorithm and Lingo.

Fig. 2 Flow of particle swarm optimization algorithm

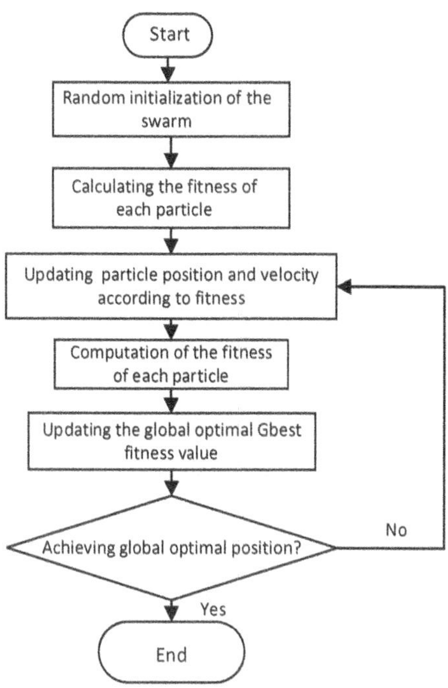

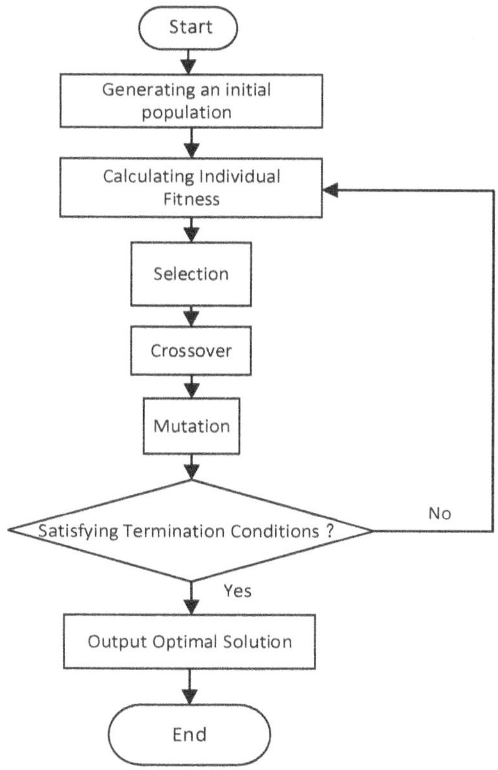

Fig. 3 Flow of genetic algorithm

4 Results of Numerical Analysis

Table 2 shows that the largest gap between particle swarm optimization (PSO) and genetic algorithm (GA). It is not difficult to find that the two algorithms have the same trend of change, which shows that the solution has not fallen into local optimum comparing particle swarm optimization (PSO) and genetic algorithm (GA) to solve the model. Both of the two algorithms and models are feasible.

From Tables 3, we can see: (1) When the environment (carbon tax) and the quality level of recycled products are stable ($q = 0.3$, $C1 = 3$), the average total cost increases with the increase of the probability of supply disruption. Once supply interruption occurs, it will bring serious losses to the enterprise—the increase of cost (shown in the Table 3 as the increase of ATC when $\omega = 0$ and $\omega = 1$) (2) Manufacturers can minimize the average total cost by adjusting the quality level of recycled products to the lowest level to meet the recycling requirements, and changing the proportion of remanufacturing and manufacturing times. (In this case, when $q = 0.1$, m:n = 1:1, the average total cost can reach the minimum value under supply disruption; when $q > =0.2$, m:n = 1:2, the average total cost can reach the minimum.)

Table 2 Gap between PSO and GA

θ	δ	m	n	q	T	ATC	q	T	ATC	GAP (%)
				By PSO			By GA			
4	0.5	3	1	0.1462	7.7849	50341.48	0.1491	7.4757	50342.24	−0.0015
	1.0	2	1	0.2380	6.8362	50814.65	0.2281	3.7857	50964.41	−0.2939
	1.5	1	1	0.3527	6.0158	50998.63	0.3538	6.7043	51018.26	−0.0385
5	0.5	3	1	0.1428	7.8051	50268.44	0.1407	7.1054	50269.32	−0.0018
	1.0	2	1	0.2283	6.8513	50649.07	0.2033	4.2545	50712.07	−0.1242
	1.5	1	1	0.3398	6.0643	50918.61	0.3342	6.6400	50930.37	−0.0231
6	0.5	3	1	0.1401	7.8142	50177.39	0.1305	7.2107	50185.33	−0.0158
	1.0	2	1	0.2019	6.8725	50538.28	0.1976	4.9052	50569.56	−0.0619
	1.5	1	1	0.3156	6.1547	50818.52	0.3112	5.8369	50821.60	−0.0061

Table 3 Optimal operational strategies (Different supply disruption probability when $C_1 = 3$)

q	ω	m	n	ATC
0.1	0	1	1	48,487.33
	0.5	1	1	52,159.83
	1	1	1	55,832.34
0.2	0	1	2	48,961.05
	0.5	1	2	52,692.92
	1	1	2	56,424.79
0.3	0	1	2	49,376.18
	0.5	1	2	53,156.65
	1	1	2	56,937.13
0.4	0	1	2	49,740.23
	0.5	1	2	53,560.56
	1	1	2	57,380.77
0.5	0	1	2	50,054.45
	0.5	1	2	53,907.29
	1	1	2	57,760.14
0.6	0	1	2	50,324.39
	0.5	1	2	54,203.91
	1	1	2	58,083.43
0.7	0	1	2	50,553.36
	0.5	1	2	54,454.72
	1	1	2	58,356.08
0.8	0	1	2	50,746.65
	0.5	1	2	54,665.89
	1	1	2	58,585.13
0.9	0	1	2	50,909.08
	0.5	1	2	54,842.96
	1	1	2	58,776.84

Table 4 Optimal operational strategies (Different carbon taxes)

q	C_1	m	n	ATC
0.1	1	1	1	49,800.18
	3	1	1	49,956.33
	5	1	2	50,073.48
0.2	1	1	1	50,297.21
	3	1	2	50,453.80
	5	1	2	50,567.90
0.3	1	1	1	50,734.78
	3	1	2	50,888.37
	5	1	2	51,002.73
0.4	1	1	1	51,116.41
	3	1	2	51,268.34
	5	1	2	51,383.55
0.5	1	1	1	51,445.18
	3	1	2	51,595.58
	5	1	2	51,711.15
0.6	1	1	1	51,726.57
	3	1	2	51,876.20
	5	1	2	51,992.46
0.7	1	1	1	51,965.07
	3	1	2	52,113.90
	5	1	2	52,230.51
0.8	1	1	1	52,166.24
	3	1	2	52,314.72
	5	1	2	52,431.88
0.9	1	1	1	52,334.57
	3	1	2	52,482.63
	5	1	2	52,600.08

As shown in Table 4, these conclusions can be draw:

1. From the aspect of government, it can increase carbon tax to promote manufacturing. With the increase of carbon tax, the cost of carbon tax for new products will increase. In order to reduce the cost of carbon tax, manufacturers will increase the number of remanufactured products and reduce the production of new products.
2. For a given carbon tax (formulated by the government), enterprises can minimize the average total cost by recovering the quality level and remanufacturing and manufacturing ratio. (In this case, when $C1 = 3$ enterprises can choose the best ratio $m:n = 1:1$ if the $q = 0.1$; choose the best ratio $m:n = 1:2$, if $q >= 0.2$, shown in Table 4)
3. We get an interesting conclusion: the proportion m:n of the lowest total average cost decreases with the increase of carbon tax, which seems to be contrary to the theory—The increase of carbon tax means that the cost of remanufactured

products is more advantageous than that of new products. Enterprises should increase the number of remanufactures if they only consider carbon tax. Thus, m:n should be increased. The reason may be that in our numerical example, the increase of carbon tax cost and inventory holding cost per unit of remanufactured products is greater than that of manufactured products. Therefore, the increase of carbon tax reduces the remanufacturing rate and manufacturing rate.

5 Conclusion

Based on the closed-loop supply chain of the manufacturer as a recycler, this paper establishes the total cost function model of the manufacturer considering the influence of external environment changes (carbon tax and supply interruption). By comparing PSO and GA algorithms, the validity of the model and the feasibility of the algorithm are proved. The results show that when the external environment changes, manufacturers can take effective measures to minimize the negative impact of change.

References

1. Shakourloo L, Kazemi A, Javad MOM (2016) A new model for more effective supplier selection and remanufacturing process in a closed-loop supply chain. Appl Math Model 40(23–24):9914–9931
2. Bazan E, Jaber MY, Zanoni S (2017) Carbon emissions and energy effects on a two-level manufacturer-retailer closed-loop supply chain model with remanufacturing subject to different coordination mechanisms. Int J Prod Econ 183:394–408
3. Wang J, Lim MK, Tseng M-L, Yang Y (2019) Promoting low carbon agenda in the urban logistics network distribution system. J Clean Prod 211:146–160
4. Zhen L, Huang L, Wang WC (2019) Green and sustainable closed-loop supply chain network design under uncertainty. J Clean Prod 227:1195–1209
5. Haddadsisakht A, Ryan SM (2018) Closed-loop supply chain network design with multiple transportation modes under stochastic demand and uncertain carbon tax. Int J Prod Econ 195.(Part B:118–131
6. Wang XY, Guo JQ (2018) Subsidy strategy model of multi-period closed-loop hybrid system under carbon tax. Comput Eng Appl 54(14):236–240
7. Hasani A, Khosrojerdi A (2016) Robust global supply chain network design under disruption and uncertainty considering resilience strategies: a parallel memetic algorithm for a real-life case study. Transp Res Part E: Logist Transp Rev 87:20–52
8. Baghalian A, Rezapour S, Farahani RZ (2013) Robust supply chain network design with service level against disruptions and demand uncertainties: a real-life case. Eur J Oper Res 227:199–215

9. Fahimnia B, Jabbarzadeh A (2016) Marrying supply chain sustainability and resilience: a match made in heaven. Transp Res Part E: Logist Transp Rev 91:306–324
10. Jabbarzadeh A, Haughton M, Khosrojerdi A (2018) Closed-loop supply chain network design under disruption risks: a robust approach with real world application. Comput Ind Eng 116:178–191
11. GUO JQ, YA G (2015) Optimal strategies for manufacturing/remanufacturing system with the consideration of recycled products. Comput Ind Eng 89:226–234

Study on Strategic Transition of E-commerce Companies Based on Capability Reconfiguration

Bo Hu

Abstract Under the background of Internet and large data, electric business enterprise how to take advantage of existing, to achieve strategic transformation, achieve sustainable development, is currently the bottleneck problem urgently to be solved. The paper analyzes driving factors of strategic transition of e-commerce companies led by Alibaba Group and JD Group. Then the paper tells in detail the method of strategic transition based on capability reconfiguration, which means to improve the six main factors under the influence of capability reconfiguration.

Keywords Capability reconfiguration · Strategic transition · Driving factors

1 Introduction

China's e-commerce has developed to the top of the world under the tide of Internet + and big data. At the same time, traditional enterprises have also transformed into e-commerce businesses. Fierce competition within the industry and cross-border competition are also common. The bottleneck period of China's e-commerce enterprises begins to appear. Driven by the mobile Internet, the e-commerce industry develops rapidly and seeks new ways to break the bottleneck, forming a new pattern of joint development of online and offline, spot and futures, wholesale and retail, urban and rural circulation markets. In this context, how e-commerce enterprises respond to the rapidly changing market environment, and when the Internet era is changing to the era of mobile Internet, it is a thorny issue for e-commerce enterprises to timely find problems, reshape their capabilities and make appropriate preparations for strategic transformation [1–3].

B. Hu (✉)
School of Economics and Management, China University of Petroleum (East China), Qingdao, China
e-mail: hb@upc.edu.cn

X. Li, X. Xu (eds.), *Proceedings of the Seventh International Forum on Decision Sciences*, Uncertainty and Operations Research,
https://doi.org/10.1007/978-981-15-5720-0_22

2 Analysis on the Causes of Strategic Transformation of E-commerce Enterprises

As the external driving factors of strategic transformation, the macro environment and industry environment force e-commerce enterprises to realize that the new external environment changes not only bring opportunities but also challenges to enterprises. In the fierce market competition environment, e-commerce enterprises have to cope with new difficulties, make timely adjustments, and find their own way of transformation [4, 5]. The internal driving factors of strategic transformation are the reflection and adjustment of enterprises. Internal and external driving factors interweave to promote the strategic transformation of e-commerce enterprises.

2.1 Macro Environmental Driven

Network and the improvement of the search engine, interactive community platform technology, the popularity of social networking tools such as QQ, WeChat, the improvement of the electronic payment, the development and application of big data, cloud services and the Internet of things such as the development of technology, for the prosperous development of e-commerce provides important technical support, and lead the electronic commerce to the direction of more efficient and convenient. In 2018, Internet coverage will be further expanded, "of network infrastructure in poor areas will be gradually open up, and the "digital divide" "will be bridged more quickly". Mobile traffic charges dropped significantly, inter-provincial "roaming" became a history, the threshold for residents to access the network was further lowered, and the efficiency of information exchange was improved. The Chinese government strongly supports the development of e-commerce [3, 6]. In 2015, the general office of the state council issued the action plan on the in-depth implementation of "Internet+circulation", promoting the "Internet+circulation" action, promoting the innovative development of circulation and the transformation and upgrading of real enterprises [5, 7].

2.2 Industry Environment Driven

Firstly, China's e-commerce sector has now passed its period of supercharged growth. Chinese e-commerce enterprises generally face the "last mile" problem of e-commerce logistics in the domestic market. Solving this problem well can provide help for e-commerce enterprises to go deep into third-tier and fourth-tier cities and develop rural e-commerce business. In the era of mobile Internet, the integration of online and offline will be accelerated in combination with the "Internet+circulation" action plan. The development of cross-border e-commerce and rural e-commerce will be the new commanding heights of the e-commerce industry. Secondly, In the aspect of cross-border e-commerce, the whole market has grown from high-speed to high-quality and centralized, and the market pattern has become stable. Traditional B2C, C2C, B2B to develop C2B, O2O. The sellers ignore the buyers' brand psychology, the vicious cycle of price competition on the Internet, the shopping gap of online shopping and other reasons make the customer-oriented market put forward higher requirements on customer experience. In addition, traditional industries have also been transformed into e-commerce [2, 3, 6]. In the face of competition, e-commerce companies with strong online business capabilities have been jointly setting up O2O platforms with offline brick-and-mortar stores to get through the online and offline business layout. With the gradual penetration of technology in the O2O field, O2O has entered a new era of technology enabling merchants.

2.3 *Enterprise Development Needs*

From the perspective of the enterprise itself, this paper analyzes the interrelation and influence among corporate vision, corporate culture, employee quality, financial status, organizational structure and other factors, and explores the internal driving factors of corporate transformation. Innovation is always the key to respond to change and enhance competitiveness in the era of mobile Internet, and how to consolidate and strengthen innovation culture is the key point that enterprises need to explore urgently. Organizational structure reform is a problem that every enterprise must face. Finding an organizational structure suitable for the current development stage and future development direction of the company is the basis for the healthy growth of the enterprise, and also an important driving force for the transformation of the enterprise [8, 9].

3 Strategic Path Selection of E-commerce Enterprises Based on Capability Remodeling

3.1 *Key Elements of the Strategic Transformation of E-commerce Enterprises*

Strategic transformation means adaptive change in the new environment, which needs to be based on management upgrading, capital operation as a means, cultural transformation as the core, to promote strategic industrial upgrading for the purpose, to improve the overall quality of employees as a guarantee. So how to achieve a successful strategic transformation, that is, what are the key factors of strategic transformation? Six key elements are required for successful

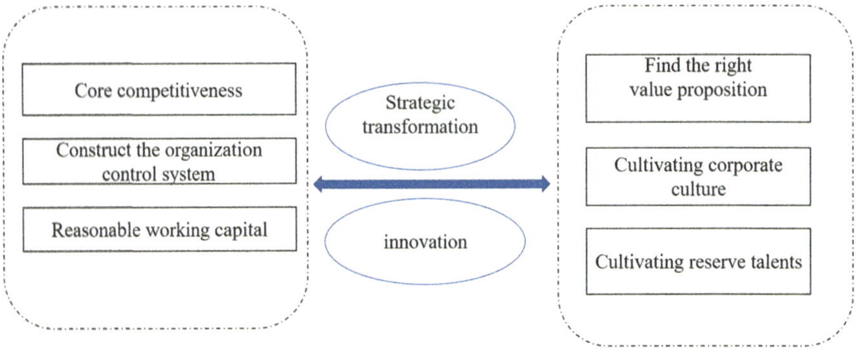

Fig. 1 Diagram of key elements of strategic transformation

strategic transformation of e-commerce enterprises [5, 7]: (1) on the premise of accurate value positioning; (2) build core competitiveness; (3) construction of organizational control system; (4) reasonable capital operation; (5) cultivate a good corporate culture; (6) pay attention to reserve talent training. These six elements are interrelated and affect each other. Strategic transformation needs to be actively adjusted under the driving force of motivation, and it is these six key elements that play a qualitative role in promoting strategic transformation in the process of implementing actions. Figure 1 show the key elements of strategic transformation.

3.2 The Strategic Transformation Path of E-commerce Enterprises

3.2.1 Remodeling Based on Risk Identification Capability

In terms of value positioning, for e-commerce enterprises, they should choose their business fields and core business scope, guard against products or services with poor quality, buyers and sellers with poor credit and investment fields with more bubbles, reduce the possibility of risks, and improve their risk identification ability. Core competitiveness, the electricity business enterprise to innovation in team effort, and in his own has the advantage of resources and capacity, on the basis of maintain or develop new superior resources and abilities, to form a stronger core competitiveness or new core competitiveness to adapt to the environment, thus reducing the risk probability and improve the ability of risk identification. In terms of organizational structure, it is an optional strategic transformation path to change organizational structure, set up relevant departments or increase the investment of relevant technical personnel for risks that need to be specifically prevented, or cancel and merge inefficient organizations, or flatten organizations so as to curb bureaucratic ethos. In terms of corporate culture, it is people-oriented, pursues high quality and excellent service, and encourages innovation, so as to reduce the problems of inferior products or services, form a positive and active team atmosphere, generate good ideas in operation, prevent risks, and improve the ability of risk identification. In terms of talent construction, friendly cooperation and healthy competition among departments are encouraged to create a good working environment and growth atmosphere for employees and attract more excellent employees. With a good talent pool, risk identification will naturally improve.

3.2.2 Remodeling Based on Offline Promotion Capability

In terms of value positioning, when choosing the core business scope, it is necessary to deeply understand and tap the needs of customers to create a good user experience, so as to reshape the offline promotion ability of e-commerce enterprises. In terms of core competitiveness, the core of O2O offline promotion is online payment. Therefore, e-commerce enterprises with conditions should strive to build core competitiveness in finance and payment, and those without conditions should create opportunities to make use of this core competitiveness [6, 7]. In terms of organizational structure, the integration of online and offline needs the joint operation of e-commerce enterprises, offline enterprises and stores, and the exploration of a new competitive and cooperative profit model. In terms of corporate culture, a performance-driven culture should be cultivated to enable employees to work actively in a good atmosphere, make efforts to expand offline business and improve offline promotion ability. In terms of personnel training, the O2O model originated from the United States and has just started its exploration in China. Therefore, in terms of personnel training, on the one hand, talents with relevant foreign work experience should be introduced; on the other hand, talents with understanding of China's O2O model should be cultivated patiently. In addition, we should also pay attention to absorbing the rich experience of excellent personnel from offline enterprises or stores, so as to lay a foundation for facing customers face to face, providing quality services and building our own brand image [6, 8].

3.2.3 Remodeling Based on Logistics Distribution Capability

In terms of value positioning, platform mode, self-run mode and self-run + open hybrid mode are the mainstream operation modes of e-commerce today. Choosing different modes means different requirements on logistics distribution ability. Choosing self-operation mode requires e-commerce enterprises to have higher logistics distribution ability. For example, JD needs to establish its own logistics and warehousing system. However, the selection of platform mode requires a relatively low level. The logistics and distribution capability it lacks should be made up by third-party logistics service providers, such as Taobao, a subsidiary of Alibaba. The choice of value orientation is closely related to the promotion strategy of logistics distribution capability.

In terms of core competitiveness, if the core competitiveness includes logistics and distribution capability, the logistics and distribution capability can be remolded by concentrating resources to maintain or improve the core competitiveness. If the core competitiveness does not include the logistics and distribution capability, the existing core resources can be used to provide logistics and distribution services, and the logistics and distribution services can be remolded without affecting the performance growth and development of enterprises, or the new core competitiveness can be cultivated and the logistics and distribution capability can be enhanced. In terms of organizational structure, self-operation requires more manpower and financial resources to be invested in organizational construction and management becomes more complex. However, the improvement of logistics distribution capability is obvious [8, 9]. If the problem of logistics and distribution is solved with the help of external forces, the organizational structure construction does not need to spend too much resources on logistics and distribution business, and the streamlined organizational structure will be more suitable for e-commerce enterprises [6, 9]. In terms of talent cultivation, it is necessary to cultivate the innovative consciousness of talents and technical talents in big data, cloud computing and other aspects, so as to make preparations for solving the "last mile" problem and promoting the development of rural e-commerce and cross-border e-commerce.

Acknowledgements This work was supported by Shandong college social science foundation (J16WF22), China.

References

1. Wang X, Yu W (2018) The interactive relationship between cross-border e-commerce development and traditional foreign trade. Econ Manage Res 2:79–86
2. Bloom N, Draca M (2016) Trade induced technical change? The impact of Chinese imports on innovation IT and productivity. Rev Econ Stud 83:87–117
3. Yi S (2019) Challenges and suggestions for cross-border e-commerce enterprises to "go global"-take Alibaba's entry into the Australian market as an example. China Dev Obs 8:60–61
4. Xiaowen T, Dunhu L, Jin X (2015) Research on the mechanism of strategic transformation process from the perspective of dynamic capability. Sci Res Manage 36(1):90–96
5. Weiding W (2015) Principles of e-commerce operation: strategies, methods and practices. China Machine Press, Beijing
6. Chen L (2014) New attempt of e-commerce logistics in "last kilometer" joint distribution. Logist Technol: Equip Ed 10:63–67
7. Ying L (2014) Alibaba model: changing the rules of the game and growing with the release of grassroots innovation. Citic Press, Beijing
8. Connolly T, Begg C (2003) Understanding dynamic capabilities. Strateg Manage 24(10):991–995
9. Agarwal R, Helfat CE (2009) Strategic renewal of organizations. Organ Sci 20(2):281–293

Identification Method of Taxi Drop-off Location Based on Combination Retrieval

Haitao Yu, Tianze Xu, and Randong Xiao

Abstract The past, the GPS locating closest to drop-off time was selected as the taxi passenger's alighting position, but due to equipment failure, urban buildings, and complicated network, the accuracy of identifying the alighting position was low. In order to solve this problem, we designed a taxi drop-off location identification system based on combined retrieval. By searching the historical database, the taxi trajectory is reckoned, and the drop-off position is calculated based on the trajectory. Experiments show that this method has higher computational efficiency, and the accuracy is significantly improved compared with the GPS position matching method.

Keywords Taxi · Drop-off location · Roads · Inverted index · Finite-state machine

1 Introduction

The analysis of residents' travel demand requires analyzing all the trip modes of OD, including taxi, online-hailing car, bus, subway, etc. [1]. Due to the relatively old equipment and the separating of ordering system from positioning system of existing taxi system, the data of each order from taxis only contains information such as time, distance and price, not including the position where passengers' get

---

H. Yu · R. Xiao
Key Laboratory of Intelligent Transportation Systems Technologies, Ministry of Communications, Beijing Transportation Information Center, and Beijing Key Laboratory for Comprehensive Traffic Operation Monitoring and Service, Beijing, China
e-mail: sy1821116@buaa.edu.cn

T. Xu (✉)
College of Software Engineering, Beihang University, Beijing, China
e-mail: sy1821116@buaa.edu.cn

X. Li, X. Xu (eds.), *Proceedings of the Seventh International Forum on Decision Sciences*, Uncertainty and Operations Research,
https://doi.org/10.1007/978-981-15-5720-0_23

off position, Only by matching the get-off time with the GPS data uploaded by the positioning system at a certain time interval can obtain the drop-off position of passengers. However, because of the interference of GPS signals by the problems of equipment and pile in the city, the GPS data quality of the taxis is poor. Some positioning data deviation is too large or the adjacent GPS data interval is too long, so the accuracy of calculating the alighting position only depending on GPS registration point is low. Therefore, to solve the problem of accurate extraction of taxi drop-off location, this paper proposes a method of taxi drop-off location identification based on combination retrieval.

2 Characteristic Analysis of Relevant Data

Since the taxi passengers' getting-off time is not synchronized with the GPS uploading time, the GPS positioning point may be far away from the passengers' drop-off position, which cannot be accurately obtained via GPS data. As shown in Fig. 1.

More than 20% of the time differences between passenger arrival times in taxi order data and the most recent GPS data were greater than 30 s. The average speed of floating vehicle in Beijing is 20 km/h. When the time difference is more than 30 s, the position deviation between GPS positioning point and actual drop-off position exceeds 150 m, so these GPS data cannot be directly used for drop-off position calibration. Therefore, only the GPS position information with a time difference of less than 30 s is matched as the passenger's drop-off position.

For the case where the time difference is more than 30 s, the drop-off position can be calculated by means of TLINK data [2]. TLINK data is based on taxi GPS data and can be used to characterize the trajectory of a taxi. It can express the track of a taxi in a certain time period. TLINK data contains Recording time, Taxi ID, Road ID, and Running Speed. The Recording time is the time when calculates TLINK data through GPS information, the taxi ID is the unique identifier of the vehicle, The road ID is the unique identification of the road in the road network, and the Running Speed is the average speed of the taxi on each road based on GPS data.

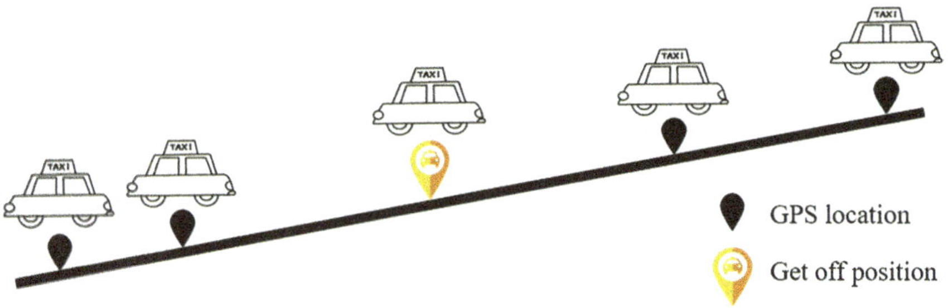

Fig. 1 GPS positioning deviation

Fig. 2 The position relationship

The roads with the same recording time and the same taxi ID constitute the driving trajectory of the vehicle.

According to the TLINK data structure, the drop-off position can be estimated from the TLINK data. Combined with road network data, the recorded time, running speed and drop-off time are matched to calculate the driving distance of the taxi on the continuous road, and then the accurate drop-off position is calculated. However, according to analysis of TLINK data, about 80% of the roads records before and after the alighting time are discontinuous, so it is impossible to directly calculate the drop-off position by the above method. Figure 2 shows the spatial relation between the discontinuous path and the drop-off location.

By filling the discontinuous roads completely, the precise drop-off position can be calculated based on the road network data. The discontinuous roads can be supplemented by the continuous roads of other vehicles in the historical database containing TLINK data. After the continuous roads is obtained, we can calculate the precise drop-off location.

3 Proposed Method

3.1 Basic Strategy

Firstly, read the taxi order data and calculate the time difference between the arrival time and the recent GPS upload time for each order data. If the time difference is less than 30 s, then the drop-off position can be directly matched by GPS registration point. If the time difference is greater than 30 s, check whether the TLINK roads before and after the order alighting time are continuous. If the path is inconsecutive, the historical data is used to complement the roads and then calculate the drop-off location [3]. Retrieve all eligible driving routes through TLINK historical data and fill in the roads with statistical driving modes [4]. It is divided into two steps to search for eligible driving paths. First, search the eligible taxis and the corresponding recording time, which often exceed thousands of vehicles. Then, the actual driving path is retrieved according to the vehicle and time, and the driving path selected by more vehicles is selected as the driving mode. The passenger drop-off position is calculated after the driving mode is applied to the discrete roads.

Theoretically, the more data, the better the effect, but it will also reduce the calculation efficiency. Moreover, according to the calculation principle of floating vehicle system, TLINK data is stored in chronological order. For the extraction of historical trajectory model, this storage method has a very large memory overhead. We design a fast search of Combination method. Firstly, we use the thought of Full-text Retrieval to establish inverted index [5]. Then the inverted correspondence between road and taxi ID is constructed. Index compression technology is used to reduce the storage overhead and quickly extract eligible vehicle number and time. For the case that the number of qualified taxis exceeds 10,000, we have designed a pattern matching machine, which can accomplish the matching of all taxis and the extraction of TLINK trajectory data in one traversal process, thus reducing the overall time overhead.

3.2 Build Inverted Index and Compression

Figure 3 shows the inverted index structure. Taking the road ID as the key word, the associated vehicles and the time passing through the road are collected into an inverted list to establish inverted index. When searching the road, only a specific list needs to be traversed, which can reduce the number of retrieval and time saving. In order to reduce the space occupied by the index itself, the index only records the necessary information. The vehicle data in the inverted list only record the taxi ID. The format of the recorded time in the historical data is YYYYMMDDHHMMSS, for example, 20191201175047, which represents 17:50:47 on December 1, 2019.

Index files for large amounts of historical data undoubtedly occupies a lot of space and should be stored after compression [6]. The D-gap compression method is to sort the records, and then use the first value as the reference [7]. Subsequent values only record the difference between consecutive values. We use D-gap method to compress the time records in the inverted index list: only the first record (date, hour, minute, and second) is saved in the sorted inverted list. For the subsequent time, the time difference from the previous time is stored. Table 1 shows a comparison of the inverted list before and after compression.

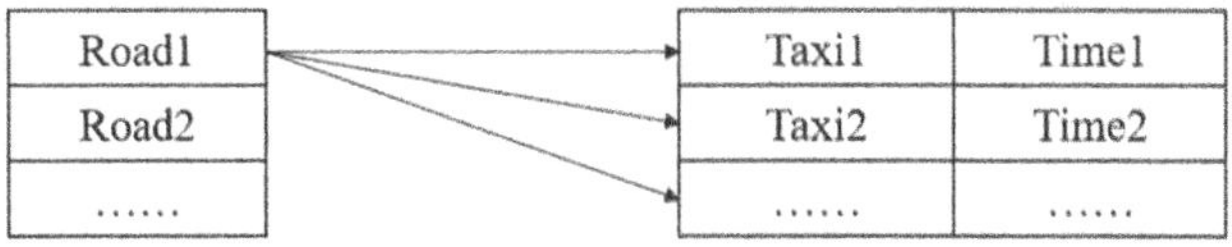

Fig. 3 Inverted index

Table 1 Compression contrast

Before compression	20191201175407	20191201175108	20191201175117	20191201175133
Compressed	20191201175407	21	9	16

3.3 Retrieval Method Based on Pattern Matching Machine

The general method of multi-keyword matching is to match each keyword with a text string. This method needs to match several times to get the matching result. The pattern matching machine based on the finite state machine. [8] can get the matching result in one traversal process and save the retrieval time.

The pattern matching machine is constructed according to the keywords K, including a set of states, state transition function $NextMove(s, a) = s^{'}$, output function $Output(s) = K^{'}$. Firstly, constructing the goto function $goto(s, a) = s^{'}$ and failure function $fail(s) = s^{'}$, and then calculate the state transition function based on the goto function and the failure function.

After building the pattern matching machine, input the text string into the machine, and search the state transition function to move to the next state according to the current state and input characters. Finally, the match result is returned based on the current state and the output function.

3.3.1 Construction of goto and Output Function

For example, suppose $K = \{NB1, HG1, HG2, MLP\}$ is the set of keywords. To construct goto function, we should construct a goto graph. Enter each keyword into the diagram by adding a directed path to the diagram starting from the state 0. A path from state 0 represents a keyword and adds state and goto functions only when necessary. Figure 4 shows an example about adding new state and path. HG1 and HG2 has been added in to goto graph. When the keyword HG2 is added, state 2 is reached from state 0 according to the goto function, since $goto(2, 2) = null$, so a new state 4 and goto function $goto(2, 2) = 4$ are created. Because 2 is the last character of HG2, create the output function $output(4) = HG2$.

3.3.2 Construction of Failure Function

Define the depth of state s as the length of the shortest path from state 0 to state s. To calculate the failure function, we first calculate the state with depth 1, then calculate

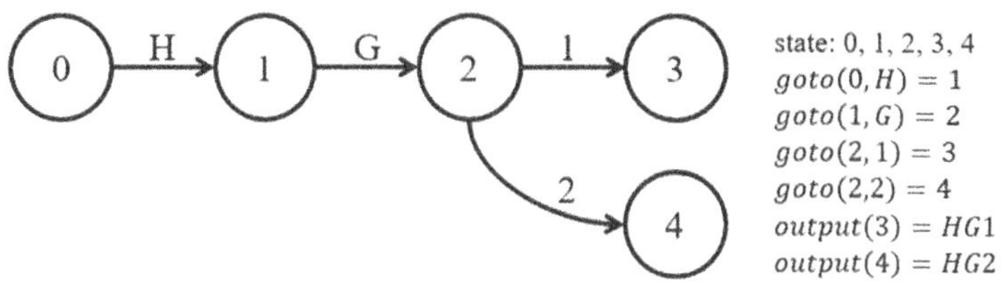

Fig. 4 goto graph

the state with depth 2, and so on. We make $fail(s) = 0$ for all states s of depth 1. In order to calculate $fail(s)$ of depth d, consider each state r of depth d-1 and calculate as follows. Define a as all the characters contained in the keywords.

1. *if* $goto(r, a) = null$, end.
2. Otherwise, for each a such that $goto(r, a) = s$.
   (a) Set $s' = fail(r)$.
   (b) Execute $s' = fail(s')$ until $g(s', a) \neq null$.
   (c) Set $fail(s) = goto(s', a)$.

3.3.3 Construction of State Transition Function

Construction the state transition function $NextMove(s, a) = s'$ based on the goto function and the failure function. Start at the state 0 in the goto graph and traversing each state in depth. Consider each state s and perform the following actions.

1. for each symbol a in keywords
2. if $goto(s, a) = s' \neq fail$.
   (a) $NextMove(s, a) = s'$.
3. Otherwise, $NextMove(s, a) = NextMove(fail(s), a)$.

4 Experimental Verification

In the experiment, 500 taxi orders from Beijing within one day were randomly selected as test cases. The historical database contains 10-day taxi GPS data and TLINK data. The size of GPS data is 81.2G and the size of TLINK data is 57.6G.

The index of improving retrieval efficiency is defined as follows:

$$\eta = \frac{1/t' - 1/t}{1/t} \times 100\%$$

η stands for the improvement rate of retrieval efficiency, t stands for the time of simple traversal, and t' represent the time of adopting the method in this chapter. Supposing the retrieval task is 1, $1/t$ represents the efficiency of simple traversal and $1/t'$ represents the efficiency of the algorithm in this chapter. The above formula can be used to measure the percentage of efficiency improvement.

Figure 5 shows the relationship between the improvement of combined retrieval efficiency and the number of vehicles retrieved. The more vehicles retrieved, the higher the retrieval efficiency.

Figure 6 shows the calculated passenger drop-off location compared to the actual drop-off position of the order. The average speed of floating vehicles in Beijing

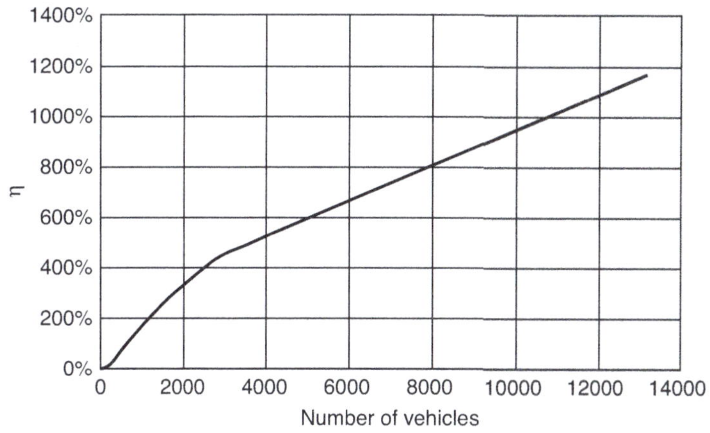

Fig. 5 Retrieval efficiency

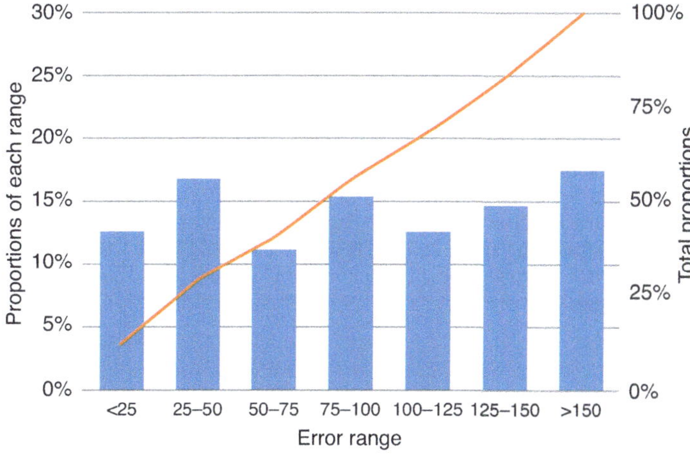

Fig. 6 Error distribution

is 20 km/h, and the maximum distance error of GPS matching is 150 m based on the calculation of 30 s. Statistics the error distance between the calculated drop-off location and the actual drop-off position of the order. The error of 84.2% of the calculation cases is less than 150 m, and good results are obtained for the discontinuous taxi alighting position. Based on the identification results of taxi drop-off location matched by GPS, the accuracy of the overall taxi passenger drop-off location identification method reached 95%.

5 Conclusion

In this paper, we studied the method of identifying taxi drop-off position based on combined retrieval. In order to calculate the drop-off location, except for the traditional GPS data matching method, the method of retrieving continuous moving tracks similar to the target is used to retrieve the travel trajectory of other vehicles stored from the historical database in the case of poor quality of GPS data. In order to balance the time complexity and space complexity of retrieval, all vehicles passing through a specific roads are first retrieved by searching inverted index, and then the multi-keyword retrieval of these vehicles is merged into a single retrieval by means of pattern matching machine, and the continuous road chain of each vehicle is obtained during single traversal. Through the statistics of roads, the driving mode of vehicles is obtained. Then, the driving mode is used to supplement the discontinuous roads. The drop-off position is calculated according to the continuous roads. As future work, first, we can continue to increase the number of historical databases and further improve retrieval efficiency; In addition, a more scientific method can be adopted to extract the driving patterns of vehicles from all the roads retrieved and construct the pattern library. By filling the discontinuity with the pattern library, the times of retrieval can be reduced and the computing efficiency can be improved.

Acknowledgements This work was partly supported by the Opening Project of Key Laboratory of Intelligent Transportation Systems Technologies, Ministry of Communications, P. R. China and partly by Science and Technology Plan Project of Beijing (No. Z181100003918010), and partly by Science and Technology Plan Project of Beijing (No. Z191100002519002), and partly by the program of Beijing Outstanding Talent Training Foundation (No 2017000021063G008), and partly by Grants from the National Engineering Laboratory for Comprehensive Transportation Big Data Application Technology.

References

1. De Fabritiis C, Ragona R, Valenti G (2008) Traffic estimation and prediction based on real time floating car data. In: 2008 11th international IEEE conference on intelligent transportation systems. IEEE, 2008, pp 197–203
2. Quddus MA, Ochieng WY, Zhao L et al (2003) A general map matching algorithm for transport telematics applications. GPS Solutions 7(3):157–167
3. Kim SW, Won JI, Kim JD et al (2007) Path prediction of moving objects on road networks through analyzing past trajectories. In: International conference on knowledge-based and intelligent information and engineering systems. Springer, Berlin, pp 379–389
4. Pei J, Han J, Mortazavi-Asl B et al (2004) Mining sequential patterns by pattern-growth: the prefixspan approach. IEEE Trans Knowl Data Eng 16(11):1424–1440
5. Zobel J, Moffat A (2006) Inverted files for text search engines. ACM Comput Surveys (CSUR) 38(2):6
6. Anh VN, Moffat A (2005) Inverted index compression using word-aligned binary codes. Inf Retr 8(1):151–166

7. Zhang J, Long X, Suel T (2008) Performance of compressed inverted list caching in search engines. In: Proceedings of the 17th international conference on world wide web. ACM, pp 387–396
8. Aho AV, Corasick MJ (1975) Efficient string matching: an aid to bibliographic search. Commun ACM 18(6):333–340

The manufacturer's authorised representative in the EU is Springer Nature Customer Service Centre GmbH, Europaplatz 3, 69115 Heidelberg, Germany. If you have any concerns regarding our products, please contact ProductSafety@springernature.com

Printed and bound by CPI Group (UK) Ltd, Croydon, CR0 4YY
30/09/2026
02225333-0003